DEVELOPING HIGH QUALITY DATA MODELS

DEVELOPING HIGH QUALITY DATA MODELS

MATTHEW WEST

AMSTERDAM • BOSTON • HEIDELBERG • LONDON
NEW YORK • OXFORD • PARIS • SAN DIEGO
SAN FRANCISCO • SINGAPORE • SYDNEY • TOKYO
Morgan Kaufmann Publishers is an imprint of Elsevier

Acquiring Editor: Rick Adams
Development Editor: David Bevans
Project Manager: Sarah Binns
Designer: Joanne Blank

Morgan Kaufmann Publishers is an imprint of Elsevier
30 Corporate Drive, Suite 400, Burlington, MA 01803, USA

Library of Congress Cataloging-in-Publication Data
West, Matthew, 1953-
Developing high quality data models / Matthew West.
    p. cm.
ISBN 978-0-12-375106-5 (pbk.)
1. Database design. 2. Data structures (Computer science) I. Title.
QA76.9.D26W47 2011
005.7′3—dc22   2010045158

British Library Cataloguing-in-Publication Data
A catalogue record for this book is available from the British Library.

For information on all MK publications visit our website at www.mkp.com

CONTENTS

PREFACE

I would like to start by explaining how I came to write this book, and to acknowledge its influences and the help I have received along the way.

I have been extremely fortunate. I have a wonderful wife and two wonderful grown-up children, and I have had all but thirty years working for Shell, which provided an environment that had stimulating challenges and opportunities to look more deeply at problems than is often the case.

I first came across computers in 1971. My undergraduate course was in Chemical Engineering at Leeds University, and we all had to learn how to write basic Fortran programs in our first year. I went on to do a PhD, which involved mathematical modeling of chemical processes and led to my developing an automatic integrator for stiff ordinary differential equations. As a result I am probably among a relatively small group of people who have started a computer by loading the bootstrap program into memory from the switches to boot up the computer.

I joined Shell in 1978 at Shell Haven Refinery on the north bank of the Thames estuary, east of London. I was immediately thrown into the implementation of a computer supervision system for the Crude Distillation Unit, which monitored the hundreds of measurements taken around the unit and warned of deviations from target performance. I spent eight years at Shell Haven, and while I had a wide range of roles, computers and computing were a recurring theme. I was, for example, responsible for the purchase of the first IBM PC on the refinery, and one of the first in Shell for engineering calculations using a spreadsheet, and at the time I left the refinery I was responsible for all the mini-computer based systems on the refinery.

My next move was to London in 1986, where I was a business analyst on one of the first relational database (DB2) implementations in Shell, the Oil Management Project. This was an information system designed to produce an overview of the planned and actual production and sales of oil products by Shell in the UK. It was here where I first came across data models in the Shell UK Oil data architecture and Bruce Ottmann, who ran the data architecture team and who became a major enabler and encourager of much of the work I have done in data management. I immediately found data models fascinating. As a chemical engineer, I was very used to a process view of the world, and data models gave a completely different perspective. I was hooked.

I spent 1989 in The Hague working for Jan Sijbrand. He had a vision for a system's and data architecture for refineries such that a common suite of systems could develop and evolve to support refinery operations. My part was to develop the data models, which was done through a series of workshops, led by Bruce Ottmann, by now leading the corporate data management group. Ken Self, later to be one of my bosses, was one of the attendees.

I returned to London in 1990 to work for Bruce in a project called the Data Management Key Thrust. Shell's Committee of Managing Directors had noticed that IT costs were rising exponentially, but it was not clear why so much money was being spent, or whether it was delivering value. They issued an edict that IT costs were to be capped and instituted a number of Key Thrusts to improve matters. The Data Management Key Thrust was one of these.

The next few years were particularly fruitful. What we noticed was that many Shell companies were developing different computer systems to do the same thing, but that these systems were not suitable for other Shell companies. When we investigated why this was the case, we discovered that the data models contained constraints that did not always apply, or meant that historical data could not be held. We looked for and discovered data model patterns that were examples of the traps that data modelers fell into, and what you needed to do to improve those data models. From this we were able to work out principles for data modeling to avoid falling into those traps. We also included a Generic Entity Framework as a high-level data model to help create data models that were consistent with each other. These documents were "Reviewing and Improving Data Models" and "Developing High Quality Data Models," and yes, that is where the title of this book comes from. This book aims to address some of the same issues as the original article, and while there is little if anything of the original documents that has not been updated, some of the same issues and principles are recognizable. Shell made a version of this publicly and freely available and I am pleased to have use of this and to significantly update and extend it.

There was much other work done by that group in information management around information quality and information management maturity that was significant in general, but I will limit myself to the data modeling story.

In 1993 I was asked to get involved in the development of a standard for the integration and exchange of engineering design data for process plants, including refineries and offshore oil platforms, joining a consortium called PISTEP, the Process Industries STEP[1] consortium, consisting of UK oil companies, contractors, and Computer Aided Design software companies. The aim was to develop a standard as part of the STEP (ISO 10303, developed by ISO TC184/SC4 – Industrial Data) family of standards to meet our needs, so that engineering design data could be handed over electronically, rather than on paper, which was the practice at that time. Some of the key people involved in making PISTEP a success were Terry Lazenby of BP who chaired PISTEP, Stuart Lord from ICI who managed the consortium, Donald Bell who provided administration, and Bill Mesley who looked after publicity and conferences. Other key contributors were David Adam, Ian Glendinning, Ian Bishop, Alan Thomson, and David Leal. We found there were a number of other industrial consortia in Europe, and I was asked to call a meeting of these to see if we could find a way to work together on a standard. From this meeting EPISTLE[2] was established as a consortium of consortia. This included PISTEP; ProcessBase, a European Commission funded project; a Dutch consortium that was to become USPI-NL; and a Norwegian consortium that was to become POSC Caesar. I became its founding Chair.

When looking for a starting point, the Generic Entity Framework I had developed for the Data Management Key Thrust and the data modeling methodology that went with it was considered to be a better place to start than the alternatives that were available at the time. Shell agreed to contribute the work to the standards process. These were developed into what became the EPISTLE Core Model, edited by Chris Angus, and another edition of "Developing High Quality Data Models"[3] published by EPISTLE, written by myself and Julian Fowler.

However, there were some niggling problems that kept recurring and to which it was not possible to find an enduring solution. So I was very interested when I met Chris Partridge at a conference and he started talking to me about an approach to ontology[4] called 4-dimensionalism that could help to explain the things that were causing problems in the EPISTLE Core Model. It was eventually agreed that we would adopt this

---

[1]STEP: Standard for the Exchange of Product model data
[2]EPISTLE: European Process Industries STEP Technical Liaison Executive
[3]http://www.matthew-west.org.uk/documents/princ03.pdf
[4]The study of what exists.

approach for the EPISTLE Core Model, and Chris Partridge's book about the 4D paradigm, which he had recently published, *Business Objects: Re-engineering for Re-use*, was a key input.

On the standardization front, there were problems emerging with making our work part of ISO 10303. The Integrated Resources, the data modeling framework for STEP, were constrained in ways that meant we could not meet our requirements in a way that was compatible with others who were developing standards as part of ISO 10303, and those who had already developed standards were unwilling to see changes made to the standard that would accommodate us, but require them to rework what they had already done. This resulted in a new standard being developed: ISO 15926 - Lifecycle integration of process plant data including oil and gas production facilities.

The first parts of ISO 10303 were also being published at this time, and it was noticeable that different parts were not actually compatible with each other, unless considerable care had been taken to make sure they were. This was a surprise to some who thought that because they were all based on the same Integrated Resources, this would be sufficient to ensure they would be compatible. Others of us knew that it was quite enough to use a data model in different ways for the two data sets likely to be incompatible. A new working group, WG10, was set up with the best brains in ISO TC184/SC4 to work out what to do about it, and what it would take to develop a suite of standards that were compatible. I was elected Deputy Convener, with Bernd Wenzel as Convener. There were two main outputs: a modular approach to developing ISO 10303 and an integration architecture.

The modular approach to developing ISO 10303 was intended to enable the construction of exchange standards out of modules, so that exchange standards for different requirements would be constructed by combining different modules. This would reduce the chance of the same model being redeveloped in different ways in different standards. David Price was a key contributor to this work.

The integration architecture was developed principally by Julian Fowler and me with input from Bernd Wenzel and David Price. It looked at what was necessary in order to be successful at integrating data from different sources. The result was ISO TS 18876 — Integration of industrial data for exchange access and sharing. ISO 15926 is a standard that conforms to this architecture.

The EPISTLE Core Model started its development by committee, with sometimes twenty or more people in the room, and not necessarily the same people at different meetings. This was probably necessary in the early stages to get a broad consensus, but it was unwieldy and unmanageable for the detail and for issue resolution. It was decided to set up a data modeling team with two technical representatives from each consortium: David Leal and I from PISTEP, Andries van Renssen and Hans Teijgeler from USPI-NL, and Jan Sullivan and Magne Valen Sendstad from POSC Caesar, plus someone to manage the process. This produced more stability and progress, but it was eventually agreed to reduce the team to just three technical members, one from each consortium, and these were myself, Jan Sullivan, and Hans Teijgeler, again with someone to manage the process.

In ISO TC184/SC4 American colleagues, including Mark Palmer, expressed concern that the data model being developed was too generic, and did not tie down enough terms for unambiguous exchange. As a result, it was decided to establish a Reference Data Library of classes and other objects to create a more specific common language. Andries van Renssen, Magne Valen Sendstad, and David Leal went on to make major contributions to the development of the Reference Data Library that accompanies and extends the data model.

My standards work brought me back into contact with Leeds University, which was also active in standards development in ISO TC184/SC4, and in 2000 I was invited to be their Shell Visiting Professor.

Finally, the data model was published as ISO 15926-2 in 2003, accidentally at almost the same time as ISO TS 18876 parts 1&2. I have used some of the slides developed by Jan Sullivan as training material for ISO 15926 in this book, and thank him for permission to do so.

It was at my first ISO TC184/SC4 meeting in 1993 that I was told that I had not developed a data model, but instead an ontology—the first time I had heard the word. I did look it up, but did not think too much more about it until I came across Chris Partridge and the 4-Dimensionalism he introduced me to, which is a particular approach to ontology. Since then I have educated myself to a reasonable extent in both the tools of ontology, namely logic, and some of the ideas from philosophical ontology, in particular a more thorough grounding in 4-Dimensionalism, objections to it, possible worlds, and other related topics. I have been particularly fortunate that Leeds University had Professor Peter Simons in its Department of Philosophy, famous for his book *Parts: An Ontology*, and an active computer science ontology group under Professor Tony

Cohn, in particular Dr. John Stell. Together with active partici-
pation in the Ontolog Forum these have provided lively stimula-
tion and challenges from an ontological perspective.

It was not all theory. There were practical implementations
as well. I was involved in a European Commission supported
project PIPPIN[5] between 1996 and 1998, which was about
developing software solutions for the problem. A consortium
that included Shell developing the Shearwater oil field in the
North Sea applied the results delivering significant practical
benefits, in a project lead by Peter Mayhew of AMEC with the
help among others of Robert Adams, Richard Marsh, Ian Bailey,
and Chris Partridge.

Meanwhile, Bruce Ottmann was applying the principles we
had developed to management information. With Chris Angus,
Andy Hayler, Andrew Davis, and Cliff Longman in various roles
and at various times they developed software to integrate data
and manage its summarization for business reporting. This was
initially developed by Shell, but eventually sold off as an independent software company called Kalido, at first under Andy
Hayler's leadership.

Around 2003/2004 Shell started a major initiative to develop
global processes and implement global systems for its downstream (oil tanker to petrol pump) business. This was a truly
massive program split into separate projects for particular business areas. Initially, I was a business information architect,
reviewing some of these projects' progress and in practice helping them to deliver the data specifications for their projects. A
critical area to ensure success in such a project is Master and
Reference Data. This would need to be managed at a global
level across Shell in order to ensure consistency of data across
the business. Frans Liefhebber was put in charge of this, and I
was asked to work for Ken Self in the strategy group responsible
for standards and architecture.

One of the things that was missing was an overall conceptual
data model of the Downstream Business, a weakness that arose
from having had to divide the overall project into smaller
pieces. I was tasked with developing one. By mid 2005 I was
able to put together a strong team for this task consisting of Jan
Sullivan, Chris Partridge, David Price, David Leal, Carol Rene,
Jenny Meader, Ian Bailey, and Tim King. Together we were able
to apply the principles we had learnt to create within a year a
consistent and integrated data model developed as separate but
integrated schemas within an overall entity framework. The

[5]PIPPIN: Pilot Implementation of a Process Plant Information Exchange

whole model was some 1700 entity types. We were fortunate to persuade David Hay to review what we had done, and he made many useful suggestions about how we could make the data model easier to digest.

This book is a distillation and development of what I have learnt about data modeling through these many experiences.

I am aware that I have only mentioned a small number of the literally hundreds of people who have contributed to what I have learnt over the years. I apologize if you are one and I have missed you. However, I have so far mostly mentioned those who contributed technically. Also as important are the managers who had the vision to support the work the technical people were doing. Some of those who were particularly important to me are Bruce Ottmann, Dalip Sud, Ian Skinner, Frans Liefhebber, Ken Self, and Tony Rowe, all managers at Shell; Stuart Lord, manager of PISTEP and PIPPIN; Nils Sandsmark, Manager of POSC Caesar; Thore Langeland, Chair of POSC Caesar; and Howard Mason, Chair of ISO TC184/SC4. It takes a clear vision of how technology can support business to make the case, and patience and persistence to pursue a difficult course in the face of adversity.

Finally, I would like to thank my editors, Rick Adams, David Bevans, and Heather Shearer, for their support and encouragement. I would also like to thank the book's project manager, Sarah Binns, and my reviewers Chris Partridge, David Hay, and Jan Sullivan for the many helpful suggestions they have made in helping me write this book.

MOTIVATIONS AND NOTATIONS

This part provides the background and motivation for the type of data model this book is about. Not all data models are the same, and things that are important for one type of data model may not be important for another. I also introduce a number of the notations I shall be using.

- Chapter 1 gives an introduction to set the scene.
- Chapter 2 presents a number of different notations that can be used for data models and instances.
- Chapter 3 looks at some of the different uses of data models, and in particular how they fit into an integration architecture.
- Chapter 4 shows how data models fit in the context of enterprise architecture.
- Chapter 5 looks at some limitations and challenges of data models and data modeling.

1

INTRODUCTION

In this Chapter I set out what I am trying to achieve with this book, describe who the target audience is, and look at some challenges in data modeling that I will address.

1.1 Some Questions about Data Models

What is a data model for? Once upon a time a data model was simply an abstraction of the table and column structure of a database that showed how the tables related to each other. (Today we would probably call this a physical data model.) It was not long before the logical data model was introduced, which would be described as "fully normalized." However this type of data model would still be related to the contents of a single database. Another popular sort of data model is the conceptual data model. There are various thoughts about what this type of model is but typically it includes no or few attributes and might be described as being about the things the data represents, rather than about the data contained in it.

Initially these were all data models associated with a single application. But what about integrating data across applications? Enterprise and other sorts of integration data models have been produced to give a single view of an enterprise's data or to support supply chain processes between enterprises in a business sector. Some have said that enterprise data models are either impossible to construct, or not worth it—or is it just that those who have said so do not know how to do it?

Then there are packages. Many said that these would be the death of data modeling. Were they right? How did they design the packages? How do you judge whether an application's data model is fit for purpose? In many cases applications need to be configured; how does this affect whether information requirements are being met, now, and in the future?

Then along comes enterprise architecture. What does this mean for data modeling? What sorts of data models do you need in an enterprise architecture? What other elements do they relate to? How does this affect change management?

Data modeling is a challenging task. It is often seen as a black art that some people seem to have a facility for. So how can you evaluate a data model that you are presented with? If you find some problems, how do you change the data model so that you remove the problem without introducing new ones? Why is it that if you look at the data models produced by different data modelers for the same requirements, it is unlikely that any two of them will be essentially the same, i.e., the same structure and meaning, and only the names of entity types and relationship types differing? How can this be? Are some of the data models wrong? If not, what chance is there for developing data models with overlapping scope that will fit together afterward? What would you need to do to ensure that this is the case?

Possibly you have read books like David Hay's "Data Model Patterns" and thought that these look like great data models, but how do you produce data models like that for other areas?

1.2 Purpose

If some of these are questions you have, then you are reading the right book because I hope to provide some answers. So the purpose of this book is to help data modelers understand the following:

- The purpose of data models in both developing an Enterprise Architecture and supporting Information Quality
- Common problems in developing data models, learning how to recognize them, and making improvements
- How to develop high quality data models, in particular conceptual, integration, and enterprise data models
  - How to achieve a consistent approach to data modeling
  - How to establish a consistent view of the world

- Some generic data model templates that are reusable in many applications and can be used to develop more specific templates

1.3 Target Audience

This book is for a range of modelers: from those who understand the data modeling basics but who are just starting to learn about data modeling in practice and who want to get on the fast track to developing good data models, through to experienced data modelers who want to expand their knowledge and skills and solve some of the more challenging problems that data modeling introduces.

1.4 What Is a Data Model?

A data model defines the structure and intended meaning of data. However, it should also be noted that a data model is restrictive rather than permissive.

Let me illustrate this with an old joke (well I've been telling it for a long time) about the differences between different European cultures. It goes like this:

"What is the difference between the British, the Germans, and the Italians?"
"I don't know, what is the difference?"
"Well, for the British it is allowed unless it is forbidden, for the Germans it is forbidden unless it is allowed, and for the Italians it is allowed especially if it is forbidden."

Well data models are like the Germans. It is forbidden unless it is allowed. So if you have not provided the necessary entity types, relationship types, and attributes, then the data cannot be held.

1.5 Why Do We Do Data Models?

Things can go wrong with data modeling; we can forget why we are doing it or not know why in the first place. The results are damaging: resources are wasted and the reputation of data models and those that create them is diminished.

So, what are data models about? In almost any enterprise, the answer is that data models are about improving the quality of information used in making decisions. The key thing here is to understand that quality does not mean ever more accurate. Quality means fit for purpose. So once it is accurate enough, or timely enough, then making it more accurate or available sooner is unnecessary and will probably increase costs without increasing benefits—and the net value of information is another property that is critical to its quality.

The good news here is that this message resonates well with management. They understand that getting decisions right is important and that good quality information is a vital input to decision making, even if they have little awareness of data models themselves. So as long as we can identify how what we are doing contributes to information quality, then we can justify what is being done. The corollary is of course that if we cannot show how what we are doing contributes to information quality, then we should not be doing it—and that is useful to know too.

Figure 1-1 shows the critical properties of information and identifies those that data models support. You will see that clarity—the meaning of data—and consistency—data having the same meaning for different parts of the enterprise—are critical contributions that data models make.

In addition, as you shall see, data models play a key role in the information lifecycle through their role in the design of databases and interfaces, and their subsequent maintenance, so

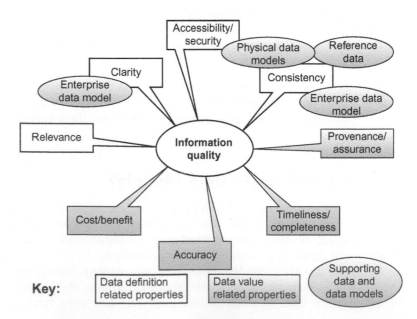

Figure 1-1 The properties of information critical to information quality and those that are supported by data models.

physical data models have a big impact on the accessibility of information.

1.6 Approach to Data Modeling

It is worth noting at this early stage that the approach I take to data modeling is not the traditional normalization approach, but an ontological one, which rather than looking at and eliminating the repeating groups in data, looks at what the data is about and uses that as a structuring basis for data.

1.7 Structure of This Book

This book is divided into three parts:
- Part 1, Motivations and Notations, covers
  - Some basics of data model notation and introduces EXPRESS, the notation I use for the framework in Part 3 and Part 4.
  - Some types and uses of data models. Data models are used for a variety of different purposes. In this part, I identify some different types of data models, explore how data models are used in data integration, and look at enterprise data models and determine when to develop them.
  - Data models and enterprise architecture. I present an information-centric view of enterprise architecture that shows the place of data models in enterprise architecture. I then introduce an approach to process modeling that incorporates identifying the information requirements of the processes as a starting point for data modeling.
  - Some observations on data models and data modeling. Data models have a number of inherent limitations, and it is worth being aware of these so that you can make good choices on how to best support the requirements of a particular data model. There are also some key challenges that data modelers face, which I indentify, and finally, I explain the ontological approach to data modeling and explain the difference between this and a normalization approach.
- Part 2 introduces some general principles for data models:
  - Introduces the principles for developing ontologically based data models
  - Looks at the application of the principles for attributes
  - Looks at the application of the principles for relationship types
  - Looks at the application of the principles for entity types

- Part 3 presents an ontological framework for developing consistent data models:
  - Develops an ontological foundation including key ontological commitments
  - Develops a high level data model for individuals
  - Develops a high level data model for classes
  - Develops a high level data model for intentionally constructed objects, and works out more detailed data models for organization, person, agreements, and representation
  - Develops a detailed data model for systems and system components
- Part 4 provides a more formal representation of the ontological framework in Part 3.

ENTITY RELATIONSHIP MODEL BASICS

This chapter introduces a number of notations for representing data and data models and considers some of the basic limitations and choices that have to be made in developing data models.

2.1 Oh, It's Boxes and Lines Again...

There are a plethora of different notations for data models, and in addition to that, we sometimes need to model data instances to get the true picture of what is going on (indeed, this is one of the secrets of successfully modeling complex domains). One of my friends and colleagues, Jan Sullivan, has been around long enough that when presented with a new diagramming convention for data models, he studies it earnestly, asks some pertinent questions, and then allows a look of comprehension to pass across his face as he exclaims, "Oh, you mean its boxes and lines again!"

I will not be using just one set of data modeling diagramming conventions and will certainly not be using all the ones I have come across, but rest assured, they are all boxes and lines! In this chapter, I shall be setting out some of the things to look for in diagramming conventions and explaining the particular ones I shall use in this book.

Although we probably all have a favorite graphical notation, in practice, we are unlikely to be able to choose the notation we use. Likely as not, it will be defined by an enterprise standard, or the enterprise standard data modeling tool, so unless you are lucky enough to be the one who sets that, you will have to be able to learn to get on with what is in use. So I think it is good practice to be familiar with a variety of notations, to help to remember that it is not the notation that is important, but how it is used.

2.2 Graphical or Lexical

At the outset it is worth noting that data models do not have to be described graphically, or only graphically. To be computer interpretable there must be a text alternative. This may be SQL, some other data definition language, or a data modeling language like EXPRESS (ISO 10303-11) that has both a lexical and graphical notation, EXPRESS-G (see Figure 2-1)—and of course UML has XMI as an XML-based notation.

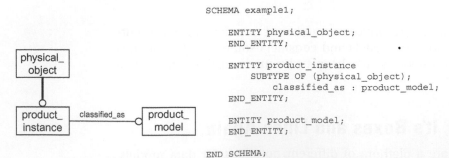

```
SCHEMA example1;

    ENTITY physical_object;
    END_ENTITY;

    ENTITY product_instance
        SUBTYPE OF (physical_object);
            classified_as : product_model;
    END_ENTITY;

    ENTITY product_model;
    END_ENTITY;

END_SCHEMA;
```

Figure 2-1 An example EXPRESS data model showing both graphical and lexical form.

However, I have always found that a graphical form is much easier to work with, and so this will be the norm.

2.3 Graphical Notations: Complexity vs. Understandability vs. Capability

When defining graphical notations, it is tempting to be overly elaborate and to have graphical symbols for everything. This is effectively the same as creating a secret code language, which only the initiates can understand. This is a bad idea when you are trying to communicate with an audience. A good graphical notation is one that makes good use of intuitive symbols, where you can still remember what they mean after six months without looking at a data model (which will be the case for many of those to whom you present your data models).

A good example of a notation that is easy to understand was developed by the CDIF (CASE Data Interchange Format) community. Since the CASE[1] tool vendors were exchanging data between their different tools, politically, they could not use a notation used by one of their tools, so they had to come up with something different. Figure 2-2 shows the same data model as Figure 2-1, but it uses the CDIF notation.

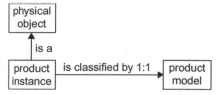

Figure 2-2 An example data model in CDIF notation.

I doubt if I even need to explain this notation. You just read in the direction of the arrows (that is all the arrow does). So "A product instance is a physical object," and "A product instance is classified by one and only one product model." The only slight complication is the 1:1, the cardinality constraint, but even this is easy to decipher for anyone with data modeling experience, and if I were presenting a model to those without data modeling experience, I would not show cardinalities in any case, since these are generally a matter of technical discovery.

Watch out for the restrictions that a notation has. An example is in the Barker methodology used by Oracle.

Figure 2-3 shows a subtype/supertype structure. A single pump can be both a reciprocating pump and an electrically driven pump, and another might be a reciprocating pump and a steam driven pump. However, the Barker method requires subtypes to be mutually exclusive. Consequently this data model is not valid.

I should say that other than this restriction, I particularly like the Barker/Oracle notation. Boxes-in-boxes is intuitive for

---

[1]CASE – Computer aided software engineering.

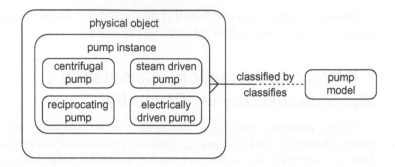

Figure 2-3 An invalid data model in the Oracle-Barker notation.

subtypes (like Venn diagrams) and the crows feet and dashed line are both easy to remember for many and optional.

So we can state the following principles for good notations. They should be

- Simple
- Memorable
- Capable

If you have a choice, these are the characteristics you should be considering.

2.4 Language and Notation Elements

In the end, any graphically based language consists of boxes and lines, or more formally, nodes and links (some may prefer the terms vertex and edge).

2.4.1 Nodes

A node is at the end of at least one link. In an entity relationship diagram, entity types are nodes, and relationship types are links, except that some notations allow relationship types between more than two things, in which case the relationship types themselves are nodes, with a link to each of the elements of the relationship type. A node can represent quite complex things, because a lot can be said about it through all the links that it has.

2.4.2 Links

A link has two ends, each of which is connected to a node. In an entity relationship diagram, binary relationship types are links. There is normally very little that can be said about a link, because it is not a first class object. That is to say that a link does not itself have other links, which limits what you can say about it to what is predefined in the metamodel. For example, with entity relationship diagrams, the name and cardinality constraints are allowed.

One still needs to be clear about the nature of the link. The link does not necessarily represent a direct link between the nodes. For example, in entity relationship diagrams, the link generally represents a class of relationship; that is, it is saying that instances of one entity type can or do have a relationship to instances of another entity type. The class of relationship is instantiated in the foreign keys of records that are instances of the entity type.

In many data modeling languages, a special relationship—the subtype/supertype relationship—is supported. When a data model is about the objects in the real world, then this is a relationship between the entity types themselves, rather than a class of relationship.

2.4.3 Rules and Constraints

Different data modeling languages allow different rules and constraints to be defined. For example, EXPRESS has a rather rich rules capability in its lexical form. However, most data modeling languages can only express cardinality constraints.

2.5 Express-G

This section deals with EXPRESS-G, which is the language in which the framework data model I develop in the latter part of this book is written. I therefore deal with it in more detail than the other notations I have covered, though my treatment is far from comprehensive.

2.5.1 Notation

The EXPRESS language is formally defined in ISO 10303-11, and it was the first data modeling language to be standardized by ISO, the International Organization for Standardization. It has a lexical form as well as a graphical form, but the focus here is on the graphical form, for which I describe some (but far from all) of its elements.

Figure 2-4 shows the main graphical elements. On the left you find a plain box for an entity type, the lines used for mandatory and optional attributes, and the subtype relationship. We

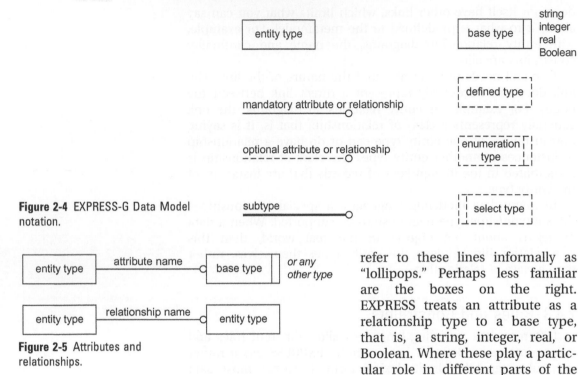

Figure 2-4 EXPRESS-G Data Model notation.

Figure 2-5 Attributes and relationships.

refer to these lines informally as "lollipops." Perhaps less familiar are the boxes on the right. EXPRESS treats an attribute as a relationship type to a base type, that is, a string, integer, real, or Boolean. Where these play a particular role in different parts of the data model, then a **defined type** can be created to represent that usage. Thus a defined type of **person_name** can be created from the base type **STRING**. An **enumeration type** is a controlled list of instances of some base type, such as a list of colors of the rainbow. Finally, a **select type** allows a member of more than one type to be allowed to play a role in a relationship type. So if you want a party to a **contract** to be able to be either a **person** or a **company**, then you can achieve this by making **party** a **select type** linked to both person and company. This is equivalent to the exclusive arc that some other notations use.

2.5.2 Attributes and Relationships

A data model is constructed by linking together types (boxes) with attributes/relationship types (lines) as illustrated in Figure 2-5. So for example, if you want to give an entity type called **person** an attribute called *name* that is of type **STRING**, then you would construct the model in Figure 2-6.

There are two useful conventions for naming attributes and relationship types: The first is to provide some connective text that reads as a sentence between the two entity types; the second is to name the attribute in terms of the role it plays in the entity type. Either of these might appear more natural in particular circumstances. The second approach is taken in Figure 2-6.

In order to save space in diagrams, EXPRESS-G allows the base type or defined type symbol for an attribute to be omitted (the case where just the "lollipop" is shown). However, even this form can lead to cluttered and potentially confusing diagrams. Therefore, I sometimes use the third option shown: This is *not* standard EXPRESS-G, but it borrows from IDEF1X and other entity-relationship notations in that it lists the attributes by name within the box that represents the entity data type.

• Each **person** has a **name** that is a **STRING**.

Figure 2-6 Attributes.

2.5.3 Reading Relationships and Cardinalities

I will now take a closer look at reading relationship types and the meaning of the various symbols around them.

Figure 2-7 illustrates the default and explicit specification of the cardinality of a relationship and Figure 2-8 shows the default cardinality for the inverse of a relationship. The relationship type between two entity types can be read in either direction as shown in Figure 2-9 and Figure 2-10.

This is often as much as is required for business use; however, the diagrams do say more about the number of entities (instances) at one end of a relationship type that may or must be involved with an instance at the other end. This is referred to as the cardinality of a relationship type. The representation of some different options is explained in Figures 2-11 and 2-12.

Optional relationship types are drawn with a dashed line as shown in Figure 2-13.

Optional relationship types are read as illustrated in Figure 2-14.

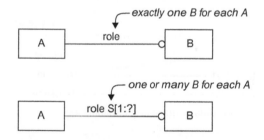

• Express-G specifies the cardinality of an attribute relationship in terms of an aggregation (SET, BAG, ARRAY, LIST).

Figure 2-7 Cardinalities.

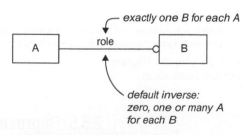

• Every relationship has an inverse.
• Default is that the inverse relationship is not named, and that the cardinality is zero, one, or many.
• Naming the inverse allows this to be constrained.

Figure 2-8 Default inverse relationships.

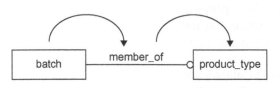

- Read in the direction of the "lollipop."
- Each **batch** is a *member_of* exactly one **product_type**.

Figure 2-9 Reading the relationship from batch to product_type.

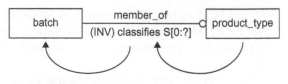

- Read the inverse in the opposite direction.
- Each **product_type** *classifies* zero, one, or many **batches**.

Figure 2-10 Reading the relationship from product_type to batch.

2.5.4 Redeclared Types

EXPRESS has an unusual feature in redeclared types. Relationships of a supertype are inherited by the subtype, but it is possible to redeclare them in the subtype. This effectively restricts the domain of the relationship to that specified in the subtype.

Figure 2-15 illustrates this. A **physical_object** may be a *member_of* one or more **class_of_physical_object**. However, in **batch**, which it a subtype of **physical_object**, the relationship is redeclared to mean that when the *member_of* relationship defined in **physical_object** is for a **batch**, then the **batch** must be a *member_of* a **product_type**, and not any other **class_of_physical_object**.

Another thing to note is that if you do not want this restriction, then you have to give the relationship a different name, something you will find I do from time to time in the EXPRESS data models, usually by adding an underscore somewhere, or perhaps a qualifying term.

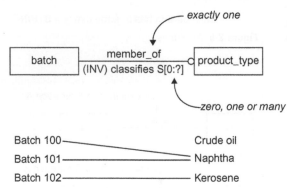

Figure 2-11 Default maximum cardinalities.

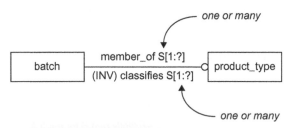

- Each **batch** is a *member_of* one or more **product_type**.
- Each **product_type** *classifies* one or more **batch**.

Figure 2-12 Reading the diagram with maximum cardinalities.

2.5.5 Representing a Many-to-Many Relationship as an Entity Type

There are times when you might want to represent a relationship by using an entity type. Some examples of this are

- The relationship itself has relationships.

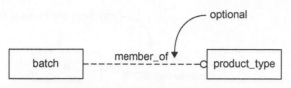

- The dashed line means that the relationship is optional for **batch**.
- If a relationship is optional, then either the relationship may or may not exist, or it is not necessary to record the relationship.

Figure 2-13 Optional relationships.

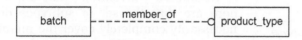

- Each **batch** may be a *member_of* one **product_type**.

Figure 2-14 Reading minimum cardinalities on an optional relationship.

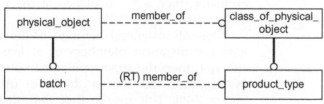

Figure 2-15 An example of a redeclared type.

- The relationship can change over time, and you want to reflect this by giving the relationship start and end dates.
- You are targeting a relational implementation, and you want to have an entity type for each table required.
- You just want to be consistent, and because you have to model some relationships this way, you model all of them this way.

Figure 2-16 illustrates how this transformation might look.

2.5.6 Subtype/Supertype Relationships

Subtypes are shown linked to the supertype by a thick line with a lollipop at the subtype end (see Figure 2-17). Thus **batch** is a subtype of **material**.

In EXPRESS an instance of a subtype is also an instance of the supertype, so it has the attributes of the supertype as well as the attributes of the subtype.

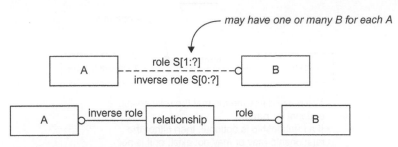

Figure 2-16 Using an intersection entity type to represent a many-to-many relationship.

• When the relationship is many-to-many an "intersection" entity type may be used to represent the relationship.

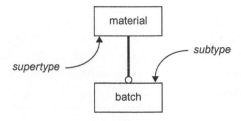

• **Batch** is a subtype of **material**.
• Each **batch** is a **material**.
• Some **materials** are **batches**.

Figure 2-17 Subtypes and supertypes.

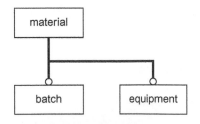

• **Batch** is a subtype of **material**.
• Each **batch** is a **material**.
• Each **equipment** is a **material**.
• An **equipment** may also be a **batch**.

Figure 2-18 And/or subtypes.

Additional conventions that are observed here are that the set of subtypes does not necessarily completely cover the membership of the supertype. The default is that subtypes can overlap in their membership (see Figure 2-18).

When the subtypes in a tree are mutually exclusive, then a "1" is placed at the root of the tree (see Figure 2-19).

When all instances/members of the supertype are instances/members of at least one subtype, then the supertype can be declared as abstract, as shown by the (AE) in Figure 2-20. This means that the supertype cannot be instantiated except through its subtypes. It also suggests that in a relational implementation, the supertype does not have to be implemented as a table.

2.5.7 Off-Page Connectors

The last element of EXPRESS-G models, used extensively in Chapter 17, is the off-page connector. In formal EXPRESS-G data models, each entity type appears on only one page, so if a relationship type is needed to an entity type on another page, rather than repeat the entity type and add the relationship type, EXPRESS-G breaks the relationship type line, and gives connector information as to where the line continues, a convention borrowed from engineering diagrams. In fact, it is not necessary for the connector to be to another diagram; if routing a relationship type line on a single diagram is difficult, off-page connectors can be used within a diagram

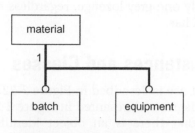

• **Batch** is a type of **material**.
• Each **batch** is a **material**.
• Each **equipment** is a **material**.
• No **equipment** is also a **batch**.

Figure 2-19 One of subtypes.

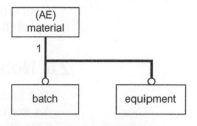

• **Batch** is a type of **material**.
• Each **batch** is a **material**.
• Each **equipment** is a **material**.
• Each **material** must be either a **batch** or an **equipment**—but not both.

Figure 2-20 Abstract supertypes.

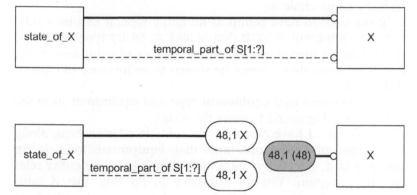

Figure 2-21 Off-page connectors on Diagram 48.

as well as between them. An example of this is shown in Figure 2-21.

The top part of the diagram shows an ordinary relationship type and a subtype/supertype relationship. The bottom part of the relationship type shows the off-page connectors (though in this case on the same page). In the top and bottom lozenge you see (48, 1 X).

• "48" is the diagram number where the entity type appears as a rectangle.
• "1" is the connector number of the other end.
• "X" is the name of the entity type at the other end.
• The grey lozenge in the middle shows (48,1 (48)) where:
  • "48" is the page number this entity type is on.
  • "1" is a sequential connector number to distinguish it from other connectors of this type on page 48.
  • "(48)" is the list of pages on which this entity type appears as a lozenge (there is just one in this case and it is the same page).

Notice that there is only one grey lozenge, regardless of how many relationship types **X** has.

2.6 Notation for Instances and Classes

The instance notation I use is described in Figure 2-22.

An example instance diagram is presented in Figure 2-23.

This diagram shows that there is an object identified as #1234. It is a member of the class pump. Pump is a subtype of equipment item and a member of equipment type. Equipment item is an instance of class of individual.

Now if we remember the constraints described earlier on what can be expressed in an entity relationship diagram, it will become clear that not all of this can be expressed, and we have to make some choices.

If we want to have **pump** as an entity type, it can be a subtype of equipment item, if that is also an entity type. However, pump cannot then be shown as an instance of equipment type, and equipment item cannot be shown as an instance of class of individual.

Let us choose that **equipment type** and **equipment item** are entity types. Figure 2-24 shows the result.

Notice that I have removed the subtype relationships, along with **class of individual**, and that **equipment item** is an instance of it, since these facts cannot be said in the entity relationship diagram. You do not have to do this, but if non-expressible elements are left, it is useful to note that they are not expressed as part of the final model. Notice that the result

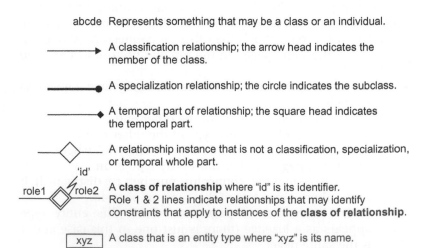

Figure 2-22 Notation for instance diagrams.

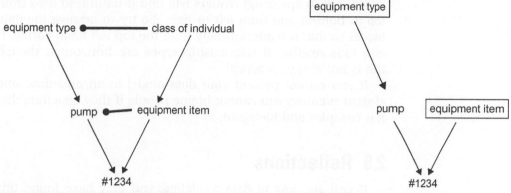

Figure 2-23 Example instance diagram. **Figure 2-24** Stage two, deciding which shall be entity types.

is a diagram in which everything that is not an entity type is an instance of at least one thing that is an entity type.

2.7 Layout of Data Models

Data models can be difficult to read for experts and almost impossible for non-data modelers, unless considerable care is taken in laying them out. For example, few could fail to find a 1700 entity type data model on a single sheet anything but intimidating. So, although I do not want to be prescriptive about how data models should be laid out, I will set out some principles that I have found useful.

2.7.1 Subject Areas for Presentation and Definition

The first principle is to try to divide the data model into sections for presentation. Most tools allow for this. Fortunately, the amount of data model that will fit on a page of A4 paper or a computer screen comfortably, about 10−15 entity types, is about the size that most people can tackle without being overwhelmed. So try to break it up that way, repeating entity types between diagrams as necessary, or using the off-page connectors of EXPRESS-G.

2.7.2 The Layout of the Page

One of the freedoms of entity relationship models is that the boxes and lines can go anywhere you want. However, you will make life easier for your audience if you remember that most of your (English speaking) readers will find it natural to read from top to bottom and from left to right. So try to arrange the data model so that it reads naturally from the top left hand corner. It also aids reading if relationship types are horizontal, though this is not always practical.

If you cannot present your data model in an organized and elegant manner, you cannot blame people if they conclude that it is complex and inelegant.

2.8 Reflections

If you are new to data modeling, you may have found this chapter a little bewildering with so many notations presented. There are, I'm afraid, even more notations than these that you may be faced with—I have not tackled one of the most popular, UML, here for example. However, the reality is that many notations are in use, and you need to get used to dealing with different notations and to realize that although we are each allowed our favorites, there is no one right way to draw data models. If you are unfamiliar with the notations presented in this chapter, study them some more; then use this chapter as a reference as you work through the rest of the book.

3

SOME TYPES AND USES OF DATA MODELS

CHAPTER OUTLINE

In this chapter I will look at some of the different types and uses of data models that can be found, what they are good for, what the differences are between them, and the sorts of data model that are the focus in this book. I will then analyze the needs of an integration architecture and the special requirements it puts on a data model.

3.1 Different Types of Data Models

One of the things you often find people arguing about is what a data model is, and what it is for. Here's one of the secrets of analysis: when you find people arguing passionately about something, try to discover why they are both right. So it is with data models. Data models have many purposes. These cause differences in both style and content, which can cause confusion, surprise, and disagreement. This section looks at some different types of data models (I do not claim necessarily to have exhausted the possibilities) and how their purposes might lead them to differ for nominally the same scope. A particular data model may be of more than one of the types identified.

3.1.1 Physical Data Model

A *physical data model* represents the actual structure of a database—tables and columns, or the messages sent between computer processes. Here the entity types usually represent tables, and the relationship type lines represent the foreign keys between tables. The data model's structure will often be tuned to the particular needs of the processes that operate on the data to ensure adequate performance. It will typically include

- Restrictions on the data that can be held
- Denormalization to improve performance of specific queries
- Referential integrity rules to implement relationship types
- Rules and derived data that are relevant to the processes of the application(s) the physical data model serves

3.1.2 Logical Data Model

There is a range of views on what a logical data model is. So I will start by talking about how I see them and then mention the divergences that I have noticed.

A *logical data model* is a fully attributed data model that is fully normalized. *Fully attributed* means that the entity types have all the attributes and relationship types for all the data that is required by the application(s) it serves. It may include

- Restrictions on the data that can be held
- Rules and derived data that are relevant to the processes of the application(s) the logical data model serves

The main difference I see from this in practice is that many data models that are described as logical actually have some level of denormalization in them, particularly where change over time is involved.

A logical data model might relate to a physical data model, but this is not the only possibility. For example, with a software application, it would be quite appropriate for a logical data model to be developed of the user view of the application through the screens, and/or the computer interfaces to and from the application. This might be considerably less flexible than the underlying database, with restrictions imposed either by the application code, or by the configuration of the application.

It should be clear from this description that a physical data model can also be a logical data model, provided it does not include any denormalizations.

3.1.3 Conceptual Data Model

As with logical data models, there are some differing opinions about what a conceptual data model is. So again, I will state the way that I understand the term and then identify some key variations I have noticed.

A *conceptual data model* is a model of the things in the business and the relationships among them, rather than a model of the data about those things. So in a conceptual data model, when you see an entity type called car, then you should think about pieces of metal with engines, not records in databases. As a result, conceptual data models usually have few, if any, attributes. What would often be attributes may well be treated as entity types or relationship types in their own right, and where information is considered, it is considered as an object in its own right, rather than as being necessarily about something else. A conceptual data model may still be sufficiently attributed to be fully instantiable, though usually in a somewhat generic way.

Variations in view seem to focus on the level of attribution and therefore whether or not a conceptual data model is instantiable.

A conceptual data model might include some rules, but it would not place limits on the data that can be held about something (whether or not it was instantiable) or include derived data.

The result of this is that it is possible for a conceptual data model and a logical data model to be very similar, or even the same for the same subject area, depending on the approach that is taken with each.

3.1.4 Canonical Data Model

In the context of data models, a *canonical data model* means a data model that is fully normalized and in which no derived data is held. So a logical data model might or might not also be a canonical data model.

3.1.5 Application Data Model

An *application data model* is (obviously) one that relates to a particular application. It may be any or all of the following data models: conceptual, logical, physical, or canonical.

3.1.6 Business Requirements Data Model

The purpose of a *business requirements data model* is to capture and reflect a statement of business requirements. For such a model, it is important that the notation is simple and easily understood. This data model will form a basis for further analysis, so it does not need to capture all the detail. It can also function as a useful framework for capturing business rules as part of the definition of the entity types.

So this type of data model is essentially a simplified conceptual data model—perhaps without cardinalities and without taking account of change over time, since most users do not understand their implications. My preferred notation for this, first introduced by CDIF (CASE Data Interchange Format) is particularly easy to read. It consists of boxes and arrows with the names of the relationship types on them, where the direction of the arrow just tells you in which direction to read the relationship type name. This is very easy and natural to read. Figure 3-1 shows an example of how such a data model might look.

The idea is that you can just read around it following the arrows, to get phrases like

- **Order** of **offering** of **product** at **price**.
- **Order** from **customer**.
- **Order** delivered to **address**.
- **Address** within **location**.
- **Delivery charge** for **product** to **location**.

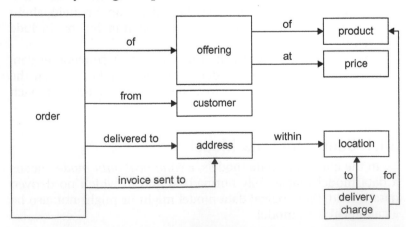

Figure 3-1 A business requirements data model for part of an order data model.

3.1.7 Integration Data Model

An *integration data model* integrates a number of separate applications. In order to do this, it needs to be instantiable. Its scope is usually either all the data for the applications it integrates or any data that is shared between at least two of these applications.

You can also use an integration data model to share data between enterprises, for example, in the supply chain.

3.1.8 Enterprise Data Model

An *enterprise data model* is a type of integration model that covers all (well, probably most in practice) of the data of an enterprise. Your Enterprise Architecture may include enterprise-wide data models that are also conceptual, logical, or physical data models.

For most types of data model, it is fairly obvious when you need to develop them. Enterprise data models, however, seem to be the exception. There are many cases where enterprise data model projects have been abandoned, or where the results have languished unused, even when what was asked for has been delivered. The reason for these failures is usually straightforward: It was not clear at the outset what questions the enterprise data model needed to provide the answers for nor was it clear what the economic imperative to answer these questions was.

Establishing the questions to be answered as the purpose of the enterprise data model is not only good because it means you have a clear purpose, it also means you know when you can stop data modeling. Otherwise it is perfectly possible and very tempting to develop the enterprise data model to a level of detail that is unnecessary, and this adds both cost and time to the exercise. It is, of course, always possible to return to the enterprise data model later and develop more detail when questions arise that require that detail.

There are two occasions when I think an enterprise data model is clearly justified. The first is when a major business re-engineering project is being undertaken and the processes of the enterprise are being fundamentally revised. In this case, developing an enterprise data model alongside the enterprise process model will deliver significant value to the re-engineering process. The second occasion arises from a bottom-up approach to enterprise architecture. As the need arises to integrate across applications, a logical data model showing the overlaps between the various systems becomes necessary. A key element of this will be master and reference data, since it is getting this consistent that enables consistency across different applications, but also the data exchanged between systems will need to be in scope. Since most transaction data is eventually transferred to data warehouses and reporting systems, it is likely that this will grow to cover most of the enterprises data.

3.1.9 Business Information Model

Business information models are a type of application data model that is used in data warehouses for reporting and slicing and dicing your transaction data. Instead of being normalized in their structure, these models are arranged in terms of "facts" (transactions, typically), and the "dimensions" (such as time, geography, or product lines) used to specify reports. The simplest structure is a "star" pattern, with a fact or group of facts in the middle, and dimensions radiating out from there. More complex structures resemble "snowflakes." There are some special rules that apply to business information models; for example, only hierarchical relationship types are allowed, otherwise as you summarize up the relationships, your data may get counted more than once. On the other hand, at different levels in the hierarchy, you may use different relationship types for summarization.

3.1.10 Data Usage Model (Data Flow Diagram)

A *data usage model* shows where data is created and used by which processes. Some examples of data usage models are CRUD (create, read, update, delete) matrices and data flow diagrams. It is these that show how the process and data models interact with each other.

One of the challenges here is that the processes in a data usage model may themselves be things about which we wish to hold information, so you need to recognize that a process in such a model may also be represented in an entity-relationship model.

3.1.11 Summary of Different Types of Data Model

You will see from the earlier descriptions that these classifications of data models are not mutually exclusive. Figure 3-2 is a Venn diagram that illustrates the combinations possible.

This now enables me to draw your attention to the focus of this book, which is conceptual and logical data models that are also enterprise or integration data models. This does not mean

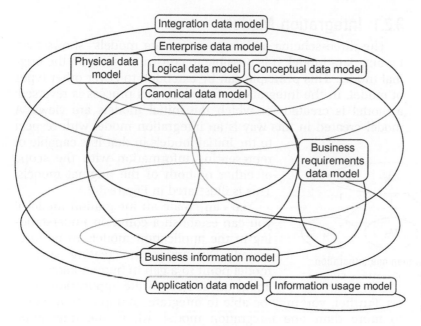

Figure 3-2 A Venn diagram showing the different types of data model.

that other types of data model will be ignored entirely, but I think this is where data modelers face the greatest challenge. Indeed, I have heard people say that enterprise data models are simply impossible, to which I would respond that the only thing you know for certain is that the person who says that does not know how to create one. I hope to show that such data models are quite achievable while pointing out some of the reasons that people fail and how you can overcome them.

3.2 Integration of Data and Data Models

In the previous sections I explained the different purposes and types of data model. In this section I am going to look in somewhat more detail at integration data models and at integrating data including an architecture and a methodology you can use for data integration.[1] The reason for this is that the approach to data modeling presented here is very much a response to the demanding requirements of data integration.

I will start by introducing the basic principles for the architecture and integration methodology presented here.

---

[1]This is largely taken from West, Matthew; Fowler, Julian. The "IIDEAS" architecture and integration methodology for integrating enterprises PDT Days 2001 (2001), which was used as the basis for ISO TS 18876 – Integration of Industrial Data for Exchange Access and Sharing.

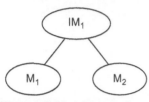

Figure 3-3 Model integration.

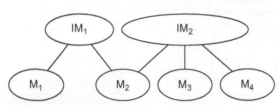

Figure 3-4 Integration into more than one integration model.

3.2.1 Integration Models

The three-schema architecture for data models[2] shows that, for any data model, it is possible to construct views on the original model. This principle can be extended to cover other types of model. In the integration of models, this process is reversed: a model is created for which the initial models are views. A model created in this way is an integration model with respect to the initial models in that it is capable of representing information with the scope of either or both of the original models. This is illustrated in Figure 3-3.

You can create an integration model if you can establish a common understanding of the application models to be integrated. Difficulties in creating such a model point to a gap in human knowledge about the subject of the application models. Further, you may be able to integrate an application model to more than one integration model, where the integration models support different ways of looking at the world (see Figure 3-4).

Integration models can themselves be integrated. This means that any arbitrary set of models can, in principle, be integrated at the cost of creating a new model (see Figure 3-5).

To have to create a new integration model each time you add a data model to the set can be time-consuming and expensive. What you want is an integration model that is stable in the face of the integration of additional models. Here stable means that the existing integration model does not need to be changed

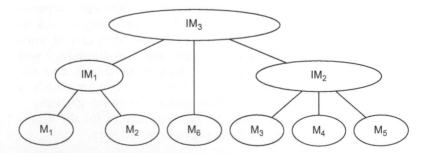

Figure 3-5 Integrating integration models.

[2]ISO/TR 9007:1988, "Information processing systems—concepts and terminology for the conceptual schema and the information base."

as more models are integrated, though extensions of the integration model may be necessary. So it is worth looking at some of the barriers that mean that the existing integration model needs to be changed, rather than simply extended.

3.2.2 Scope and Context

The scope of a data model is defined by the processes supported by its actual content. The context of a data model is the broadest scope that it could be part of without being changed.

When you create an integration model, its scope and context must be no smaller than the combined scope of the application models being integrated. Figure 3-6 shows the relationship between the scope and context of an integration model where the context is hardly larger than the scope.

If an additional application model needs to be integrated that falls outside the context of the existing integration model (see Figure 3-7), then a new integration model will have to be developed to integrate the existing integration model with the additional application model.

However, you can choose for the initial integration model to have a wide model context. This means that it can support the information needs of many different applications, even though its initial model scope is limited to that of the models that it integrates, as shown in Figure 3-8.

You can then integrate further application models by extending the integration model—enlarging the model scope within the broad model context.

It turns out that the main barrier to having a broad context is the implementation of rules that apply in the narrow context of the original use and intention of the data model but that do not apply in a wider context.

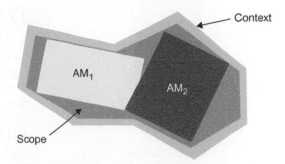

Figure 3-6 A limited integration model.

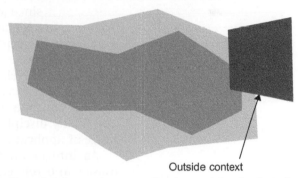

Figure 3-7 Integrating an application model and a limited integration model.

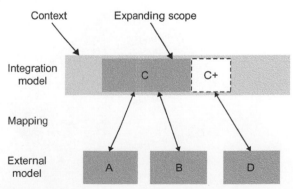

Figure 3-8 Using an integration model with a broad model context.

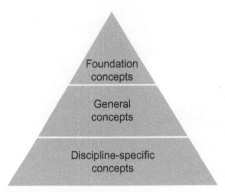

Figure 3-9 Primitive concepts.

3.2.3 Integration Model Content

The content of an integration model can be divided into primitive concepts and derived concepts. *Primitive concepts* are those that cannot be defined in terms of other concepts in the integration model, are in turn the building blocks for the definition of other concepts, and can be further divided into foundation concepts, general concepts, and specific concepts as represented in Figure 3-9.

Discipline-specific concepts depend on general concepts that depend on foundation concepts, since all the lower concepts rely on the existence of one or more higher level concepts. For example, without the foundation concept of classification, relatively little can be said about anything.

At the top level, an integration model might have foundation concepts like classification, connection, and composition. General concepts might include agreements and organization, and finally discipline-specific concepts that are limited in their range of application, such as pumps and valves.

An integration model is not just a data model. It includes master and reference data that adds detail, particularly about the detailed kinds of things that are of interest.

3.2.4 A Full Integration Model

A full integration model, as illustrated in Figure 3-10, is more than just primitive concepts; it includes derived concepts—useful and valid combinations of primitive concepts. You only need to record derived concepts that are of interest, since their existence is implicitly recognized.

A primitive concept is not necessarily primitive forever. If a concept that is initially thought to be a primitive concept turns out not to be, then you can identify and add the concepts it is derived from, and add the derivation, so that it becomes a derived concept away from the front face of the pyramid. This allows flexibility to reflect an improved knowledge of the world, rather than reflecting knowledge of the world that is

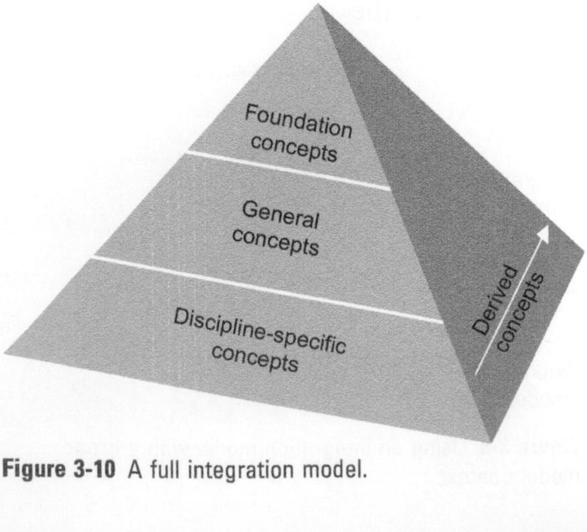

Figure 3-10 A full integration model.

constrained by a modeler's knowledge at a point in time. This is one of the ways that you will need to maintain and extend an integration model.

3.2.5 Mapping Specifications

Mapping specifications specify the transformations that determine how the instances of one model can be represented as instances of another model.

When you create a mapping specification, it is important to note that

- New concepts or constraints are not introduced in the mapping specification; that is, mapping specifications are limited to transformations of structure, terminology, and encoding.
- A complete mapping specification is bidirectional. However, the transformations of the first model to the second model may have to be specified separately from those of the second model to the first model, and the mapping in one direction need not be derivable from the mapping in the other direction.
- Before you can support a bidirectional mapping, you may need to make explicit some of the context of the data model being integrated.

3.2.6 Overview of the Model Integration Process

The model integration process takes a number of application models and an integration model. It ensures that all the concepts of the application models are represented in the integration model, and it develops a mapping specification between the integration model and each of the application models.

There are three possible cases for the integration process:

1. The integration model and the application models both exist before the integration process starts.
2. The application models to be integrated exist before the integration process starts, but the integration model does not.
3. The integration model exists before the integration process starts, but the application model needs to be developed from some statement of requirements.

The process of integrating an application model with an integration model is illustrated in Figure 3-11. The goal of this integration process is to allow the same information that is represented in the application model to be represented in the integration model without losing any meaning and to allow transformations between these representations. The result of

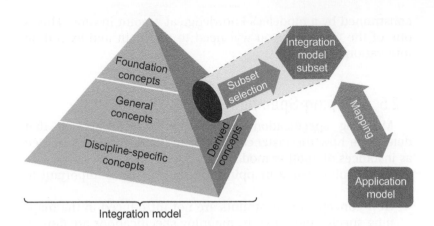

Figure 3-11 Integrating application models with an integration model.

the integration process is a mapping specification between the application model and a part of the integration model. In order to define this mapping, you may need to extend the integration model so that it precisely represents the concepts found in the application model.

The process of integrating application models with an integration model is divided into a number of steps, as follows:

1. Analyze the application models and identify the equivalent concept of the integration model, including any constraints that apply (see Figure 3-12). Most application models have a context within which the model has to be understood but which is not explicit in the model itself. Usually it is inappropriate to add this information explicitly to the application model. In this case, you should capture these requirements in the mapping specification as part of the integration process.

2. If necessary, extend the integration model so that it includes all the concepts found in the application models (Figure 3-13).

3. Identify the part of the integration model that represents the concepts in each application model (see Figure 3-14).

4. Create the mapping in each direction between each application model and the appropriate subset of the integration model (see Figure 3-15).

5. Specify any structural transformations, terminology transformations, or encoding transformations that apply within the mapping.

6. Specify any transformations that are necessary between model representations. For

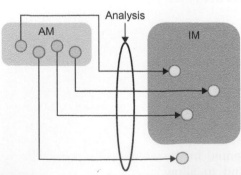

Figure 3-12 Analyzing the application models.

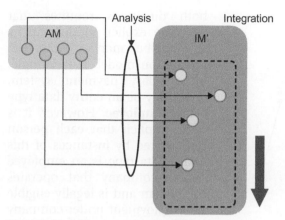

Figure 3-13 Adding any missing concepts to the integration model.

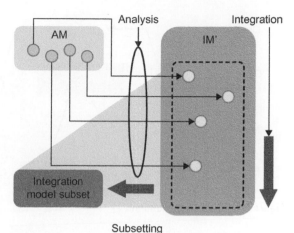

Subsetting

Figure 3-14 Identifying the subset of the integration model.

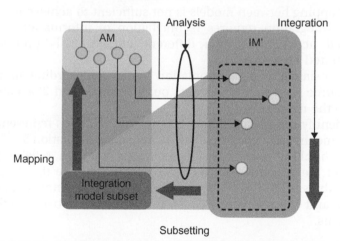

Subsetting

Figure 3-15 Creating the mapping between the integration model subset and the application model.

example, if an application model is specified in the XML Schema definition language and the integration model to which it is mapped is specified in EXPRESS (ISO 10303-11), a transformation between these languages will be necessary to map between different representations of the same concepts.

7. Repeat this process for all other application models to be integrated.

Most application models have a context within which the model has to be understood but which is not explicitly represented in the application model itself. Mapping successfully in

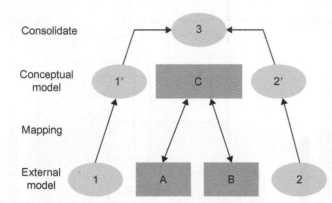

Consolidate

Conceptual model

Mapping

External model

Figure 3-16 Data consolidation.

both directions requires that both the explicit model and its context be mapped into the integration model. For example, in a salary payment system, there may be an entity data type called **employee**. However, it is often implicit that each person represented by instances of this entity data type is an employee of the company that operates the system and is legally eligible for employment under company and government policies.

3.2.7 Data Mapping and Consolidation

Mapping between models is not sufficient to achieve integration. Integration requires reconciliation of information represented according to the different models. This process is illustrated in Figure 3-16.

- Translate the data population 1 and 2 according to their source models into the data populations 1′ and 2′ according to the model C.
- Identify which data elements in the two data sets represent the same things, and consolidate them in data population 3.

It should be noted that this requires a common, reliable, persistent identification mechanism. This will enable the different ways the same object is identified in different systems to be captured and effectively provide a translation service between those systems.

3.3 Concluding Remarks

In this chapter I have looked at the different types of data model that you can find, and in particular at the business of data integration. You will have noticed that data integration presents some particular challenges, and that the desirable characteristics of integration models are not necessarily the same as those developed for other purposes. In particular it is desirable that they are stable and extensible. Parts 2 and 3 of this book are largely about a way to achieve this.

4

DATA MODELS AND ENTERPRISE ARCHITECTURE

These days data modeling is (or should be) done in the context of Enterprise Architecture. So here I will try to say just enough about Enterprise Architecture to clarify the way data models fit into an Enterprise Architecture and how they relate to other elements.

You hear a lot of different ideas about what Enterprise Architecture is for. For some it is rather technical and about things like service-oriented architecture (SOA), for others it is principally about the enterprise itself, the processes it performs, and the roles that perform them. However, I think that a more pragmatic view of Enterprise Architecture is that it supports linking information technology to the enterprise it is supposed to serve.

Enterprise Architecture provides a map of the business, including the information and systems that support it. The Enterprise Architecture functions as a significant diagnostic tool for identifying the source of problems that arise and for planning improvements. As such, it supports the management of change in the information technology–supported business environment so that the impact of changes can be understood, rather than change bringing unintended consequences.

The transformation of business requirements into information technology requirements and implementation has a checkered past, often resulting in business requirements being driven by information technology rather than information technology requirements being driven by the business. Inasmuch as

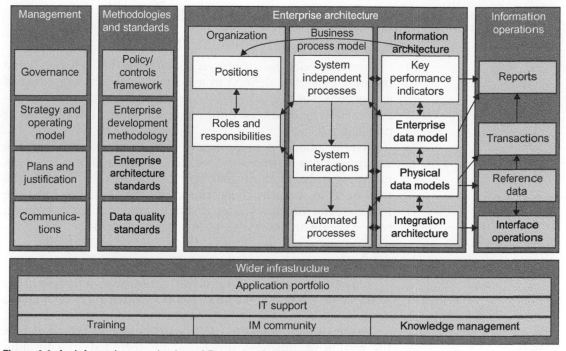

Figure 4-1 An information-centric view of Enterprise Architecture.

Enterprise Architecture is a response to this problem, it is, in my view, a good thing. However, like many things, Enterprise Architecture can become an end in itself, rather than a means to an end. If you suspect this is the case where you are, try asking those responsible what Enterprise Architecture is for. Unless there is an immediate answer (and it is essentially what I describe here) then you should be worried.

So we should again remind ourselves that linking information technology to the business is about making sure that the business has the information it needs to support the decisions that need to be taken, as well as automating those decisions that are sufficiently well defined. It follows, therefore, that Enterprise Architecture has a significant role in improving information quality; that is, getting the right information to the right people at the right time and at minimum cost.

Figure 4-1 shows a view of Enterprise Architecture that, although simplified, shows in particular, the way that data and data models fit into an overall Enterprise Architecture. Key elements and relationships are given in the following sections.

4.1 The Business Process Model

4.1.1 System Independent Processes

A *system independent process* is a process that achieves some business objective, defined in a manner that is independent of any system that might be used to support the process. The process creates or changes things that are either information or physical objects.

System independent processes are used to define how the enterprise does business so that people in the enterprise know how to get things done and how to identify the information they need to support those processes. (See Section 4.9, "The Process/Data Balance," later in this chapter for more help on how to create an enterprise-wide process model.)

4.1.2 System Interactions

A *system interaction* is a process that involves a person interacting with a computer system, such as when he or she enters data.

System interactions are used to define the workflow of how the results of business processes are recorded in computer systems.

4.1.3 Automated Processes

An *automated process* is a process that is carried out by a computer system or some other means of automation.

Automated processes are used to document and define the processes performed by computer systems.

4.2 Information Architecture

4.2.1 Key Performance Indicators (KPI)

A *key performance indicator (KPI)* is a measure of the performance of a business process.

KPIs are used by the business to assess the businesses performance of some process.

4.2.2 Enterprise Data Model

An *enterprise data model* is a data model independent of any implementation, and at a canonical level (no derived data). It is documented in the terms of the enterprise, rather than the terms of the systems used.

The enterprise data model may include both conceptual and logical data models and support views that are subject-area or process-area related.

An enterprise data model is used to document the information requirements of an enterprise as a basis to establish where different applications represent the same things, and to establish the gap between the information requirements of an enterprise and the support provided for those requirements by the applications it uses or is thinking of using.

4.2.3 Physical Data Models

A *physical data model* is a data model of how some system stores data. Where the true table structure is obscure, a data model of how the system is perceived from human and automatic interfaces may also be appropriate.

Physical data models provide the underlying structure of data from which queries are supported to provide information to the enterprise. They are also used to identify how the available data structures can be used to meet the information requirements of the enterprise data model and to provide the basis for developing interfaces between different computer systems.

4.2.4 Integration Architecture

An *integration architecture* consists of the interfaces between systems and the data model of the interfaces.

An integration architecture is used to understand the impact of a change in one system on the interfaces between systems and the consequent changes to the interfaces and perhaps other systems.

4.3 Information Operations

4.3.1 Reference Data

Reference data (some call this master data) is data that is about the key things in the business and the static data used to describe things such as units of measure.

Reference data is used to identify transactions, to summarize and report transactions, and to index documents.

4.3.2 Transactions

Transactions represent the execution of an activity and the information that describes it.

Transactions are used to record the business conducted by the enterprise.

4.3.3 Reports

A *report* is a record of performance that may include summary or calculated data.

A report may be complex, such as a pivot table or cube that can be used to slice and dice data.

Reports are used to provide information to the enterprise to support decision making processes and enterprise improvement.

4.3.4 Interface Operations

An *interface operation* is the movement of data from one system to another using a defined interface.

4.4 Organization

4.4.1 Positions

A *position* is a place in an organization.

A position is used as a collector of the roles and responsibilities that the person in the position has.

4.4.2 Roles and Responsibilities

Roles and responsibilities are the authority to perform an activity and the duties involved in carrying it out. They are used to allocate particular groups of computer and business functions to the positions that perform them.

4.5 Methodologies and Standards

4.5.1 Policy and Controls Framework

The *policy and controls framework* is the framework of controls that governs the way the enterprise operates.

A policy and controls framework is used to define the standards of behavior required of members of the enterprise.

4.5.2 Enterprise Development Methodology

The *enterprise development methodology* is the methodology for making changes to the enterprise and information technology architecture.

The enterprise development methodology is used to ensure that changes to the enterprise are performed properly, with appropriate consideration for the impact and consequences of the change.

4.5.3 Enterprise Architecture Standards

Enterprise Architecture standards are the standards that enterprise and information technology architecture deliverables must conform to.

Enterprise Architecture standards are used for quality assurance of the Enterprise Architecture.

4.5.4 Data Quality Standards

Data quality standards are the standards that data values must conform to.

Data quality standards are used for quality assurance of data.

4.6 Management

4.6.1 Governance

Governance consists of the process, roles, and responsibilities for the Enterprise Architecture.

Governance is used to define decision making and control. Without governance, different parts of an enterprise can make independent decisions about the same things, which leads to inconsistency and inefficiency.

4.6.2 Strategy and Operating Model

A *strategy and operating model* shows the way that the enterprise is to be structured and located to perform the processes.

A strategy and operating model is used to guide the direction the enterprise is taking.

4.6.3 Plans and Justification

The *plans and justification* are the plans for the development of the enterprise and information technology architecture and the justification for them.

Plans and justification are used to gain acceptance of the proposed direction.

4.6.4 Communications

Communications are used to ensure that the strategy and direction of the enterprise are understood and supported at all levels in the enterprise.

Communications are used to get the whole enterprise pointing in the same direction.

4.7 Wider Infrastructure

4.7.1 Application Portfolio

The *application portfolio* is the suite of applications used to support the business and their management.

The application portfolio is used to variety manage the applications used by the enterprise.

4.7.2 Information Technology Support

Information technology support is the support services provided to users of hardware and software in the enterprise.

4.7.3 Training

Training provides suitable training to people so that they have the skills they need to perform their roles.

4.7.4 IM Community

The *IM community* is the community of information management practitioners who can share best practice and encourage professional standards.

4.7.5 Knowledge Management

Knowledge management is the acquisition and active management of relevant knowledge about information management, which ensures that the knowledge is available to those who need it, when they need it.

4.8 Enterprise Architecture Mappings

In addition to the primary elements in an Enterprise Architecture, there are also a number of mappings that are important. Some of these are shown in Figure 4-1 and are described in Table 4-1.

Table 4-1 Important Mappings between Primary Enterprise Architecture Elements

Mapped Element	Mapped Element	Description
System independent processes	Roles and responsibilities	A mapping of the role that performs an activity in a process. Used to identify the roles needed to conduct the business of the enterprise.
System independent processes	System interactions	A mapping of what system interactions are required in the performance of a business process. Used to determine the impact of changes to system independent processes.
System independent processes	Enterprise data model	A mapping of what things and data associated with them are created, used, changed, and destroyed by what processes. Used to identify the information requirements for a process and whether all the processes needed to support the lifecycle of something are in place.
System interactions	Physical data model	A mapping of what data is created, used, changed, or deleted in a system interaction. Used to ensure that all the processes needed to support the lifecycle of some data are in place.
System interactions	Roles and responsibilities	A mapping of what system interactions are allowed by a role. Used to control access to computer functions.
Position	Roles and responsibilities	A mapping of what roles and responsibilities in various processes are held by a position. Used to control permissions to perform system interactions.
System interactions	Automated processes	A mapping of the automated processes triggered by a system interaction. Used to assess the impact of changes to system interactions or to the underlying applications.
Automated processes	Physical data model	A mapping of the data created, used, changed, or deleted by an automated process. Used for change management of the application design and usage.
Automated processes	Integration architecture	A mapping of the interfaces that are triggered by an automated process. Used for change management of the integration architecture.
Enterprise data model	Physical data model	A mapping of how the requirements in the enterprise data model are met in the physical data model. Used to define how information requirements are met in the physical data model. The mapping will also reveal information requirements that are not met and any constraints the systems impose upon the enterprise.

(Continued)

Table 4-1 (Continued)

Mapped Element	Mapped Element	Description
Physical data model	Integration architecture	A mapping of the data structures that an interface takes data from or delivers data to. Used to support change management of the interfaces and computer systems.
Enterprise data model	KPIs	A mapping that defines the KPI in terms of a query on the enterprise data model. Used to define the KPI in business terms.
KPIs	Positions	A mapping of what KPIs are used by a position. Used to identify usage and stakeholders in a KPI as well as report delivery.
KPIs	System independent processes	A mapping of which KPIs reflect the performance of which processes. Used to identify which KPIs indicate the performance of which processes.
KPIs	Reports	The KPIs that define a report.
Enterprise data model	Reports	The definition of a report in enterprise terminology.

4.9 The Process/Data Balance

In many organizations you will find either a tension between those who have a data focus and those who have a process focus, or you may find that a "war" has been won by one side or the other. Data models and process models show very different ways of looking at a situation, and it is likely that for any individual, one way will feel more natural than the other. I trained as a chemical engineer, which is very much about processes for chemical reactions. As a result, I had a process-based view of the world. So when I first came across data models I was fascinated that such a different view of the world might exist, and I spent a lot of time exploring what that different view could do. However, others might just find the difference off-putting and confusing.

My experience is that most people find process models more natural and that data models are then seen as "difficult." One common response to things that are difficult is to restate the problem to avoid/ignore what is difficult or claim that it is not

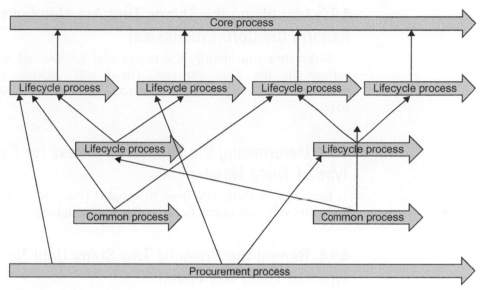

Figure 4-2 Finding your processes.

important (how can it be if I don't understand it?). This can lead to unfortunate consequences later on.

Having said this, it is important to remember that the purpose of information is to support decision taking in processes, so you need to know what your process is before you can know what information you need to support it. Thus it is essential that you see the process and data models as mutually supporting. The following description provides a systematic approach to identifying processes and the information required to support and manage them illustrated in Figure 4-2.

4.9.1 Finding the Core Processes

The first thing you need to do when you are developing an enterprise process model is find the core process(es) that the organization performs. In a commercial organization, this will usually be the process that starts with a customer making an enquiry, that includes delivery of a product or service, and that ends with payment being received. In public administration, you may need to adapt this to determine what it is the organization exists for. There is usually, but not necessarily, only one core process. Remember to include the activities performed by third parties in the process.

4.9.2 Identifying the Things That Are Needed to Perform the Core Process(es)

Make sure you identify the things that are needed for each activity in the core process. These will include people, resources, assets, equipment, products, services, methods, and so on.

4.9.3 Determining the Lifecycle Process for Each Type of Thing Needed

Each type of thing you need to support your core process(es) has a lifecycle that needs to be managed throughout.

4.9.4 Repeat the Previous Two Steps Until No New Types of Thing Are Found

Each lifecycle process may throw up new types of things whose lifecycles need to be managed. Although you may out-source some processes, remember that you are vulnerable to their failure, so you need to assure their quality.

4.9.5 Identifying Common Processes

Common processes are ones that are repeated as components of other processes. Common processes enable standardization of best practice and process simplification. A particularly important common process is procurement.

4.9.6 Adding a Process Improvement Process

You need to monitor and improve the execution of all processes. This means you need to measure the operation of each process, identify where defects are occurring, and eliminate the source of defects.

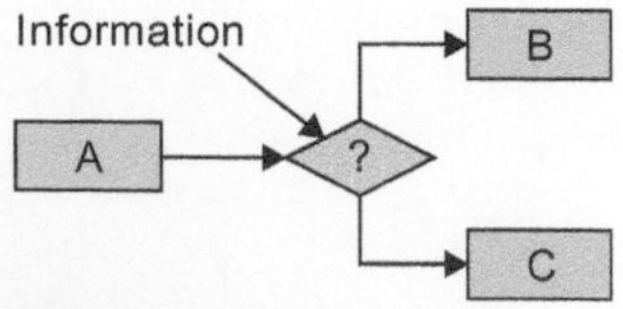

4.9.7 Identifying the Information Requirements to Support the Processes

Figure 4-3 illustrates how information is required to support a decision that happens after process step A to choose between B and C as the following process step.

The information you need to support a process will include the information you need to make decisions involved in the

Figure 4-3 The purpose of information is to support decision making.

process and records of the execution. In addition, the process improvement process will require KPIs for the processes.

4.9.8 The Importance and Meaning of Scope and Governance and Standards in Enterprise Architecture

One of the key aspects of Enterprise Architecture in general and data modeling in particular are the issues of scope and governance. These two interrelated things have a significant impact on the effectiveness of what can be achieved.

Scope here means the part of the enterprise over which an Enterprise Architecture—including standards, methods, and a corporate process—and data model are deployed. Having *governance* means that within some part of the enterprise, there is an authority structure so that when someone does not want to follow the standard, methods, corporate process, and data models, there are controls in place to ensure compliance. I like to describe this as being able to say to someone who wants to do their own thing, "Why do you think anyone cares what you think?" and "Do you enjoy working here?" You have governance if people understand that you have the necessary authority to say this.

Of course, this does not mean that if the standards, methods, corporate process, and data models are wrong that they cannot be changed; it just means that there is a proper process by which to make the improvements, and that individuals (people, projects, parts of the organization) cannot just do things differently unilaterally.

Understanding scope and governance is important, because clearly, if parts of the organization can do what they like, then there is little value in an Enterprise Architecture. So the corollary here is that if you have been assigned the task of establishing an Enterprise Architecture or enterprise data model and you can see that governance does not exist for the scope intended, you need to either

- Establish governance for the scope you have been assigned, or
- Reduce the scope to one for which governance does exist.

It is of course better to establish governance for the largest practical scope. However, the scope that can be achieved depends on the degree of business integration that exists between the parts, not to mention the size of the enterprise. Some enterprises are simply dysfunctional, with stove pipes and informal organizations that undermine any attempt at governance. In this case, it is best to understand and accept the situation. It is better to institute governance and architecture successfully on (at minimum) a project-by-project basis, or on a department-by-department basis, than it is to fail to introduce governance and architecture across the whole enterprise. If you achieve success on a small scale, some may see the benefits of replicating that on a larger scale.

5

SOME OBSERVATIONS ON DATA MODELS AND DATA MODELING

5.1 Limitations of Data Models

Entity relationship models are limited in what they can express. It helps to be aware of the limitations up front, since they can affect the choices you make as to how you represent the enterprise you are modeling.

5.1.1 One Entity Type Cannot Be Shown as Having Another as an Instance

I will talk about classification—when something is a member or instance[1] of a class—more generally later. Here you need to understand what is explicit in the entity relationship paradigm.

---

[1] I use these terms interchangeably and tend to use "instance of" when the class is also an entity type and "member of" when it is not.

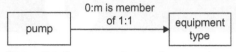

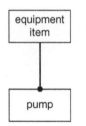

Figure 5-1 Can one entity type be a member of another?

Figure 5-2 An example subtype/supertype relationship.

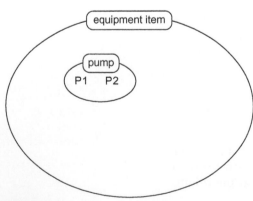

Figure 5-3 Venn Diagram of **pump** as subtype of **equipment item**.

The only classification that the entity relationship paradigm supports directly is records/objects being instances of entity types. For example, if one entity type happens to be an instance of another, there is no way to say this in an entity-relationship diagram. At first glance, this seems counterintuitive. Surely, I can just create a data model like the one in Figure 5-1 to say that **pump** (the entity type) is a member of the entity type **equipment type**?

The problem with this is that the lines that we sometimes call relationships are really classes of a relationship. This data model actually says:

*"Each **pump** is a member of exactly one **equipment type**."*

So, according to this data model, it is not the entity type **pump** that is an instance of **equipment type**, but an instance of **pump** that is a member of an instance of **equipment type**. It is the set of these that is represented by the relationship type line.

There is, however, one type of relationship that is between entity types, and that is the subtype/supertype relationship.

Figure 5-2 shows a subtype/supertype relationship using the EXPRESS notation. You read it as follows:

*"**pump** is a subtype of **equipment item**."*

or

*"Each **pump** is also a member of **equipment item**."*

This is a relationship between the entity types; however, it is not a classification relationship, it is a specialization relationship. This can be made clearer by comparing a Venn diagram for real-world pumps and equipment.

In the real world, P1 and P2 are directly members of both the class **pump** and the class **equipment item**, as illustrated in Figure 5-3.

A slight complication is that the situation is slightly different when we are talking about data records. Figure 5-4 shows some possible tables that might be used to represent instances of the real world **pump** and **equipment item** classes. The key thing to note is that there is a record in *each* table that represents the pump, whereas in the Venn diagram (and the real world) there is one pump that is a member of

equipment item

Inventory no.	Manufacturer's serial no.	Manufacturer	Model	Date of manufacture
P1	P01456	ACME Ltd	M345	2007/06/31
P2	AE45F	Bloggs & Co	467	2009/03/10
...	...	...	...	...

pump

Inventory no.	Net positive suction head (m)	Nominal flow rate (water) (m^3/hr)
P1	10	0.5
P2	5	2.5
...	...	...

Figure 5-4 Tables for **pump** and **equipment item**.

two classes. Thus, when a data model is of *data* that represents a pump, then the subtype/supertype relationship is saying that for each record in the **pump** table there is also a record in the **equipment item** table that represents the same pump.

The consequence of this is that when we use data models to talk about objects in the real world, then a subtype/supertype relationship is a relationship instance between the entity types; however, when it is a model of the data structures in a database, then it is a class of relationship, where the relationship is one of the records in the two tables representing the same thing.

It is a very desirable characteristic of data models that they can be developed as models of things that exist in the real world but then be used as models of data records. However, this example makes it clear that you need to make sure in which way you are using the data model since its meaning is subtly different under different interpretations.

5.1.2 An Entity Type Cannot Be Shown as Having an Instance of Any Entity Type as a Subtype

Continuing with the equipment example, let us take a look at another limitation. You cannot show a subtype relationship between an entity type and an instance of any entity type in the data model. This ought to be fairly obvious, because the only relationship that is supported between entity types and instances is being an instance (member) of the entity type. Figure 5-5 illustrates this issue.

This model allows an **equipment item** to be classified by an **equipment type**. Pump is an example

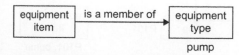

Figure 5-5 Unexpressable subtype relationship.

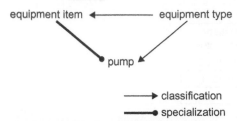

Figure 5-6 The relationships between **equipment item**, **equipment type**, and pump.

instance of **equipment type**. We already saw in the Venn diagram of Figure 5-3 that pump is a subtype of **equipment item**. However, there is no way to show this in the data model when pump is represented as an instance of **equipment type**. That is, there is no way to link the pump instance of **equipment type** to the entity type **equipment item**. The full set of relationships is illustrated in Figure 5-6, but this is not an entity-relationship model.

By the way, **equipment item** is also an instance of **equipment type**, and this cannot be shown in the entity-relationship diagram either. However, you can make an instance of **equipment type** that replicates the entity type **equipment item**, and then you can add a specialization relationship to **equipment type** and show at the instance level that pump is a subtype of equipment item, just as at the data model level you can add an entity type called **pump** as a subtype of **equipment item**.

5.1.3 Understanding the Limitations

It is important that you understand the limitations I just described. They will influence how you choose to model a particular situation so that you are able to say the things that are most important.

5.1.4 Data Model vs. Reference Data

A key choice then is in deciding which things are represented as entity types, and which things are represented as instances of entity types. Of course only classes (things that have members or instances) can be entity types, but you can model classes either as entity types or as instances of entity types. Deciding where to draw the line is an important decision, since it can significantly impact how understandable your data model is and how flexible it is (how stable it is in the face of changing requirements).

As an example, Figure 5-7 shows two ways in which you can show that P101 is a pump. In the first case, P101 is an instance of the entity type **pump**. In the second case P101 is classified by an instance of **equipment_type**.

Notice that there is no way in the second case to show that pump is a subtype of the entity type **equipment_item**. You can also see that the entity

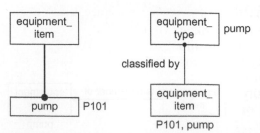

Figure 5-7 The difference between representing pump as an entity type or as reference data.

type, **equipment_type**, is essentially part of the metamodel for the first case. This means this style of data model can have an unfamiliar feel. On the other hand, the second case is easy to extend with other equipment types as reference data, even after the system has been built. The choice between these two approaches will depend on the purpose of the data model. Indeed, an important design choice when designing database systems is where to place the divide in the ontology between what part is in the data model and what part is in the master and reference data.

One of the techniques we used in developing the ISO 15926-2 data model was to start by developing a composite model of instances and classes without making commitments, and then to decide which classes would be entity types after we had explored the problem space. This turned out to be the fastest way to do the analysis, since it significantly reduced the number of mistakes we were making, even though initially it looked like extra work.

I introduced a way to model classes and instances together in one diagram in Section 2.6 and used in Figure 5-6, which allows you to defer the choice of which classes will be entity types. It is based on, and almost identical to, the conventions we used in developing the ISO 15926-2 data model.

5.2 Challenges in Data Modeling

One of the key challenges data modelers face is that the characteristics of a good data model depend on the purpose. So something could be appropriate in the context of an application data model, but not in the context of an enterprise or integration data model. As stated earlier, I shall be looking at what makes a good enterprise or integration data model. This means, among other things, that I will look at what it is in some application data models that may mean they are not directly suitable as integration data models, and why an integration or enterprise data model cannot be constructed simply by aggregating together the available application data models.

5.2.1 Key Requirements for Information Systems

To manage information, you need to be able to meet the following requirements:
- Know what information exists and what it is about.
- Extract portions of the information suitable for a particular purpose.

- Exchange data between organizations and systems.
- Integrate information from different sources, resolving what information is about things they already have information about, and what is about new things.
- Share the same data between applications and users with different views.
- Manage the data, including history, for life.

It is not unusual for meeting some or all of these requirements to be difficult and expensive. So it is worth looking at the underlying causes of why this is so.

5.2.2 The Reality of Computer-Based Information

You may find a number of problems as a result of the way information systems hold data:

- Arbitrary or inappropriate restrictions are placed on the data that can be held because of the data structures and constraints imposed.
- Historical data cannot be held because the data structure is designed to hold the current state only, and because it replaces the previous state with the current one when it changes.
- False data may be introduced to overcome restrictions. When data requirements are not supported by a system, users may use fields for unintended purposes. This will mean that usage will not match that intended by the data model. Sometimes more than one group will use the same field for different purposes, which means that not only does the usage not match the intention, but the usage is inconsistent.
- Uncontrolled redundancy of data arises from the same data occurring and being updated in multiple systems. This requires subsequent reconciliation of different versions.
- Difficulty may arise in integrating data from different sources because of incompatibility in the definitions and format of data. Indeed, consistency between systems can only be expected if positive action was taken at the outset to ensure consistency.

All of these problems either restrict the way a company does business or add to the cost of doing business. Here are some financial and time penalties incurred when these problems are encountered:

- Translating data is expensive. The cost of interfaces to translate the meaning of data from one system to another can account for 25 to 70 percent of the total cost of a system development project.

- The need to translate data means that users of different systems can often only share data sequentially, and not concurrently. This can extend the time required for critical business processes.
- There is a slower response to the need for change in systems. Interfaces cost time as well as money to change.
- Quality suffers. Uncontrolled replication of data invites errors, which may lead to inferior business decisions.
- Staff time is wasted trying to locate and reconcile data.

5.2.3 The Role of Data Models

Data models, and especially integration and enterprise data models, support data and computer systems by providing a single definition and format for data. If this is used consistently across systems, then they can achieve data compatibility. An integration data model or enterprise data model provides the definition and format applications need in order to exchange and integrate data. Each application knows how fields are to be used because of the way they are mapped to the integration or enterprise data model. The results of this are shown in Figure 5-8.

However, systems and interfaces often cost more than they should to build, operate, and maintain. They may also constrain the business rather than support it. A major cause of this is that the quality of the data models implemented in systems and interfaces is poor.

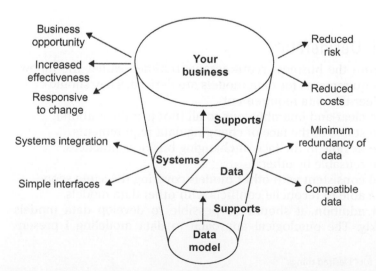

Figure 5-8 How data models deliver benefit.

- Business rules, specific to how things are done in a particular place, are often fixed in the structure of a data model. This means that small changes in the way business is conducted lead to large changes in computer systems and interfaces.
- Entity types are often not defined or incorrectly defined. This can lead to replication of data, data structure, and functionality, together with the attendant costs of that duplication in development and maintenance.
- Data models for different systems are arbitrarily different. This is because each system was approached independently, without regard for how the data might be shared in the future. The result of this is that complex interfaces are required between systems in order to share data.
- Fixing the data model of the physical database is not sufficient to ensure compatibility. Some organizations have standardized on a particular application in order to fix the data model and ensure compatibility. Later, however, they discovered that different implementations of the system were incompatible because of the way that they had been configured and used.
- Data cannot easily be shared electronically with customers and suppliers because the structure and meaning of data has not been standardized. For example, product catalogs and engineering design data and drawings for the process plant are still sometimes exchanged on electronic paper.

The reason for these problems is a lack of appropriate standards that will ensure that data models will both meet business needs and be consistent.

5.2.4 Desiderata[2]

From the business requirements outlined earlier the following requirements for data models are derived. They should

- Meet the data requirement.
- Be clear and unambiguous to all (not just the authors).
- Be stable in the face of changing data requirements.
- Be flexible in the face of changing business practices.
- Be reusable by others.
- Be consistent with other models covering the same scope.
- Be able to reconcile conflicts with other data models.

In addition, it should be possible to develop data models quickly. The ontological approach to data modeling I present

[2]Latin for "Desired things"

here is aimed at producing data models that meet these desiderata.

5.2.5 Some Key Issues for Data Models

Systems sometimes cost more than they should. Some of the reasons for this are attributable to how data modeling is done (or the lack of it) and these are illustrated in Figure 5-9.

Sometimes apparently small enhancements to a system cause major rework in the system or interfaces. This problem points to inflexibility in the original data models.

This is also a major cause of the repeated development of essentially the same system. If "how things are at some time and place" is built into a system, then any restrictions imposed by the system must be accepted by anyone wishing to use it. Otherwise the system will be misused or rejected. This is the challenge faced by those who build packages.

System interfaces account for 25 to 70 percent of the development and support costs of current systems. The primary reason for this cost is that these systems do not share or are not mapped to a common data model. If data models are developed and implemented on a system-by-system basis, then not only is

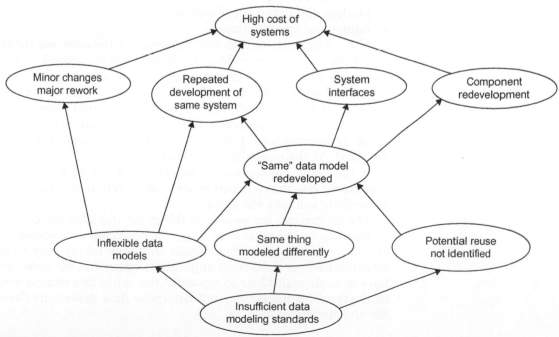

Figure 5-9 Some issues for data models.

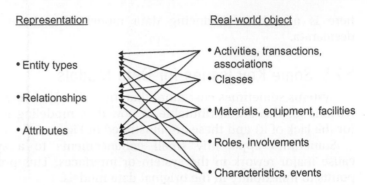

Figure 5-10 Some mappings of real-world objects to entity-relationship concepts.

the same analysis repeated in overlapping areas, but further analysis must be performed to create the interfaces between them. The physical data model development may be done with packages, but how the data model is used and how it is mapped to the corporate or integration data model will determine the degree of consistency in definitions. This in turn will provide the basis for exchange and integration of data.

Most systems contain the same basic components redeveloped for a specific purpose. For instance the following can use the same basic classification model as a component:
- Materials catalog
- Product and brand specifications
- Equipment specifications

The same components are redeveloped because we never notice they are the same thing. An integration framework would show they are examples of a more abstract or general pattern.

A lot of the inconsistency that arises between data models is because of the different ways in which real-world objects are represented in entity-relationship diagrams. Figure 5-10 shows some representations I have found in data models I have reviewed. All the possibilities are covered.

If the same concepts are modeled in different ways, then there is no way that you can expect that different models of the same thing will look the same.

The differences between how things get modeled are caused by building models that have a specific application viewpoint or specific rules and constraints built in. Since others may have different rules or a different application viewpoint, we know we have to understand how to represent the world in a neutral way so the resulting integration and enterprise data models are flexible and stable.

GENERAL PRINCIPLES FOR DATA MODELS

This part introduces general principles for data models developed on an ontological basis independent of the particular ontological framework that is chosen. The application of these principles and the consequences of not applying them are shown through a series of examples. The chapters of this part

- Introduce the principles, including an explanation of the difference between an ontological and normalization approach
- Show how to apply the principles to attributes, including examples of how applying the principles can be used to improve data models
- Show how to apply the principles to relationship types, including examples of how applying the principles can be used to remove inappropriate restrictions from data models
- Show how to apply the principles to entity types, including examples of how applying the principles can help recognize patterns that can lead to more flexible and reusable data models

6

SOME GENERAL PRINCIPLES FOR CONCEPTUAL, INTEGRATION, AND ENTERPRISE DATA MODELS

In Part 1, I looked at a number of notations, and pointed out some of the built-in limitations of data models, and also some of the problems that face those trying to build flexible, stable, consistent, and coherent data models, such as integration data models or enterprise data models. In this chapter, I look first at the difference between a normalization approach and an ontological approach to data models, and then I examine general principles that you can apply from ontology and the basic structure of the modeling components that are available to help you achieve those aims. In particular, the principles presented here are independent of any particular ontological framework you might choose. In Part 3, I will introduce a four-dimensional ontological framework as a particular way of producing consistent and coherent data models, as well as a number of principles that can be used when adopting that framework.

6.1 Data Modeling Approach

There are two approaches that you commonly see in data model development:

1. Look for repeating patterns and anomalies in the data, and eliminate them by creating additional entity types—this is usually referred to as *normalization.*
2. Look at the things in the enterprise about which we want to hold data as a basis for structuring data—this is referred to as an *ontological approach.*

This book is distinguished from most other "how to" books on data modeling in that it takes an ontological[1] rather than traditional normalization approach on how to develop data models. If you want to understand normalization thoroughly (I will only cover it briefly here), several books are available that cover the subject in detail, and I see no point in repeating their good work. I recommend Simsion and Witt[2] as a clear and thorough text.

Books are available that use an ontological approach to data modeling, such as David Hay's Data Model Patterns books.[3] However, these do not explain how to develop data models in this way. It seems to be a matter of intuition, and the quality of your intuition seems to determine the quality of your data models. The rest of this book looks to plug this gap. In particular, I intend to

---

[1]An *ontology* is a theory of what exists, including the sorts of things there are and the rules that govern them.

[2]Simsion, Gaeme C. and Witt, Graham C. Data Modeling Essentials, 3rd Edition, Morgan Kaufmann, San Francisco, 2005.

[3]Hay, David C., Data Model Patterns— A Metadata Map, Morgan Kaufmann, San Francisco, 2006.; Hay, David C., Data Model Patterns— Conventions of Thought, Dorset House, New York, 1995.

provide you with a set of tools, templates, and techniques that will enable you to develop high-quality data models that are in 6th Normal Form, without ever having to think about the normalization process.

6.1.1 The Difference between Normalization and the Ontological Approach

The big difference between an ontological and a normalization approach to data modeling is in the questions you ask as you are doing the analysis. In a normalization approach you look for the underlying structure by trying to find and extract repeating groups. An ontological approach is quite different. It looks at the data and asks the question, "What does this represent?" and then it structures the data around that.

A very simple example is given in Table 6-1.

If we accept that the small data sample is representative, then a normalization approach will be quite happy to accept that **EQUIPMENT** is a single entity type with two attributes: *ID* and *type*. However, an ontological approach will not. It will ask the question of each attribute, "What does this represent?"

In the case of the *ID* attribute, you will conclude that each value represents a piece of equipment. In the case of the *type* attribute, you will find that each value represents an **equipment type**. Therefore we have two entity types and not one. There is an important difference to note here. In traditional analysis, after you identify your main entity type, you then think of the attributes that *describe* the instance of the entity type. In ontological analysis, you go on to ask what those attributes themselves *represent*.

Why does this matter? Well if you are designing an isolated application with a limited and well-defined scope, then it probably does not. However, if you are trying to create an enterprise data model as the basis for integrating data across multiple applications, then that integration is going to depend on the

Table 6-1 A Simple Example

EQUIPMENT	
ID	*Type*
P101	Pump
E321	Heat Exchanger

values in the Type column being used consistently across different applications. In this case, that might mean they are being used across data sheet, CAD, procurement, commissioning, operations, and maintenance applications. If the list of types is to be controlled so that all these applications use the same values, then this will require an entity type to hold them. An ontological analysis immediately provides this.

6.1.2 Normalization

Although I am not going to describe normalization techniques in detail, I do need to say a little about normalization, since it is inevitably the benchmark against which data models are judged. Mostly, however, I want to dispel fears about being esoteric when achieving high levels of normalization.

A normalized data model is good because it does not contain duplicate data and is free of certain insertion, update, and deletion anomalies that can lead to a loss of data integrity. If you have data modeling experience, it is likely that you are familiar with it being considered good practice to develop data models to 3rd Normal Form, but that it is not really worth bothering with higher levels of normalization, which are quite hard to understand (at least 4th and 5th Normal Form). However, the reality is a little different; the vast majority of data models that are in 3rd Normal Form are also in 4th and 5th Normal Form, simply because the cases that give rise to having to perform those levels of normalization are very rare.

As for 6th Normal Form, it is possible that you have not even heard of this because it is a relatively recent development.[4] 6th Normal Form arose from noticing that many data models are developed as current state models; that is, when change happens, the knowledge of the previous state is thrown away and replaced by the data about the new current state. Table 6-2 is an example of such a table.

When you notice that it is undesirable to throw away the historical data, you might add a date field and perhaps a version number to the table to allow the history to be held as well as the current state. This is illustrated in Table 6-3.

However, this also denormalizes the data model. So you are not in 6th Normal Form unless your data model takes account of change and is in 5th Normal Form. Of course, if you understand the need to account for change over time, and you

[4]C.J. Date, H. Darwen, N.A. Lorentzos, Temporal Data and the Relational Model, Morgan Kaufmann, San Francisco, 2003.

Table 6-2 A Current State Table of Payroll Data

Name	Dept	Salary
John Bright	Distribution	$35,000
Henry Watts	Sales	$45,000
Helen White	Purchasing	$40,000

Table 6-3 A Table with Date and Version Added— Note the Shaded Repeating Group

Name	Dept	Salary	Version	Date
John Bright	Distribution	$35,000	1	2008-11-27
John Bright	Distribution	$37,000	2	2009-12-03
Henry Watts	Sales	$45,000	1	2008-03-14
Helen White	Purchasing	$40,000	1	2009-06-13

develop your data model to 3rd Normal Form, the chances are that your data model is already in 6th Normal Form.

6.1.3 Ontological Approach

An ontological approach looks at the things the data is about and uses them as the basis for the structure of the data. If you correctly identify the things that are important to the business, and the relationships between them, then you will have developed a data model in 6th Normal Form. The goal is to represent one thing once and control duplication to maximize data quality.

That still leaves the small matter of understanding what the things are, how they relate to each other, and how change impacts them. I will focus on this in the other chapters of Part 2 and Part 3. I will try to give you a way to look at the world that will enable you to gain insight into how to identify things of interest, and how to understand the different ways in which they relate to each other, and indeed what those relationships are really about.

As a word, "ontology" is in danger of reaching buzz word status. However, it is not a word that is a recent invention. It has a long and honorable history going back at least to Aristotle. In its original philosophical context, *ontology* is the part of metaphysics that is the study of what exists. However, the word has also been used in philosophy and computer science as a noun for the results of conducting ontology. So in philosophical terms, *an* ontology is a theory of what exists; that is, the sorts of things that exist and the rules that govern them. Most recently, in computer science, an ontology has been used as a term to mean a computer-interpretable set of terms, axioms, and propositions over which reasoning can be performed. This usage originates in the artificial intelligence community, who use logic to perform reasoning tasks. However, SQL is essentially a logical language. The structure and constraints of a database represent axioms and some terms. Data in a database represent propositions and other terms, and queries perform reasoning over these. Indeed, relational databases represent by far the largest and most widely used ontologies, and some people are starting to make the link between the very pragmatic everyday work of databases, and the philosophical and computer science work on ontology to see what benefit can be gained. I will be presenting the results of my experience in doing this in the remainder of Part 2 and Part 3 in order to help you understand how work done in philosophical ontology can help you be more productive in your daily work.

I claim that applying such ontological principles to data model development makes them more rigorous, and as a result, where data models are developed with the same ontological commitments, consistency is likely to be easier to achieve.

6.2 General Principles

In this section I set out some general principles for data models, most of which would apply whether you are taking an ontological or normalization approach to data modeling.

6.2.1 Ensuring That the Statements and Rules a Data Model Makes Are Always True

As shown in Chapter 2, data models can be read as a series of statements. These often incorporate rules that apply to the instances of the data model. An important check you need to make on a data model is that all the statements it makes are true—always. A common fault to find in data models is that a data model is true, but only most of the time. This just means it

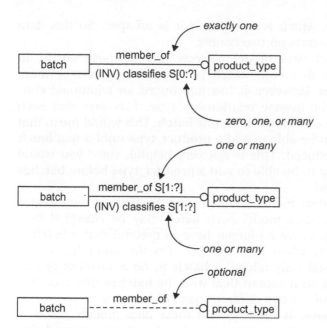

Figure 6-1 Different models of the **batch** and **product_type** relationship type.

is wrong. It just cannot deal with the times when it is not true, and this either means that some information cannot be captured, or the data model has to be used in an unintended way to capture the information. A particularly common failure is for a data model to make statements that are true at a point in time, but not true over time.

In Chapter 2, I presented a series of example data models of the same basic scenario to illustrate the EXPRESS data modeling notation. They are repeated in Figure 6-1. Let us look and see which, if any, is correct. I should point out that the purpose of the examples was to illustrate the cardinality notation, rather than to necessarily be correct, so it will be interesting to see whether or not they are.

The first model says that each **batch** is a *member_of* exactly one **product_type**. This example comes from the oil industry, so the kind of batch intended is a batch of some oil product in a tank. Most batches will be of just one **product_type**. However, there are two types of kerosene: aviation kerosene for jet engines and burning kerosene for use in cooking. It is quite possible that a **batch** will meet both specifications, so it will be a *member_of* more than one **product_type**. So the first model is not true for all batches. Another problem with this data model is what do you do with a **batch** that is off-spec? This data model insists that *each* **batch** is a *member_of* exactly one

product_type, which is not true if it is off-spec. So this data model is inaccurate on two counts.

The second data model corrects one of these errors, in that it allows that each **batch** is a *member_of* one or more **product_types**. However, it has introduced an additional constraint with the inverse relationship type. This says that each **product_type** *classifies* at least one **batch**. This would mean that you would not be able to add a **product_type** until a first **batch** had been produced. This is not very helpful, since you would generally want to be able to add a **product_type** before **batches** of it are created.

The third data model addresses the problem of the off-spec **batch**. In this data model each **batch** may be *classified_by* a **product_type**, so we no longer have to pretend that a **batch** is kerosene really when it is off-spec. On the other hand, this data model still only allows a **batch** to be a *member_of* one **product_type**, so it cannot deal with the **batches** that meet the specification of the two different types of kerosene.

So the answer is that none of these data models can deal with all the situations that can arise. So, if you spotted this when you were reading through Chapter 2, well done. In any case, it is good practice to try to think up examples that break the data model, as I have done here.

6.2.2 Definitions

Definitions are how the terms we use to name entity types are related to the things in the real world: the definitions allow us to understand what the terms mean. I have seen many definitions that were not actually definitions; instead, they were perhaps just some examples, or even a discussion that skirted around the term without actually defining it. Here I will give some guidance on what I have found useful when defining terms:

- Definitions should be in terms of the real-world object represented, rather than in terms of the data record.
- The definition should be expressed in terms of an instance of the entity type.
- It should start by referring to the supertype(s) of the entity type.
- It should provide the features that distinguish the members of this entity type from others of the same supertype.
- Some explanatory notes may be provided; for example, the source of the definition, how instances are used, and so on.
- Some examples should be given of instances of the entity type; occasionally it might be useful to give examples that are not instances of the entity type.

Here is a template for a definition:

A <**supertype1**, and a **supertype2**...> that/where <distinguishing features>.

Note: An <**entity type**> is used to....

Examples: <such and such> and <so and so> are examples of <**entity type**>.

For example:

Debt—An **agreement** where one **party** borrows money from another.

From these examples you might infer that all entity types have at least one supertype, except, of course, for the one at the top of the hierarchy. You would be right in thinking this. Placing entity types in a subtype/supertype hierarchy is a key element in how you achieve integration across a wide scope, so it is an important principle.

There are some who prefer the definition to be a phrase rather than a sentence, so they would leave out the initial indefinite article (a, an) and the full stop. Thus:

Debt—**agreement** where one **party** borrows money from another

The advantage of this is that the definition can be substituted for the term in a sentence and the sentence should still parse. However, I have found that this occasionally leads to ambiguity, so I tend to prefer the sentence form.

6.2.3 Meaning, Model Theory, and Intended Model in Formal Ontology

Since I have touched on meaning with definitions, it is worth looking at this in a bit more detail by giving a brief informal introduction to the subject of model theory, on which whole books have been written.

The meaning of a data model is divided into two parts: the formal meaning of the theory, and the intended interpretation of the theory.

The formal meaning, or theory, is just the meaning of the cardinality constraints in the data model if all the entity type names are substituted for meaningless codes. This is the part that is computer interpretable (the computer does not understand the names of the entity types either). The theory is satisfiable if there is a valid population of it. In model theory this population is known as a model. In data model terms, this means that if you have a data model that can be turned into a database that you can validly instantiate, your data model is satisfiable. Different valid populations are different models of the theory it represents. This might be as simple as implementing a personnel database with one company's data or another company's data, or it might be using the data structures to hold another sort of data entirely.

The intended interpretation of the theory is the mapping between the elements in the theory (in our case the entity types and relationship types) and what they are intended to stand for. This is where useful names and definitions come in.

Model theory is a major issue in the field of ontology in general, because theories are often thought of in the abstract. The good news for data modelers is that it is something we do not have to worry about too much, because we start with an intended interpretation and with the aim of being able to populate it.

6.2.4 Rules

Over the years I have noticed a range of opinions on the extent to which rules should be included in a data model. These range from implementing rules to the maximum extent possible, including things that you expect to change, through to only including rules that are basic to data integrity. I fall at the latter end of that spectrum. So my view is that you should only include rules necessary for data integrity, or rules about the world that cannot change, but nothing that can be changed at management discretion. This principle applies to data models that are going to be implemented either as application models or as integration models. There is no problem in capturing rules in say, a requirements data model, provided that they are going to be filtered out as part of the analysis process. My rationale for this is that if rules are implemented in the data structure, then when the rules change, the data structure has to change, and this is very expensive. In any case, only a relatively small proportion of rules can be implemented in the data structure, so you are going to have to use code for most rules in any case.

The application of rules in a data model is usually restricted to cardinality constraints, and these are quite limited. For example, a reasonable rule that you might want to put in a data model is that if A is a part of B, then B cannot be a part of A. But this just cannot be expressed with cardinality constraints alone. So for example, in Figure 6-2 you see that the **composition** entity type, which represents a real-world relationship, must have both a *whole* and a *part*. It just is not a **composition** relationship without them—recording a **composition** relationship with just a *whole* or just a *part* does not make sense.

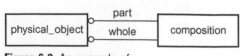

Figure 6-2 An example of basic integrity constraints.

6.2.5 Naming Conventions

The discussion surrounding the naming of entity types is surprisingly contentious with a number of strong opinions. So I will start by reminding you that entity type names are just labels, and they don't actually mean anything in their own right. It is the definitions of the entity types that are the arbiters of meanings, not the names. So if you have two data models with the same data structures and in one you find

physical_object
A **possible_individual** that is a distribution of matter, energy, or both.

and in the other you find:

E1035
A **possible_individual** that is a distribution of matter, energy, or both.

then they mean exactly the same thing. Now the first name is much kinder than the second, since it hints as to the meaning, but if the name is ambiguous in some way, then in the end, it is your job to read the definition. Having said that, where possible, it is good practice to use names that suggest the definitions and to try to eliminate ambiguity rather than encourage it. When different uses of the same word are used in the enterprise concerned, it reduces confusion to add a qualifying term to the name to make it unambiguous.

One area where ambiguity needs to be addressed is in the distinction between individuals[5] and classes. A problem in the way we commonly use the English language is that we frequently use the same word when we are talking about both a class (a type of thing) and an individual (one you can touch). So for example, we talk about business processes both when we design them—a specification for a class of activities—and in the process execution—the performance of a specific activity. The confusion that can be caused is significant.

In designing the ISO 15926-2[6] data model, we made a choice to distinguish these two cases by using the simple word for the individual, and prefixing "**class_of_**" to the classes. So you will find **activity** and **class_of_activity**, and **physical_object** and **class_of_physical_object**. As long as you are aware of the

---

[5]*Individual* is the term I use for things that exist in space and time, such as physical objects and activities, in contrast with classes, which are timeless. It is not used as an alternative to person.
[6]http://www.tc184-sc4.org/wg3ndocs/wg3n1328/lifecycle_integration_schema.html

convention, this will keep you straight. However, there are exceptions. In some cases, a specific term is unambiguously a class. The particular example we found was **property**, where there is no ambiguity because properties are **classes**. Similarly with **status** there was no ambiguity. Initially, we did add **class** to these names so it was clear that these too were classes, but this turned out to be confusing in its own right. So the moral here is not to try to be more consistent than the English language.

6.3 Understanding Relationships

6.3.1 Relationships in the Real World

In the real world a relationship is what one thing has to do with another. You might want to say something about a relationship such as when did the relationship start and when did it finish. Then there might be someone responsible for the relationship, and you want to record that, which requires a relationship between the relationship and the person. These are not requirements that can be met by a relationship type in an entity-relationship model.

So by now I hope I've convinced you that real-world relationships do not automatically align with the lines in entity-relationship models, and since it would be confusing to use the word "relationship" for both of them, I will use the term *relationship type* for lines in a data model and the term *relationship* on its own for relationships in the real world.

6.3.2 Relationship Type as a Data Model Element

I have already pointed out a basic limitation of the entity-relationship technique: relationship types (lines) are second-class objects, in that they are dependent on what they relate. You can say nothing about them beyond a name, perhaps a definition, and what they relate to (well, your tool may allow some additional metadata, but it will not allow the relationship type to have relationship types, or attributes).

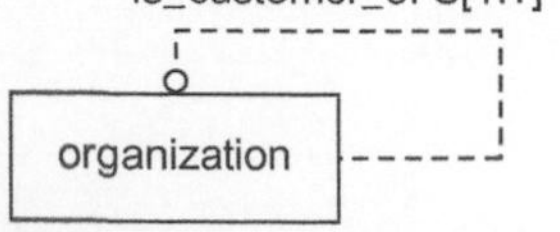

Figure 6-3 An example of a relationship type we may wish to say something about.

6.3.3 Turning a Relationship Type into an Entity Type

If we need to say something about a relationship type, then we need to turn it into an entity type. Let us take a practical example of a customer-supplier relationship (business sense), as shown in Figure 6-3. What I am talking about here is a business relationship that is recognized as being important to a company and that needs to be managed in its own right.

Now one might wish to ask quite a number of things about such a business relationship:

- When did the relationship start?
- When did the relationship finish, or is it current?
- Who manages the relationship?

None of these things can be represented if this business relationship is represented as a relationship type. So let us take the next step of turning the relationship type into an entity type, often referred to as *reification*. This is shown in Figure 6-4.

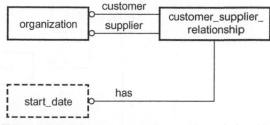

Figure 6-4 Reifying the customer_supplier_relationship type.

6.3.4 Where Do You Stop?

Help! I started with one relationship-type line, and now I have three; I also have two entity types and a defined type instead of one entity type! This all looks much more complicated than the model I first had. If I now look at the three new relationship types, I can presumably turn each of those into an entity type and two more relationship types, and so on. Where does it all end?

Well yes and no. The first data model really was not fit for purpose. It might have been possible to add a lot of stuff as attributes, but the resulting model would have been heavily denormalized, and what we are trying to do is to produce normalized data models for integration.

The good news is that there is really only one step further to go with this data model. The *customer* and *supplier* relationship types shown here now represent roles that different organizations play in the **customer_supplier_relationship**. These are also things that you might want to say something about. For example, each party might have someone assigned to manage their role in the relationship. Since either could have **customer_ supplier_relationships** with other organizations, you cannot simply place this with the **organization**. So you need to represent the role as an entity type too. This is shown in Figure 6-5.

A common mistake is to use a subtype/supertype relationship for the ones I have labeled as *role_of*. Surely, the **customer** is the same thing as the **organization**? The problem is that an organization can have multiple **supplier** or **customer** roles, whereas the rules of the subtype/supertype relationship type

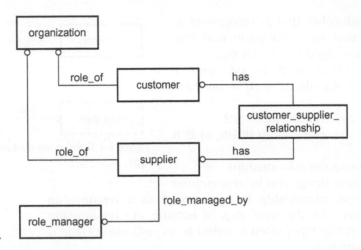

Figure 6-5 Reifying roles.

say that each different **customer** role is a different organization. So the nature of the relationship between a role and the thing playing it is more complex than simply being the object playing it. We will return to this issue in a later chapter.

You will also notice that most of the names of the relationship types in this diagram are getting much simpler and have very little content. There is good news behind this. I have not found a situation where there was something to be said about what the *role_of* and *has* relationship types in this diagram represent beyond what they relate. So this is where we can stop. This does not apply to the *role_managed_by* relationship type, which could be further analyzed. Again, we will return to the nature of these relationships in a later chapter.

6.3.5 Activities

A common misconception is that activities belong in process models and the things the activities act on belong in data models. This is not the case. Activities are things we might want to hold information about, and indeed a whole class of entity types, transactions, does precisely this. Individuals, and changes to them, are brought about by activities, and although sometimes the results of the activities are all we need to hold information about, it is surprising how often we also need to recognize the activities as well.

6.3.6 Structural vs. Semantic Subtypes

In the world of object orientation it became very popular to talk about inheritance through subtype/supertype relationship types. This tended to be used to inherit methods and attributes, rather than to reflect the nature of the thing represented. This led to unintended effects, which in turn lead to some object-oriented languages restricting subtype/supertype networks to a single hierarchy to prevent these unintended problems.

However, if subtype/supertype hierarchies are constructed strictly on the basis of the nature of the things being represented, rather than on convenient inheritance of methods and attributes, then these problems do not occur, and multiple inheritance will give no problems. So if you see problems with inheritance in a subtype/supertype hierarchy, suspect that the subtyping is not true subtyping.

6.3.7 Identifiers

When I was talking about definitions, I mentioned that entity types should be part of a subtype/supertype hierarchy. I usually call the supreme supertype **thing**, and one of the things I have found is that it participates in quite a few relationships; classification and representation are examples that come to mind. This means that there is a need for an identifier for **thing**, which can only sensibly be an attribute designed solely for this purpose. The advantage is that this is then inherited by all its subtypes, which guarantees that there is a unique system identifier for each **thing**. This does not, of course, prevent alternative identifiers from being set up, either for data integrity, or external reasons.

6.4 Principles for Data Models

Sections 6.2 and 6.3 are captured as the following six principles. All but one of these (number 4, which has been modified for this version) were in the version of "Developing High Quality Data Models" published under the auspices of EPISTLE (European Process Industries STEP Technical Liaison Executive).

1. Entity types should represent, and be named after, the underlying nature of an object.
2. Entity types should be part of a subtype/supertype hierarchy in order to define a universal context for the model.
3. Activities should be represented by entity types (not relationship types).
4. Relationship types (in the entity/relationship type sense) should only be used to represent things about which there is nothing to say. Take a consistent approach to what is represented by entity types and relationship types to help with

consistency over the longer term and with independently developed data models.

5. Candidate attributes should be suspected of representing relationships to other entity types.

6. Entity types should have a single attribute as their primary unique identifier. This should be artificial, and not changeable by the user. Relationship types should not be used as part of the primary unique identifier (they may be part of alternate identifiers).

6.5 Naughtiness Index

It was Cliff Longman who first introduced me to the idea of a Naughtiness Index. Given a set of principles, the Naughtiness Index tells you whether you have been a goody-two-shoes or somewhat lax.

The most important thing I have noticed is that these principles exhibit graceful degradation. So if you follow them a little bit, you see small improvements in your data models. If you follow them a lot, you see much bigger improvements. The choice, of course, is yours.

APPLYING THE PRINCIPLES FOR ATTRIBUTES

In this chapter, I look at some practical examples of problems that arise with attributes in data models and how the principles set out in the previous chapter can help overcome or avoid these problems, because they lead to data models that are more stable and regular in their structure.

The two principles related to attributes are

- Candidate attributes should be suspected of representing relationships to other entity types.
- Entity types should have a single attribute as their primary unique identifier. This should be artificial and not changeable by the user. Relationship types should not be used as part of the primary unique identifier (they may be part of alternate identifiers).

7.1 Looking for Attributes Representing Relationships

Attributes are traditionally the things we want to know about an entity type. Sometimes these attributes really represent relationships to other entity types. Entity types with attributes that hide other entity types are *complex entity types*. Failing to recognize these attributes as relationships can have the following consequences.

Consequences

Imposing restrictions through the data structure means:

- Arbitrary or inappropriate restrictions are placed on the data that can be held.
- History data about a relationship cannot be held.
- Data may be replicated to overcome the restrictions in the data structure. The different versions must be reconciled.
- The entity type will only work within the context defined. A change in business rules may require a change in the database structure.
- The resultant system is harder to share.

    Failing to correctly recognize entity types means

- The same data may be replicated.
- The same data structures may be replicated.

7.1.1 An Example—Sales Product

Figure 7-1 gives an example of a complex entity type.

The clue to look for is a relatively large number of attributes or unexpected attributes. This means that a particular business view is being modeled rather than the underlying nature of the problem.

The process that you follow when resolving a complex entity type is to examine each attribute in turn, discover what it means, and determine whether it is really an attribute *of* the entity type in question. The key question is, does the attribute directly describe the entity type, or does it represent a relationship to another entity type that is perhaps unrecognized?

First look at the entity type. What is it about? **sales_product** is a classification of the products, materials, and possibly services an enterprise sells.

The first attribute is *product_code*. This appears to be the identifier for the **sales_product** and is appropriate. Likewise the *product_name* appears to be a textual description of the **sales_product** and is also appropriate.

However, this is not the case for *stock_item_code*. "Code" is a word that is usually used in attributes that are entity type identifiers. So if *product_code* is the identifier for **sales_product**, then what is *stock_item_code* the identifier for?

If you are familiar with Sales and Stock systems, you will understand that there are two different views

• What does the stock_item_code mean?

Figure 7-1 A complex entity type.

of the product that are important. One is the view of what is stocked or made; the other is the view of what is sold. This is necessary because the same product is sometimes sold under different names into different markets, or the same **sales_product** is supplied from products with different specifications. Now the **sales_product** entity type is clearly the view of what is being sold, however, the *stock_item_code* attribute is referring to the view of what is held as stock. This is illustrated in Figure 7-2.

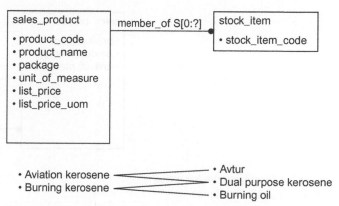

Figure 7-2 Identifying the different views of **sales_product**.

Note that the relationship type is many-to-many, as illustrated by the example of the different types of kerosene held and sold. The original model could not have catered for Aviation kerosene possibly being supplied from either Avtur or Dual purpose kerosene, or Burning kerosene being supplied from either Burning oil or Dual purpose kerosene.

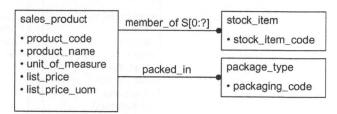

Figure 7-3 Identifying **package_type** as a separate entity type.

Let us consider the *package* attribute next. This refers to the type of material used to pack the **sales_product**. Again this is really representing a hidden entity type: this time, those materials that are used to pack other materials. Again a new entity type is created with a relationship type to **sales_product**. Here I will assume that if the same **sales_product** is sold in a different **package_type**, then it is deemed to be a different **sales_product**, but I will return to the accuracy of this in a moment. Figure 7-3 shows the resulting model.

The next attribute to consider is *list_price*. The *list_price* can change over time, and it is not unusual to have several *list_prices* at the same time when the business is selling into different markets. The current model means that only one *list_price* at a time is allowed and that the history of what the *list_price* has been cannot be held. Thus the **list_price** should be represented as a separate entity type, with a one-to-many relationship type, as illustrated in Figure 7-4.

You will notice that some additional attributes are appropriate to indicate the period over which a **list_price** is valid, and to

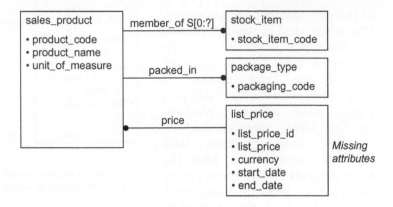

Figure 7-4 Identifying the **list_price** entity type and its attributes.

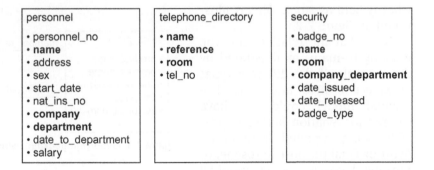

Figure 7-5 Entity types from three different systems.

allow for prices to be quoted in different currencies, but even this model does not support different prices in different geographies.

An apparent disadvantage here is that the number of entity types has increased. This is a temporary phenomenon. As the model grows in size, these simpler entity types get reused in different contexts. An example that starts to illustrate that follows.

7.1.2 An Example— Personnel and Security

The entity types in Figure 7-5 came from three different systems. As you can see from the attributes in bold, much of the data is repeated between the systems. Furthermore, each of the entity types is complex.

There were many problems caused by these systems. First, when people joined the company or worked on contract, they had to provide the same data several times. Any changes to the data also required multiple updates, with a high chance that one of the systems would get out of date. In addition, three

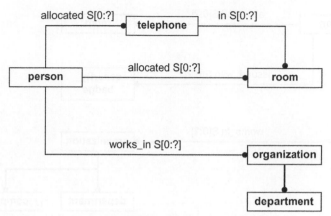

Figure 7-6 Resolution of the **telephone_directory** entity type.

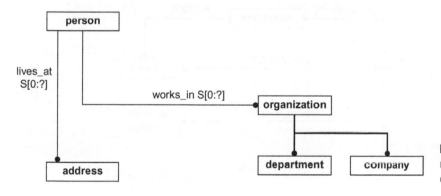

Figure 7-7 Partial resolution of the **personnel** entity type.

different systems were created and maintained to manage the same data.

Figure 7-6 shows the partial analysis of the **telephone_directory** entity type as a complex entity type.

Figure 7-7 shows the partial analysis of **personnel** as a complex entity type, where it overlaps with the **telephone_directory** and security entity types, as a complex entity type.

Figure 7-8 shows the partial resolution of the **security** entity type as a complex entity type.

Now that these original entity types have been analyzed in more detail, it is easy to see how they fit together without interfaces or data duplication. Figure 7-9 shows the result.

This does not complete the analysis of this example, but the purpose is to show the approach and its effect, rather than to complete the analysis.

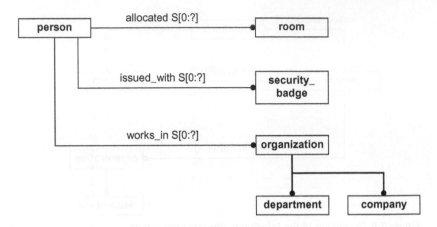

Figure 7-8 Partial resolution of the **security** entity type.

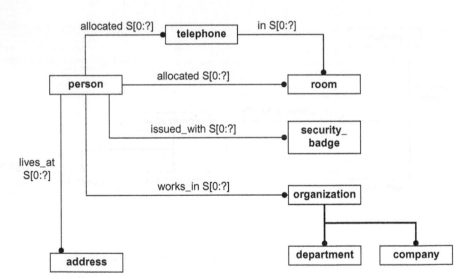

Figure 7-9 Entity type duplication/complex entity type resolution.

7.2 Identifiers

There are two levels at which identification of things is important:

1. Internal, within a file or database
2. External, across a number of independently managed files, databases, or organizations

7.2.1 Internal Identification

The purpose of an internal identifier is so that computer systems can efficiently and effectively manage data about something. Within a database or file, it is important that each object represented has a unique surrogate that is not used for anything else so that information about the object can be grouped together. In a database, this might be provided by a column derived from an attribute.

If you use a relationship type as part of the internal identifier, this makes recording the existence of the object dependent on the relationship type, and hence it makes existence of information about the object dependent on knowing information about the object it is related to. This can lead to problems, because even if there is a real-world dependence, it does not necessarily translate into data dependence. For example, just because I must have two parents does not mean that you must know who my parents are to know me. In any case, if your data model has a complete subtype/supertype hierarchy, your identification will be inherited from the **thing** entity type, or whatever you have called your supreme supertype, and no relationship types at that level could be part of the identifier for all its subtypes. It is always possible to have alternative unique identifiers based on combinations of relationship types.

Another problem that can arise is when the relationship types may be necessary dependencies, but together they may not form a unique key. An example of this can be with an intersection entity type resolving a many-to-many relationship type, when the same relationship type can occur between two objects on more than one occasion. The combination of foreign keys is not sufficient for a unique identifier.

So it is prudent to provide objects with an identifier attribute as the primary key so that you are not a hostage to fortune. This has the advantage of always working and giving a level of consistency to your data model.

7.2.2 An Example of Inappropriate Choice of Unique Identifier—Ship

In the real world things don't necessarily come with a convenient number stamped on them for identification. Sometimes we have to give things an identifier, and often we refer to things indirectly— "the one I ordered last week"— and rely on the context. It is tempting to carry over this indirect identification of objects through the relationships or attributes they have and into data models where it can cause problems.

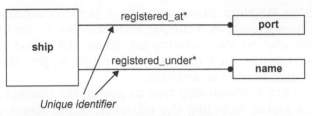

Unique identifier

Figure 7-10 Inappropriate choice of a unique identifier.

Consequences

Imposing restrictions through the data structure means

- Arbitrary or inappropriate restrictions are placed on the data that can be held.
- Fudge or false data may be introduced to overcome the restrictions in the data structure. This may have to be programmed around.
- The entity type will only work within the context defined. A change in business rules may require a change in the database structure.
- The resultant system is harder to share.
  Failing to correctly recognize entity types means
- The same data structures may be replicated.

Figure 7-10 shows an example of this.

The entity type **ship** has as its primary unique identifier two relationship types, **ship** *registered_at* **port**, and **ship** *registered_under* **name**. This depends on the context for ships: that ships are normally registered at a port under a name. However, this provides no way to identify a **ship** before it is registered or if it is reregistered. Either fudge data or another entity type would be required to show this information.

In addition, using the relationship types to **port** and **name** as the unique identifier means that those relationship types have to be mandatory and unchanging. This means that using the relationship types as the unique identifier places restrictions on the business. In this case, it is quite common for a ship to be reregistered, particularly when ownership changes. This cannot be recognized by this data model; you effectively have to pretend that there are two ships, rather than one ship whose name has changed.

This problem arises from modeling the data, rather than what the data is about. The temptation is to think that you are restricted in your choice of unique identifier to the attributes and relationships that the user is interested in.

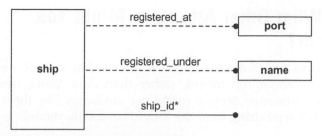

Figure 7-11 Getting the unique identifier right.

The solution is disarmingly simple. If there is not a single attribute that never changes over the life of an entity, create one to act as a surrogate for and to identify instances of the entity type. If they are important enough to hold information about, they deserve to be given their own identifier. It is further worth noting that the user should not be able to change the values, and indeed the user does not necessarily ever have to see them.

In this case an attribute *ship_id* could be added. The entity type with its new identifier is shown in Figure 7-11. A ship is always a ship!

7.2.3 External Identification

The purpose of external identification is so that computer systems, people, and organizations can know what information is about in a broader context than the local computer system or organization. This is particularly important when you are integrating data from different systems. Take for example the unit of measure kg. If one system calls it "kg" and another "kilograms," then they will not be able to exchange data. A weight of 30 kg in the first system would be meaningless to the second system.

The first thing to understand about external identifiers is that there can be many of them. For example, I have an employee number, a driving license number, a National Insurance number, a National Health number, and so on. The next thing is to understand that each of these identifiers is issued by an authority, which manages them so that an identifier is only issued for one person, and that a person only has one identifier (of a type, at a time).

The consequence of this is that external identification is best dealt with as part of the overall data model, and so it is not dealt with further here, but in Part 3.

7.3 What Other Attributes Might You Expect?

It turns out that most of the attributes that are left are actually data about the record, rather than data about what the record represents. So you might get attributes like these from the entity type **thing** from the ISO 15926-2 data model:

record_copy_created	The date and time when this copy of the record was created in the current system. This attribute shall have a value only when the current system is not the originating system.
record_created	The date and time on which this record was first created in its originating system.
record_creator	The person, organization, or system that first created this record in the originating system.
record_logically_deleted	The date and time that this record was logically deleted.
why_deleted	The reason why the record was logically deleted.
	Note: Logical deletion means that although the record is still available in the system as a matter of historical record, it is no longer considered a valid statement. That is to say it is considered that it was never true.

7.4 Concluding Remarks on Attributes

A key consequence of this approach to attributes and identifiers is that data is broken down into small elements. This is particularly useful for data models aimed at data integration. You cannot control the granularity of the data models you will need to integrate, but if your integration data model has the finest granularity, then the data from other data models will always be able to be broken down to that level, and you will have the pieces to reassemble for more coarsely granular data models.

8

GENERAL PRINCIPLES FOR RELATIONSHIPS

CHAPTER OUTLINE

In this chapter I give some examples of the traps found with relationship types in data models, and I show how you can apply the general principles from Chapter 6 to help resolve and avoid these issues. Applying the principles will make your data models more consistent, and they will be more likely to support the data you need, rather than just the data you first thought of.

The principles for relationship types are as follows:

- Activities should be represented by entity types (not relationship types).
- Relationship types (in the entity/relationship sense) should only be used to represent things about which there is nothing to say. Take a consistent approach to what is represented by entity types and relationship types to help with consistency over the longer term.
- Cardinality constraints on relationship types should be true always.

8.1 Example of Inappropriate Cardinalities—Batch and Product Type

Understanding how to represent the world is best done by looking at an example. In Figure 8-1, I have reproduced the

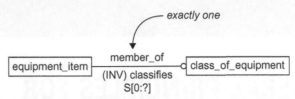

Figure 8-1 An example of a relationship type.

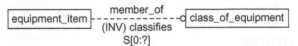

Figure 8-2 **equipment_item** with constriants removed.

model I used to explain the EXPRESS-G notation for entity-relationship diagrams in Chapter 2, and later in Chapter 6, when we were considering the truth of statements made by a data model.

This model is already better than many you will see. Often relationship types are not named, or are given meaningless names like "has" and "for" when there is real meaning to be expressed. The key thing to notice is that the entity types at both ends of the relationship type are independent entity types. That is, they exist independently of the things around them. An **equipment_item** is a **physical_object** designed to perform some task, and a **class_of_equipment** is a way in which it might be classified.

The data model in Figure 8-1 says that I can't have an **equipment_item** unless it is a *member_of* a **class_of_equipment**. It also says that an **equipment_item** can only be a *member_of* one **class_of_equipment**, and it says that the classification can never change (or I lose the history of how it was classified if I do change it). Now, this will be true for much of the time. If the only classification of an **equipment_item** is its equipment type, such as screwdriver, or pump, then generally only one equipment type will apply, and it will not change. However, in a workshop, you might well make a one-off **equipment_item** for which there is no equipment type, and in any case, an **equipment_item** might have a number of classifications beyond its equipment type, such as its maintenance regime, or its material of construction. This data model would not support these requirements.

Making the data model more general is relatively easy. We simply remove the constraints that may not always be true. The result is shown in Figure 8-2.

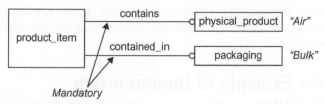

Figure 8-3 Inappropriate cardinalities.

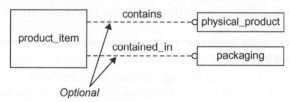

Figure 8-4 Getting the basic cardinalities right.

8.2 Example of Inappropriate Cardinalities—Packed Products

The model in Figure 8-3 shows **product_item** as the types of things sold. The cardinalities in the model say that each **product_item** *contains* exactly one **physical_product**, and that each **product_item** is *contained_in* exactly one **packaging**.

The problems caused by this data model are those that result from the restrictions the cardinalities place on the business. In this case fudge and false data need to be introduced. This problem arises because in the description of the entity types, it is explained that sometimes a **physical_product** is sold in bulk form, without **packaging**, and sometimes **packaging** is moved or sold without any contents. To get around this, a **physical_product** of Air was introduced, and a **package** of Bulk. This works around the fact that the cardinalities of the two relationship types are incorrect. They have been made mandatory, when they should be optional.

Introducing the fudge data to overcome the incorrect cardinalities can have expensive consequences. Because Air is not really a **physical_product**, it becomes necessary to introduce into the code that uses the table things like "for all the **physical_products**... except Air...." This is expensive to design, build, check, and maintain. It is also unnecessary.

Figure 8-4 shows an improved model with the cardinalities corrected and made optional.

Again, the correct cardinalities arise from modeling the underlying nature of the problem, rather than the perception of the problem.

8.3 An Example of Inappropriate Cardinalities—Ship

Sometimes cardinalities are set to one-to-many, meaning one at a time, when the cardinalities are really many-to-many over time because the relationship type is transferable.

Consequences

Imposing restrictions through the data structure means
- Arbitrary or inappropriate restrictions are placed on the data that can be held.
- Historical data about a relationship cannot be held.
- The entity type will only work within the context defined. A change in business rules may require a change in the database structure.
- The resultant system is harder to share.

Here I pick up on the ship example from the previous chapter. Figure 8-5 shows that each **ship** is *registered_at* exactly one **port**, and *registered_under* exactly one **name**.

However, what happens if you reregister a **ship**? How do you know what it was previously sailing as? The same applies to the **name**. If it changes, you do not know that it refers to a vessel that you had blacklisted, or if it was an old friend.

Figure 8-6 shows the correct relationship-type cardinalities as many-to-many, which recognizes that a one-at-a-time relationship type is potentially many-to-many over time. The problem was caused by modeling a business perspective: that we normally refer to a **ship** by its **name** and **port** of registration, rather than looking for what underlies that view.

Resolving the many-to-many relationship types into entity types leads to a data model as illustrated in Figure 8-7.

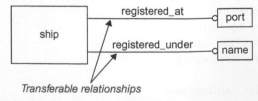

Transferable relationships

Figure 8-5 Transferable relationships.

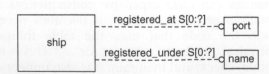

Figure 8-6 Correct cardinalities for transferable relationships.

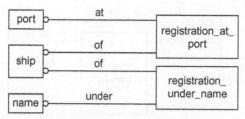

Figure 8-7 Resolution of many-to-many relationships.

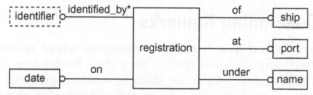

Figure 8-8 Understanding that activities cause relationships.

Now that we have resolved the two many-to-many relationships, an interesting thing emerges. The two relationships are really part of one activity, the **registration** of the **ship**. This means we can have one instead of two entity types representing the ship's registration as shown in Figure 8-8.

Notice that the **registration** entity type does not use the relationship types as its unique identifier, but has its own **identifier**. Each **registration** is *of* exactly one **ship**, *at* exactly one **port**, *under* exactly one **name** on exactly one **date**, and *identified_by* exactly one **identifier**.

8.4 A Good Example of Applying the Principles for Relationships—Transfer and Storage

In Figure 8-9, each **storage_of_material** is *of* exactly one **material**, *in* exactly one **facility**. Each **physical_transfer** is *of* exactly one **material**, *from* exactly one **facility**, *to* exactly one **facility**. Further, each **physical_transfer** *ends* exactly one **storage_of_material** and *starts* exactly one **storage_of_material**.

Notice that the sticks on the lollipops only occur on entity types that represent activities (**physical_transfer**) or relationships (**storage_of_material**) and that an activity or relationship is at one end of *all* the relationship types.

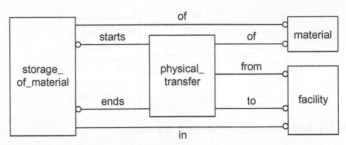

Figure 8-9 Transfer and storage of material.

8.5 Concluding Remarks

I have looked at a number of examples where relationship types have imposed constraints on a data model that are not always true and are therefore likely to cause a problem for an enterprise or integration data model. I have also shown the result of removing those constraints, and the kind of data model pattern that emerges when you do this.

9

GENERAL PRINCIPLES FOR ENTITY TYPES

In this chapter I present some examples of problems you can encounter with entity types and how to apply the principles for entity types from Chapter 6 to resolve them.

One of the biggest problems in managing data is identifying what is being talked about. That is, what is a sound basis for identifying and naming entity types? In order to be able to hold data about something, we need to identify what sort of thing *it* is. In order to be able to share and integrate data about something from different sources, we need to have a consistent view of what *it* is about, independent of the context for a particular use.

When data is context dependent, this means that the data could mean something else in another context, or data that is part of the context is missing. In order to make such data independent of its context, the context must be made an explicit part of the data, rather than something assumed.

Two principles that help to achieve this are

- Entity types should represent, and be named after, the underlying nature of an object.
- Entity types should be part of a subtype/supertype hierarchy in order to define a universal context for the model.

9.1 An Example—Combined Entity Types

Figure 9-1 shows a data model using the Merise notation that focuses on the entity type **SITE**. When you look at the

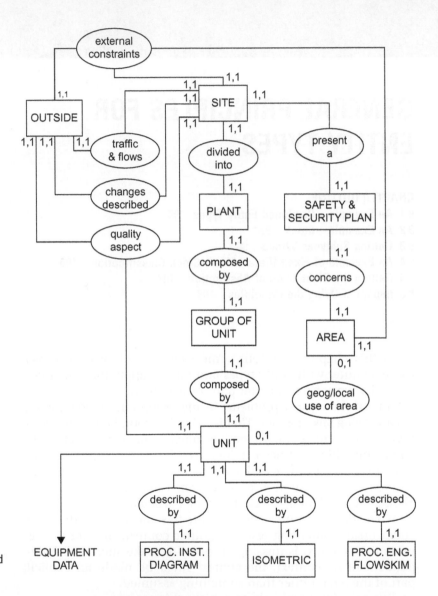

Figure 9-1 SITE—A combined entity type.

relationship types that **SITE** has to other entity types, it becomes clear that it represents many things, or at least an aggregate of many things.

First, **SITE** can be decomposed into a number of **PLANTS**, which in turn can be decomposed into a number of **GROUPS OF UNITS**, which can be decomposed into **UNITS**. This is about the manufacturing systems and their parts; it uses the names commonly used in the process industry–where this example comes from.

Second, **SITE** presents a **SAFETY AND SECURITY PLAN**. Clearly, this is about the **organization** responsible for the **SITE**, rather than the **SITE** itself.

Finally, there are **TRAFFIC & FLOWS** with **OUTSIDE**. This suggests that **location** is also wrapped up in **SITE**.

This combination of things was possible because in the place where this model came from, there was a 1:1:1 relationship between these things that allowed them to be modeled together, and the word **SITE** was sufficiently ambiguous that it could be used to name each of them. Combining these things gives a model that others may not be able to use and that may not apply given changing circumstances.

9.2 An Example—Stock

Entity types can get named inappropriately. This sometimes happens because of the indirect way in which we often describe things. Then when we describe the same object from a different perspective, we can be fooled into thinking it is something different.

Figure 9-2 shows an example where this has happened.

Here, a **stock_item** is a type of thing that is held in stock, the **storage_facility** is where the **stock_item** is held, and **stock_item_in_storage_facility** indicates the amount of the **stock_item** held in the **storage_facility**.

The misunderstood entity type is **stock_item_in_storage_facility**. If you examine the name literally, it suggests that some

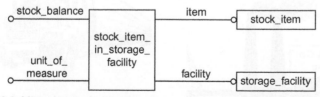

Figure 9-2 Misunderstood entity types.

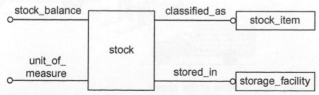

Figure 9-3 A more appropriate name for the entity type.

stock_items are in a **storage_facility**. Now **stock_items** are classes of material, so at best, putting **stock_items** into a **storage_facility** might mean putting specification sheets into a tank. This is clearly not what is intended, so we have to look for the missing words. Common sense and the attributes tell us that the entity type is about the **stock** of material that is in a **storage_facility** and is classed as being of a **stock_item**. A more appropriate name for the entity type then is simply **stock**, because we know about the **stock_item** and **storage_facility** through the relationship types. This is illustrated in Figure 9-3.

In fact, this now suggests that **stock_item** is inappropriately named as well. If **stock** is some stuff in a tank, and **stock_item** is the sort of stuff that it is, then a more appropriate name would be **class_of_stock**, or perhaps **stock_type**. The name **stock_item** suggests a type of hunk rather than gunk.

There are other problems with this model, but they are not dealt with here.

9.3 Getting Subtypes Wrong

The way we see things is often determined by the role something plays in a particular business context. This is illustrated in Figure 9-4.

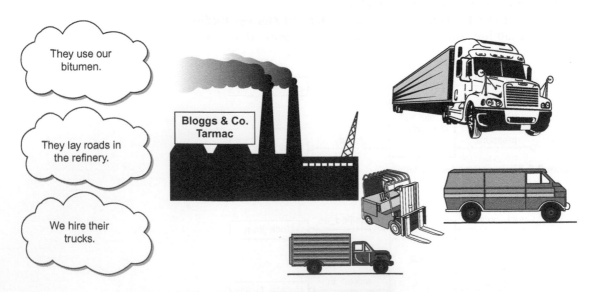

Any one company can do any, one, or none of the above.

Figure 9-4 Different roles played by the same company.

Sometimes these roles get turned into entity types, like **customer**, **supplier**, or **agent**, and since the same **organization** can play each of these roles, they are made subtypes of **organization**.

This is illustrated in Figure 9-5. It seems quite natural to say that a **customer** is an **organization**, but is it really?

In Figure 9-6 I have added some date attributes to the entity types. Now let us consider how this data model might be populated for our mythical company Bloggs & Co.

Bloggs & Co. has been around in the tarmac laying industry for a long time, and was founded in 1967, which is the start of the **organization**. They first became a **customer** of ours in 1975, which is the start of the **customer**. Bloggs & Co. did very well and saw the opportunity to sell bitumen on to others who bought it in small quantities, and they became our **agent** in 1985. In 1990, we needed some roads laid on our site, and so they became a **supplier**. However, in 1995 they were able to negotiate a better deal with one of our competitors, so they stopped being either a **customer** or an **agent** until 2001, when we were able to win back their business.

Let's look at how well the data model supports this story. There are a number of issues:

- What is really the *start* of Bloggs & Co.? The **organization** was founded in 1967, but it only became a **customer** in 1975, but if **customer** is a subtype of **organization**, then it is the same thing, and presumably it has to have the same start date. So this cannot be right. The same problem arises with the start date for the other roles the company plays.

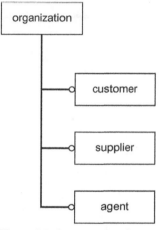

Figure 9-5 An example of inappropriate subtypes.

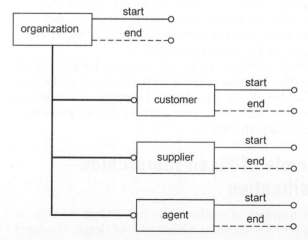

Figure 9-6 The problem with making roles subtypes of what is playing the role becomes apparent.

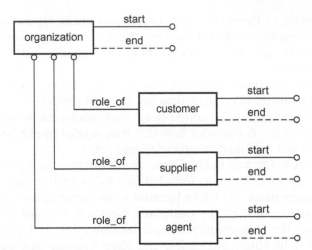

Figure 9-7 A revised data model of the roles played by an organization.

- Bloggs & Co. becomes a **customer** and an **agent** twice. Now if **customer** and **agent** are subtypes of **organization**, then each **customer** is also a distinct **organization**. So since I have two Bloggs & Co. **customers**, I should have two Bloggs & Co. **organizations**. Since there is clearly only one Bloggs & Co., something must be wrong. I could prevent there being more than one Bloggs & Co. **customer**, but then I have to overwrite the start and end dates of the customer, and I have lost history.
- I have been merrily going along in this story saying "our" **customer**, **supplier**, and **agent**, but the existence of Bloggs & Co. does not depend on them being our **customer**, or **supplier**, or **agent** (though that may determine our interest in them). Subtyping needs to depend on nature, not interest.

The answer is, of course, that these entity types are not subtypes of **organization**, however tempting that looks. A more appropriate data model is shown in Figure 9-7.

This data model is still not complete because I have not yet made the link to who the **customer** is a customer of, and so on. I did look at that briefly in Chapter 6; however, I will return to this again, and explain just what sort of things **customer**, **supplier**, and **agent** are, in Part 3.

9.4 An Example of Fixed Hierarchies— Stock Classification

Sometimes a number of entity types are linked by one-to-many relationship types showing a hierarchy of detail. However, this construct can cause considerable difficulty to the business because it allows only one hierarchy to be represented. This does not reflect the real world, and as a result, it can cause unnecessary and inappropriate restrictions on the business. In fact, it is the combination of entity-type partitioning and restrictive cardinalities.

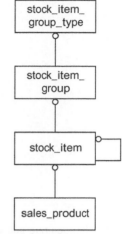

Figure 9-8 A fixed hierarchy.

Consequences

Imposing restrictions through the data structure means
- Arbitrary or inappropriate restrictions are placed on the data that can be held.
- Fudge or false data may be introduced to overcome the restrictions in the data structure. This may have to be programmed around.
- Data may be replicated to overcome the restrictions in the data structure. The different versions must be reconciled.
- The entity type will only work within the context defined. A change in business rules may require a change in the database structure.
- The resultant system is harder to share.
  Failing to correctly recognize entity types means
- The same data structures may be replicated.
- The same functionality may be replicated.

An example is given in Figure 9-8.

Each **stock_item** *must* belong to one and only one **stock_item_group**, which *must* belong to one and only one **stock_item_group_type**. An example of the kind of restriction this can place is that you might have Naphtha as a **stock_item**, and you might have Feedstock, Intermediate, and Finished Product as **stock_item_groups**. This model restricts you to allowing Naphtha to be only classed as one of those, even though it can be all three.

The first step is to check that the entity types are of the same type. By comparing each of the entity types, you can see that all the entity types are classes of stock or material, so the entity type **class** is a supertype to them all, as shown in Figure 9-9.

The next thing is to check that all the relationship types are the same. In our case, the three relationship types indicated in Figure 9-9 are of the same type, indicating that an instance of the entity type at the one end is a generalization of an instance of the entity type at the many end. On the other hand, the relationship type between **stock_item** and **sales_product** is indicating that one is sold as the other, which is a different type of relationship type. This being the case, we can simplify the model and add flexibility at the same time by

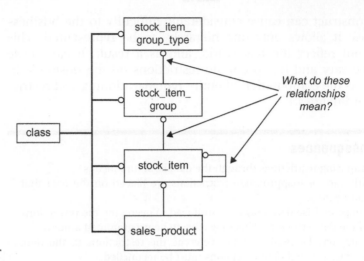

Figure 9-9 Recognizing subtypes.

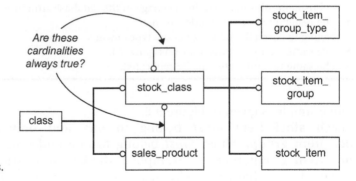

Figure 9-10 Removing some restrictions.

introducing a supertype to **stock_item**, **stock_item_group**, and **stock_item_group_type** of say, **stock_class**, and move the one-to-many relationship type to the supertype. This gives the situation in Figure 9-10.

This removes the restriction on what levels you have, but it allows you to classify any stock class as being one of its three subtypes. However, we still have to consider the cardinality of the relationship types. The cardinality of the relationship type between **sales_product** and **stock_item** was dealt with in the previous chapter and should be many-to-many. From the example used in the first paragraph of this example it is also clear that the relationship type on **stock_class** should also be a many-to-many relationship type. This leads to the situation in Figure 9-11.

Now we have a general pattern that is widely applicable. If we wish, we can still put back our restrictive relationships

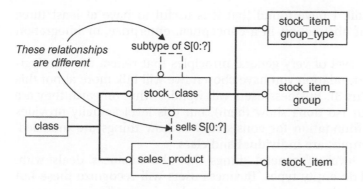

Figure 9-11 Removing more restrictions.

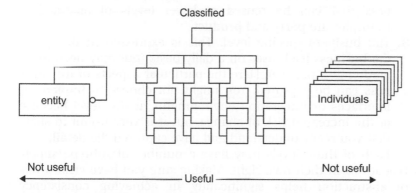

Figure 9-12 A subtype/supertype hierarchy must be at the right level to be useful.

for the special case of **stock_item**, **stock_item_group**, and **stock_item_group_type**, but now if we do, we have a flexible model that will still support the business when these restrictions do not apply.

9.5 Getting the Right Level of Abstraction

In the stock classification example in Figure 9-11, you start to see part of a subtype/supertype hierarchy emerging. Placing all your entity types in a subtype/supertype hierarchy is the best way to ensure that the same entity type is not created twice, since if it is the same, it should end up in the same place in the hierarchy, and it will be close to similar entity types.

Another consideration is what level of detail to develop your data model to. Figure 9-12 shows that you must take care to ensure that subtyping is taken to an appropriate level. Too high a level of subtyping means that entity types could mean almost anything; too low a level of subtyping means that you get lost in the detail. I have found that it is useful to have at least three levels of abstraction in a conceptual, enterprise, or integration model:

1. The level of very general principles that reflect the ontological foundation you have chosen (we will talk more about this in Part 3). Business users will wonder what on earth they are about (so don't show them), but this level actually provides the foundation for consistency in how things are modeled. Examples are **individual** and **class**.

2. The level of general things that the business deals with: generic entity types. Business users will recognize these but will think you are being a bit unclear for not being more specific. This level is useful for defining general patterns of business that can be reused at lower levels of abstraction. Examples are **party** and **product**.

3. The business-specific level. This is expressed in the terms the business itself uses on a daily basis (but may need to be made more precise). Here the particular aspects of the business can be captured. You might not choose to implement interfaces or integration environments at this level because of the increased risk of change, but it is very useful to show that you really understand and have captured the detail.

Each of these levels may have a number of subtype/supertype levels in their own right. Making sure you have clear levels of abstraction helps significantly in achieving consistency across a broadly scoped data model.

9.6 Impact of Using the Principles

In Chapter 5, I set out some desiderata for data models:
- Meet the data requirement.
- Be clear and unambiguous to all (not just the authors).
- Be stable in the face of changing data requirements.
- Be flexible in the face of changing business practices.
- Be reusable by others.
- Be consistent with other models covering the same scope.
- Be able to reconcile conflicts with other data models.

In addition, it should be possible to develop data models quickly. I hope I have been able to show that by following the principles outlined in this part you can improve existing data models and develop new data models that achieve these desiderata.

AN ONTOLOGICAL FRAMEWORK FOR CONSISTENT DATA MODELS

Part 2 introduced general principles for data models that if followed, will prevent many of the problems found in data models. However, the problem they do not solve is how to limit the variability in data models produced between different data modelers. This requires a common view of the world and a common approach to modeling it. This is a real issue for data modeling teams who are responsible for different parts of large conceptual, integration, or enterprise data models.

Part 3 introduces an ontological framework that has two objectives:

1. When working within it, you should be able to model anything that is valid.
2. Although you can model anything, the conventions of the framework are as restrictive as possible so that different people modeling the same thing should produce the same data model.

To make this happen, three things are required:
1. A rigorous ontological framework (a particular way of looking at the world and analyzing it)
2. Examples of using the ontological framework to analyze many common situations
3. A particular way of representing the results of the analysis in an entity-relationship paradigm

These issues are addressed in Part 3. The data model developed in Part 3 is more formally and completely documented in Part 4 as both an EXPRESS-G (graphical) and EXPRESS (lexical) data model.

10

MOTIVATION AND OVERVIEW FOR AN ONTOLOGICAL FRAMEWORK

In this chapter I will explain why an ontological framework is valuable in data modeling, and I will introduce the broad sweep of the four-dimensional framework I use, which is based on the work done by myself and others when we developed the data model for ISO 15926-2.

10.1 Motivation

In Part 2, I introduced some general principles that, if followed, will help prevent many of the problems found in data models, especially those intended to be conceptual, integration, or enterprise data models. There is, however, one problem that these principles do not resolve. If two people create a data model of the same thing, it is unusual if they come up with the same data model, even if we discount differences in the names they choose.

At first glance, this might seem surprising. After all, there is just one real world that these are models of, so you might expect that models would tend to be the same to reflect that.

However, both experience and theory show that considerable variety is possible.

Given this reality, the question is how do you provide a framework for analysis that will allow different people to come up with essentially the same data model when they are confronted with the same requirements, but one that does not restrict what they can model?

10.2 Ontological Foundation

Unfortunately, there is more than one way of looking at the world, so in developing a consistent approach to ontological data modeling, you need to be aware of the underlying view of the world that you are adopting, that is, the kinds of things that exist and their representation, which links to the principle of modeling based on the underlying nature of the things involved. Adopting different views in different parts of a data model or different data models may immediately give rise to inconsistency. Strangely, this is something that is rarely paid attention to in data model development. Those of you without a background in philosophy may find this chapter a new and perhaps surprising experience.

What this is not, though, is a philosophical work. Philosophical ontology is full of arguments about why a particular ontological theory is good, and even more about objections to alternative theories. My approach here is to recognize that data models are inevitably ontologies and that rather than bury your head in the sand and pretend that philosophical ontology is irrelevant, you need to apply a few selected and tested ideas from philosophical ontology that can make the data analysis process much less mysterious and much more reliable. I will leave the philosophical arguments to philosophers, and for those of you who are interested in pursuing such things, I'll give you references to a few key sources.

The most basic choices we make in how we model things are called ontological commitments. In this section I outline the key commitments I have made in this framework. For each I give one or two alternatives and the reason for my choice. All of the commitments I mention, both those chosen and rejected, are ones that are established choices in philosophical circles. That means that you can find philosophers who will argue strongly for and against each of them. None of them are my own invention, though I am not aware of them having been brought together in quite this combination before.

I claim that applying such ontological principles to data model development makes them more rigorous, and as a result, where data models are developed with the same ontological commitments, consistency is likely to be easier to achieve. Of course, you do not have to make the same choices that I have done here, but then you have to work out what your choices are and the consequences for a similar framework.

I will start by looking at the most basic kinds of things:
- *Individuals*—things that exist in space and time
- *Classes*—things that have members rather than parts
- *Relationships*—what one thing has to do with another

10.2.1 Individuals

By *individuals* I mean things that exist in space and time, and that are not set-like; that is, they do not have members (for example, you and me, but not person).

There are two main approaches that can be taken to modeling individuals, with on the whole minor variations, that dominate the philosophical literature. I will call these the three-dimensional paradigm and the four-dimensional paradigm. The differences between these paradigms are illustrated in Figure 10-1 and are really about how time and change are taken account of and not strictly about whether time and change are taken into account.

The three-dimensional paradigm says, for example, that all of me exists now, and that I pass through time, and therefore I

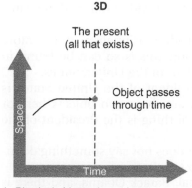

3D

The present
(all that exists)

Space

Object passes
through time

Time

1. Physical objects do not have temporal parts.
2. Different physical objects may coincide (non-extensional).

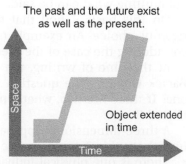

4D + Extensionalism

The past and the future exist as well as the present.

Space

Object extended
in time

Time

1. Individuals extend in time as well as space and have both temporal parts and spatial parts.
2. When two individuals have the same spatio-temporal extent, they are the same thing (extensionalism).

Figure 10-1 Three-dimensionalism compared to four-dimensionalism.

do not have temporal parts.[1] The four-dimensional paradigm says that I am extended in time as well as space, and that I have temporal parts as well as spatial parts.

The way that history and change is dealt with is therefore different; a 3D approach takes a statement and adds the time or times at which it is true. However, when this temporal indexing is not added, then you get a current state assumption. A 4D approach has time built in; the statement is true for some temporal part of the individual.

The three-dimensional paradigm needs to say that two intuitively distinct objects can coincide—say, for example, a cup and the piece of plastic it is made from—or deny that one of them exists. In the four-dimensional paradigm, the piece of plastic and the cup exist for different periods in time and are thus different because they have different spatio-temporal extents.[2]

An important thing to note here is that it is necessary to choose. You cannot choose to be both three-dimensional and four-dimensional at the same time; to do so would be to say that an individual both has and does not have temporal parts.

It may be noted that much of natural language seems to favor the three-dimensional paradigm. I conjecture that perhaps this is because much of natural language is about the here and now, and so it has become tuned to be efficient for that. However, it is perfectly possible to speak four dimensionally.

There are many reasons for making a choice one way or another, so it is perhaps worth recalling the objective of the framework in making the choice here. The objective is to tie down, as tightly as possible, the way that things are modeled so that consistency is easy to achieve—provided that is done without limiting what can be said.

On this basis, I find that four-dimensionalism is the more rigorous choice. An example of how this is so can be found in considering the case of the President of the United States.

At the time of writing, the President of the United States is Barack Obama. The question is, are there two objects here or one? If there are two, what kind of thing is the President of the United States?

A three-dimensional approach does not say something definitive about this. I could choose to say that

- There is one physical individual, Barack Obama, and there is a physical social role that is President of the United States, and they are coincident while Barack Obama is the President.

---

[1]A temporal part of me is all of me spatially for a particular period of time.

[2]A *spatio-temporal extent* is some 4D piece of space-time.

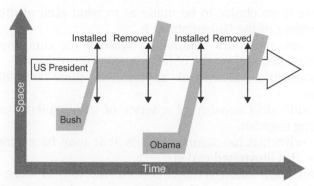

Figure 10-2 The President of the United States.

- There is one physical individual, Barack Obama, and there is an abstract[3] social role that is the President of the United States, and there is some relationship between the two.
- There is one physical individual, Barack Obama, and there is a class that is the President of the United States, and presently Barack Obama is a member of that class.

I have seen each of these approaches taken in different places. The problem here is not that any one of these choices could not be made to work; the problem is that there is a choice, and therefore different choices can be made. I want to eliminate the need to make choices.

Now compare this to the four-dimensional analysis illustrated in Figure 10-2.

Here it is quite clear. There are two spatio-temporal extents, one for Barack Obama, and one for the President of the United States. Both are physical things. You can clearly see that the President of the United States consists of temporal parts of a number of people—those who have held the office of President of the United States. At the time of writing, it is a temporal part of Barack Obama that is also a temporal part of the President of the United States. So at present Barack Obama and the President of the United States are coincident, though this was not so in the past, and will not be so for all time in the future.

Notice two things here:

1. The explanatory power that four-dimensionalism brings to the analysis.

---

[3]*Abstract* means that something does not have physical reality in some sense; either it does not exist in space and time, like a class, or if it is an individual, then it is not something you can put your hands on in some sense, as here.

2. There is no choice to be made as to what kind of thing the President of the United States is.

For me, these are compelling reasons for choosing four-dimensionalism, given the objectives set out previously.

Within four-dimensional approaches, there are still two options:

1. An individual consists of a series of instantaneous stages,[4] strung together.
2. An individual has temporal parts that may be extended in time[5] (as illustrated earlier).

In an information systems context, the first of these is just unworkable because of the very large number of stages you might need to consider, so I adopt here the second option of parts extended in time as well as space.

10.2.2 Extensional Basis for Identity of Individuals

When two objects coincide, how do we know if we have one object or two? This is essentially the problem we just looked at with the President of the United States. Was the President one and the same thing as Barack Obama, or not? This is a real question for three-dimensionalists because the President and Barack Obama wholly exist at each point in time and they are coincident. Under a four-dimensional treatment, we could see that the spatio-temporal extension of these two was different, so it was possible to distinguish between them. But what if two objects coincide under four-dimensionalism?

Consider a vase and the clay it is made from. Ordinarily, the clay exists before the vase is formed from it, and when it is made into a vase, there is still a piece of clay as well; so the spatio-temporal extents are different, thus the vase and the piece of clay it is made from are different objects. However, what about the case when the vase is made from two pieces of clay that are brought together to make the vase at the same time. Now the spatio-temporal extent of the vase is the same as for the piece of clay. So do I have one object or two?[6]

The answer is that you can choose. If you want to have two objects, you have to say something to the effect that an object can only exist at one level of reality (where an object and what the object is made out of are at different levels of reality), or

---

[4]Some writers refer to this as a *stage theory.*
[5]This is referred to as *perdurantism* by at least some writers.
[6]This is a standard test case in philosophical ontology.

you have to use some other rule that tells you when you have to discern two objects in a single spatio-temporal extent.

The alternative is to say that there is only one object for one spatio-temporal extent. This is known as *extensionalism*, since the identity basis of a spatio-temporal extent is its extent.

The advantage of extensionalism is that it is simple. There are no other rules to consider (and levels-of-reality although a useful idea, is a bit vague in comparison). But surely, now I have to choose whether my spatio-temporal extent is a vase or a piece of clay? No. There is no such rule that prevents a spatio-temporal extent from being both a vase and a piece of clay, though it is unusual. What about the properties, these will now apply to both the object as vase and the object as piece of clay? Yes. So what? Because they belong to the same spatio-temporal extent, this is just accidently the case and causes no problem.

So my choice here is for an extensional basis for identity of individuals. It is simple and rigorous, and so it best meets our objectives of minimizing wiggle room.

10.2.3 Possible Worlds

One of the challenges in data modeling is to distinguish between historical fact and plans for the future, especially since we can have more than one plan. This is an example of what is known in philosophy as *modality*.

Modality is about distinguishing between what is the case (happens to be the case), what is necessarily the case (it could not be otherwise), and what could possibly be the case. What happens to be the case is just a simple fact. What is necessarily true is a rule that holds in all circumstances. What is possibly the case is something that might (or might not) be, have been, or become a fact.

The choices here include some kind of modal logic,[7] or modal realism—or more popularly, possible worlds.[8] Possible worlds supports a number of things, including allowing worlds where the basic laws of physics might be different, and allowing alternative views of history or the future to be explored. This means that in principle, there are an infinite number of possible worlds. Fortunately, we only need to care about those that are of interest to us.

---

[7]*Modal logic* adds operators for possibility and necessity to a standard logic.
[8]This idea was first introduced by David Lewis in *On the Plurality of Worlds*. A possible world should more properly be called a possible universe, but I shall not rename David Lewis's idea here.

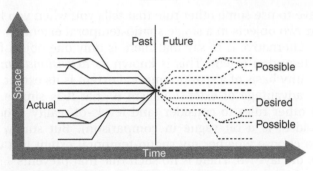

Figure 10-3 Possible worlds.

In business, the practical use of this approach is for planning, where each plan is a part of some possible world, and the outcome belongs to the actual world,[9] so that comparison can be made between them. It can also be useful in contracts when you are considering contingent situations. It is for this reason that I have chosen an approach based on possible worlds.

Figure 10-3 illustrates how this can work. With a spatio-temporal approach to individuals, possible worlds can be allowed to intersect and branch,[10] with temporal parts of individuals being shared across possible worlds. This works because the possible world would pick out a particular scenario—past or future—and this would be unique even though parts were shared between scenarios.

A philosopher might criticize this choice on the grounds that it is ontologically extravagant because it admits into existence all these possible worlds, and many philosophers would actively look to minimize the commitments they make. I am more pragmatic. I look for value for the commitments I have made, and I have found this one to deliver good value, as we shall see in just a moment.

A final comment is about whether allowing these possible worlds to exist means that they are real, which in turn means we have to distinguish between existence and reality.

On the one hand there are concrete things that we can kick, and on the other hand there are abstract things like properties, sets, and types, such as the color blue, which we cannot kick. Roughly, therefore, things exist if we can sensibly talk about them (and our ontological framework admits them).

---

[9]The actual world is also a possible world, so in the unlikely event of things turning out exactly as planned, they are the same world.
[10]This is the point at which I depart from Lewis for whom there was no sharing across different possible worlds.

So accepting possible worlds into our framework means that we accept that they exist. A separate question is whether these possible worlds are real or actual in the sense that the world we inhabit is real or actual. David Lewis, who first introduced the idea to philosophy clearly thought they were real; he called his theory *modal realism*.

We do not have to agree with him, and I certainly do not claim to know if possible worlds are real or not. As it happens, it does not matter whether they are real or not for any practical purpose, so you may make your own choice. It is, however, interesting to note that in physics and cosmology, the possibility that possible worlds are real is given serious consideration. In cosmology they have calculated that the universe is large enough that somewhere far away there is probably another you doing just what you are doing. In quantum physics, the problem of particles being in more than one place at the same time is solved by them being in different places in different universes.[11] So it is not simply outrageous to consider these possible worlds as real.

10.2.4 Extensional Identity for Classes/Sets

A *class*[12] is an abstract thing that has members, as opposed to an individual (something that exists in space-time) that has parts. The members of a class may be other classes or individuals (or both). The most useful classes tend to be those that group things by similarity, for example, red cars.

As with individuals, the key question is the one of identity. How do I know whether two classes are the same or different?

There are two answers that can be given to this:

1. **Extensional:** two classes are the same when their membership is the same (similar to the extensional definition of identity for individuals).
2. **Intensional:** two classes are the same when they have the same definition (or the definitions are provably equivalent).

I should say that this is a matter of identity and not definition. There is no problem with a set having an intensional definition, so long as it leads to a set of unchanging members. Indeed this is necessary for large sets, such as the set of real

---

[11]An overview of the different sorts of parallel universes from a physics/cosmology perspective is given in: M. Tegmark, Parallel Universes, in J.D. Barrow, P.C.W. Davies, and C.L. Harper, (Eds.), Science and Ultimate Reality: From Quantum to Cosmos, Cambridge University Press, Cambridge, UK, 2004.

[12]I shall use the word class because it is relatively familiar. I might have used the words type, set, or category. All of these words have specialist meanings that have become lost and blurred in common usage.

numbers, and they can be positively useful since you can use logic to work things out (perform reasoning) based on those definitions.

For those who choose three-dimensionalism, extensional identity can lead to considerable difficulty because the membership of a class will change over time. If I ask, "How many cars are there?" in 1700, the answer is zero, today it will be a lot more, and tomorrow, the answer will again be different. So they *need* to use intensional identity for classes, but they will still need to talk about the extension of the class (usually at a point in time) and that will be a set. So they need to have both intensionally and extensionally defined kinds of classes, often called types and sets, respectively.

However, for a four-dimensionalist the choice is real. When I ask, "How many cars are there?" I ought to get the answer, "All the cars there ever were or ever will be." This is because it is not only the present that exists in a four-dimensional approach. How many cars exist today, is a different question, as is the number of cars that exist tomorrow, or in 1700.

Let us look at the difference with an example. Let us take sheep, four-legged sheep, and two-eyed sheep as our intensionally defined classes. Now as a farmer, when I look in my field, I find I have twenty sheep; I have twenty sheep that have two eyes; and twenty sheep that have four legs. So extensionally I have just one class, but intensionally I still have three classes. Now the reason I have three classes intensionally is that although I actually only have one extension, that was not necessarily the case. It is possible that one or more of the sheep could have had three legs or one eye, in which case they would have been different. This is also the basis on which you would want to do your reasoning. So, in fact, the question is: are there extensional classes that perform this role of what is possible? Hopefully you have already picked up the clue in the word "possible" and remember the previous section on possible worlds. Even if there were no three-legged or one-eyed sheep in this world, there will be some possible world in which there are.[13]

A similar example is the case of unicorns. There are no unicorns in this world, so extensionally, unicorn would equate to the empty set. However, there are possible worlds in which unicorns do exist. So we can talk about the class of unicorns across possible worlds. This class will be extensional (alright, it will also be uncountable, but that is a different matter). If I had

---

[13]Although it is very likely that somewhere in this world there are one or more three-legged or one-eyed sheep, we cannot actually guarantee it.

taken a different approach to modality, I might not have had this choice.

This means that as a four-dimensionalist with possible worlds, I can choose an extensional identity for class and have classes that are equivalent to the intensionally defined classes. This is the choice I make. So classes have an extensional identity basis, and when I want classes that have a definition that is about what is possible, then I use classes across possible worlds. The advantage this gives us is that set theory, which is very well understood, applies to classes in a straightforward way.

10.2.5 Relationships and Their Representation[14]

Relationships represent a trilemma of confusion. Not only is there the usual confusion between relationships as members and relationships as classes, but there is also confusion about the representation of relationships, with relationships sometimes being represented as lines (relationship types) in entity-relationship models, and other times being represented as intersection entity types, with relationship types representing apparently something else. Figure 10-4 shows two different ways that **aggregation**/*part_of* can be represented in an entity-relationship model.

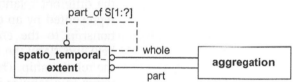

Figure 10-4 Different ways of representing a relationship.

So let us consider the anatomy of a relationship. I will start at the bottom with a relationship instance, and I will take the simplest case of a relationship between two objects, A and B. A relationship instance between two objects can be shown diagrammatically as in Figure 10-5 using the notation from Figure 2-22. The diamond represents the relationship instance, and the lines link to the related objects.

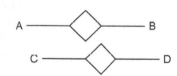

Figure 10-5 Two relationship instances.

However, I know nothing more than that two objects are related. I also need to know what kind of relationship it is. So I add this in Figure 10-6. Let me suppose that both these are **aggregation** relationships, as represented in Figure 10-4. The arrows mean that the relationships are members of the kind of relationship represented by the double diamond. The lightning strike (see Figure 10-6) links to the name of the kind of relationship—aggregation.

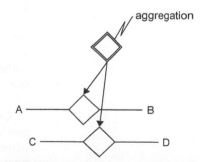

Figure 10-6 Two aggregation members.

---

[14] I take a different approach here from that taken in ISO 15926.

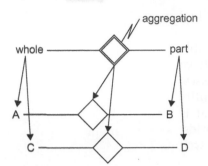

Figure 10-7 Adding roles to the anatomy of a relationship.

Well, I am a step further on, but I still do not know whether A is a part of B or if B is a part of A. I still need to know what roles the objects play in the relationship, and that having objects that play these roles is what makes an aggregation relationship what it is. Figure 10-7 shows the roles of the kind of relationship added as arms to the double diamond, and arrows showing again which objects play which roles.

Now I have all the information. I know that the relationship is an aggregation, and that in the first, B is the part and A is the whole, and in the second, that D is the part and C is the whole.

It is interesting to look at how that information is captured in the different relationship forms of Figure 10-4. The relationship represented by an entity type gives the name of the kind of relationship to the entity type and names the relationship types between it and the related object in terms of the roles they play in the relationship. This will also give convenient names for the columns in a tabular implementation of the entity type. The many-to-many relationship type version names the relationship in terms of the role one end plays toward the other, in a particular direction. Which is the whole and which is the part is implicit in the direction of the relationship type. The role in the other direction is not given, and is also implicit (though it could be stated).

I don't wish to suggest there is anything right or wrong about these two different approaches, just that you should be aware of what is left implicit.

There are four main groups of relationships:
1. Relationships between spatio-temporal extents
2. Relationships between spatio-temporal extents and classes
3. Relationships between classes and classes
4. Relationships of relationships

When you're following the 4D paradigm, it turns out that a characteristic of all relationships is that there is only one relationship of a particular kind between any two objects. This makes relationships between spatio-temporal extents timeless, since it is states that are related, and any temporal aspect is contained in them. This makes relationships themselves very simple.

Consider my car. If at one time I swap my spare for the front passenger's side wheel, and make the front passenger's side wheel the spare, and then some time later the wheels are swapped back, then under the 3D paradigm, the same wheel, which has passed through time, is part of the car on two different occasions. This does not happen under 4D. Here it is a state of the wheel that is on the car, another state that is the spare, and a third state that is the wheel on the car the second time. It is not the wheel for the whole of its life, but the states of the wheel that are parts of the car, so each is only related once.

A similar story applies with relationships between classes and individuals. In the case where the classes are accidental properties something might have from time to time, like a door being open or closed, for instance, it is a state of the door that has this property; in such a case, the state has the property for the whole of its life, rather than the door having it for the whole of its life. So again, the same object does not have the same property twice.

Relationships between classes are in any case timeless, since classes are timeless; any relationship that is true between them is always true: it will not apply at one time and not at another.

The conclusion I draw from all this is that in a four-dimensional framework, relationships are abstract objects like classes; that is, they do not exist in space-time.

Figure 10-7 shows that a kind of relationship has a signature that is a collection (strictly a bag[15]) of roles, and a relationship instance is an instantiation of that collection of roles where there is a particular thing that plays each role. The collection is a bag because a role may occur more than once in the kind of relationship. For example, in a relationship where two objects overlap, there are two overlapped roles in the kind of relationship.

It also follows that the identity criterion for a kind of relationship is the collection of roles, and the identity criterion for a relationship is the collection of classifications that are the things playing the particular roles that make up the signature for its kind of relationship.

When you are designing systems, it will probably be convenient to represent a relationship as a relation[16] (for example, tables). However, when this is the case, the order in the relation (ordering of the columns) should be seen as convenient rather than distinguishing a different relationship.

10.3 A Data Model for the Ontological Foundations

Figure 10-8 is a data model that reflects most of the ontological commitments made in this chapter.

---

[15]A *bag* is so called because it is what you get as an unordered collection when you draw numbered balls from a bag, replacing the ball each time after making the draw.
[16]A *relation* is a set of tuples that are in turn an ordered set of elements. Significance attaches to the place in the relation that an element has. A SQL table is an example of a relation.

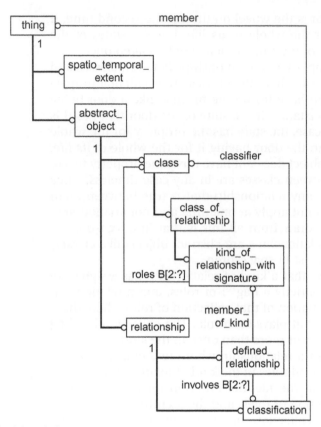

Figure 10-8 The ontological foundation.

The thick black lines show subtype/supertype relationships, with the lollipop at the subtype end. So each **spatio_temporal_extent** *is a*[17] **thing**, and each **abstract_object** *is a* **thing**. The "1" at the root of the subtype tree means that nothing can be both a **spatio_temporal_extent** and an **abstract_object**; that is, they are mutually exclusive. This is not too surprising since a **spatio_temporal_extent** is something that exists in space-time, whereas an **abstract_object** is something that exists outside space-time.

A **class** *is an* **abstract_object** and a **relationship** *is an* **abstract_object**. Once again, the "1" at the root of the subtype/supertype tree means they are mutually exclusive. A **class_of_relationship** *is a* **class**, and a **class_of_relationship_with_signature** *is a* **class_of_relationship**. A **classification** *is a* **relationship**, and a **defined_**

---

[17]"*Is a*" are the usual words to describe a subtype/supertype relationship.

relationship *is a* **relationship**; a **classification** may not also be a **defined_relationship**.

The thin lines are named relationship types. In the text, I will show the names of relationship types in the model in italics. The default cardinality for a solid thin line is that each thing at the sharp end of the line must be related to one thing at the lollipop end. A thing at the lollipop end may be related to one or more things at the sharp end. If the line is dashed then each thing at the sharp end may be related to at most one thing at the lollipop end.

A **classification** *is a* **relationship** where a **thing** is a *member* of a *class*. Each **classification** must have exactly one **thing** that is the *member* in the **classification**. Each **classification** must have exactly one **class** that is the *classifier* in the **classification**.

A **defined_relationship** *is a* **relationship** that is a *member_of_kind* of exactly one **kind_of_relationship_with_signature**. Each **kind_of_relationship_with_signature** must have two or more **classes** that are its *roles*. The cardinality is defined by the *B[2:?]* after the relationship type name. The "B" stands for bag, as opposed to set; where in a set each object can only occur once, in a bag each object may occur multiple times. In this case it is possible for a **kind_of_relationship_with_signature** to have the same role more than once. For example, in a connection, there are two things that are connected, so we need to have two connected roles in the signature.

Each **defined_relationship** *involves* a bag of two or more **classifications**, where the **class** in the **classification** corresponds to a **class** that is a role in the **kind_of_relationship_with_signature** that it is a *member of*, and the *member* is the **thing** playing the *role* in this **defined_relationship**.

An interesting feature of this data model is that it is sufficient, at this level of abstraction, to model how things are for "life, the universe and everything."[18] Note that I have not dealt with cardinalities here, however, we are already well into meta-model territory, so I will leave this relatively simple extension to the reader.

10.4 Closing Remarks

I have made a surprisingly small number of ontological commitments in this chapter:

1. Individuals exist in space-time and may be extended in time as well as space.

[18]D. Adams, The Hitchhikers Guide to the Galaxy, Pan Books, 1979.

2. The identity of individuals is defined by their spatio-temporal extent; that is, if two individuals have the same spatio-temporal extent, then they are the same individual.
3. There are other possible worlds as well as the one we inhabit, and we can talk about things that are possible but not necessarily actual by referring to the possible world in which that is the case.
4. Classes are objects that do not exist in space-time and have members.
5. The identity of a class is defined by its membership; that is, if two classes have the same members, then they are the same class.
6. A relationship is a collection of things that play particular roles in the relationship, defined by a signature that is a bag of roles.

However, together they provide a cohesive and rigorous ontological framework with which one can analyze the world to bring useful insights, which leads to more accurate data models. This we shall pursue in the following chapters.

I think it is only fair to warn you that as you work through the consequences of these commitments, it is quite possible you will come across things that make you think "but it is not like that, surely?" This will be because you have your own internal ontology of the world that is different[19] from that presented here. What I need to do is ask you to set that aside when looking at the framework I present here. The rules of your personal ontology may well not apply within a 4D framework. It is of course quite reasonable to ask whether or not what is presented is capable of supporting, and being extended to support, the information integration requirements you have. If you find problems there, then I look forward to hearing from you.

Much of this framework has already been used to develop a data model for an ISO (International Organization for Standardization) standard, ISO 15926-2:2003,[20] which I was involved in developing, and also a conceptual data model for Shell's downstream[21] business. In later chapters, I will take some examples from the work done in developing these data models, and from some of what has been learned from its practical use.

---

[19]I carefully do not say "wrong." Remember, there are a large number of possible view points, and many may be fit for purpose.
[20]http://www.tc184-sc4.org/wg3ndocs/wg3n1328/lifecycle_integration_schema.html
[21]In the oil industry downstream is from oil tanker to petrol pump.

11

SPATIO-TEMPORAL EXTENTS

In this chapter I will talk about spatio-temporal extents and some of the basic kinds of spatio-temporal extents that are commonly found. I will follow through on the ontological commitments of the previous chapter and show what some of the consequences are. In particular, I examine the space-time patterns that different kinds of spatio-temporal extents exhibit, and I look at the key relationship of one thing being a part of another that can exist between individuals. Indeed, you can use the spatio-temporal patterns that spatio-temporal extents exhibit to identify the kinds of individuals there are.

11.1 Parts

The most important relationship between spatio-temporal extents is that of one being part of another. I call this *aggregation* when the whole is the sum of the parts. Unless the aggregation is also a member of a subtype of aggregation, then the whole will be of the same kind of thing as the parts.

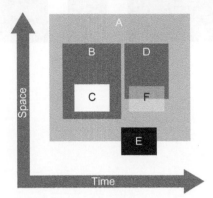

Figure 11-1 An example of an aggregation relationship.

Figure 11-1 illustrates the relationship. Important things to remember about aggregation are

- Nothing is a (proper[1]) part of itself.
- If B is a part of A, then A is not a part of B (asymmetry).
- If B is a part of A, and C is a part of B, then C is a part of A (transitivity).
- If A has parts (is not atomic—in the original sense of the word, i.e., not physics), then it has at least two nonoverlapping parts (for example, B and D in Figure 11-1).
- If there is a part of E that is not a part of A, then E is not a part of A.
- In the sum of overlapping parts like D and F, any overlapping parts only count once.
- If a part of F is a part of D, then D and F overlap.

Sometimes, the whole is more than the sum of its parts. The parts compose something that has emergent properties that result from the way that the parts are arranged—for example, a watch. This I shall call *composition*. Finally, there is the case where the part is the full spatial extent for a period in time; that is, the part is a state of the whole. This I will call *temporal composition*.

The subject of mereology (the study of parts) is itself the subject of whole books. I certainly do not intend to cover the subject in such detail here.[2]

11.2 Individuals and States

Figure 11-2 illustrates the key kinds of spatio-temporal extent. *State* is something for a period of time. A state might be a state of a car, or a state of a person, or a state of a factory. Now for some states, the period that they are for is the whole of the life of something. These I shall call *individuals*. Examples of individuals include cars, persons, atoms, activities, and brooms.

States are useful in two different ways. They are the temporal part of an individual to which some property applies, and they

[1]There are versions of *mereology* (the study of wholes and parts) where spatio-temporal extents are (improper) parts of themselves. I will stay with the more everyday understanding of being a part.
[2]If you are interested in finding out more about mereology, an excellent text is P. Simons, Parts—A Study in Ontology, Oxford University Press, 2000. I have also coauthored a paper on 4D mereotopology: J. G. Stell, M. West, A 4-Dimensionalist Mereotopology, in A.C.Varzi, L. Vieu, (Eds), Formal Ontology in Information Systems, IOS Press, 2004, 261—272.

are the temporal part of an individual that participates in an activity or association.

The naming convention I will follow is that when I refer to an individual for the whole of its life, I will use the usual noun, that is, person, pump. For states, I will use the term state of person, state of pump, and so on, remembering that an individual is itself a state.[3]

A state, whether or not it is an individual, has a temporal boundary (strictly it may be spatio-temporal, but we will deal only with the simple case here) that marks its beginning and end. We call these boundaries events. An event is the change in state, not what brings about the change. So event is used here for something instantaneous.

Figure 11-3 provides an EXPRESS-G data model of what has just been described.

I will start by walking through the subtype hierarchy. A **spatio_temporal_extent** is any **thing** that exists in space-time. An **event** *is a* **spatio_temporal_extent** that has zero temporal thickness, and is usually part of a point in time. A **state** *is a* **spatio_temporal_extent** that is an **individual** for a period of time. An **individual** *is a* whole life **state**. That might seem

Figure 11-2 Spatio-temporal extents, individuals, states, and events.

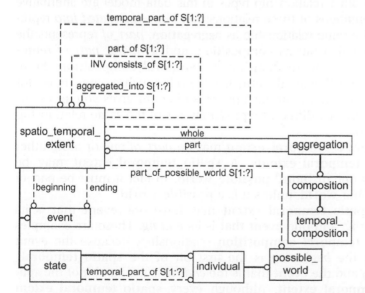

Figure 11-3 A data model for individuals, states, and events.

---

[3]For those familiar with ISO 15926-2:2003, it should be noted that a different convention was used there. In that case, for example, **physical_object** was used where **state_of_physical_object** is used here. Whole life individuals were simply also members of the entity type **whole_life_individual**.

counterintuitive, but really an **individual** is just a special kind of **state** where the period of time that it exists for is the most it can be. Finally, a **possible_world** *is an* **individual**. A **possible_world** is a complete possible history of the universe, which is why it is a subtype of **individual**.

An **aggregation** *is a* **relationship** where one **spatio_temporal_extent** is a *part* of another such that the *whole* is the sum of the parts. This means that unless the **aggregation** is also a member of one of its subtypes, the *whole* will be the same kind of thing as the *part*. For example, if I take two cups of water and pour them into a jug, the *whole* is still some water. You have to be a little careful the other way round. If I consider the *parts* of a glass of water, eventually, around the molecular level, I get something that is no longer water.

Each **aggregation** has exactly one **spatio_temporal_extent** that is the *part* in the **aggregation**. Each **aggregation** has exactly one **spatio_temporal_extent** that is the *whole* in the **aggregation**.

A **composition** *is an* **aggregation** where the *parts* are arranged in such a way that the *whole* is more than the sum of the *parts*. A car is an example of such a *whole*. A **temporal_composition** *is a* **composition** where the *part* is the entire *whole* spatially, but only *part* of the *whole* temporally.

The other relationship types in this data model are alternative representations of these relationships. Thus *aggregated into* represents the same relationship as **aggregation**; *part_of* represents the same relationship as **composition**; and *temporal_part_of* represents the same relationship as **temporal_composition**. From here on I will generally only use the relationship types (lines) for these and other relationships. This diagram gives you an example of how the different representations of the same relationship compare.

A **spatio_temporal_extent** may be *part_of* one or more other **spatio_temporal_extents**. A **spatio_temporal_extent** may be *part_of* one or more[4] **possible_world**. In fact it must be part of a **possible_world**, unless it is a **possible_world**.

A **spatio_temporal_extent** may have one **event** that is its *beginning*, and one **event** that is its *ending*. These are examples of the **temporal_composition** relationship, because the **event** that is the *beginning* is the first bit of the **spatio_temporal_extent**, and the **event** that is the *ending* is the last bit of the **spatio_temporal_extent**. Although every **spatio_temporal_extent** does have an event that marks its *beginning* and *ending*, we

---

[4]It is because possible worlds can branch that a **spatio_temporal_extent** can be *part of* more than one.

may not know what they are, which is why the relationship types are optional.

You will quickly notice that nearly all the relationship types between **spatio_temporal_extent** and its subtypes are some kind of *part_of* relationship type.

11.3 Inheritance of Properties by Substates

If I have a state of a car from 2003-08-11 to 2007-11-21 that is red, then that means that at all times between these two dates the car is red. So, if I have a state of that car from 2004-01-30 to 2006-05-23, then that state is also a red state. The property is inherited by its temporal parts. This is very similar to inheritance by subtypes of the properties of the supertype in classes. However, it is not the case that all classes are inherited. For example, the property of being a whole life object is not inherited by substates of the car. When a class is inherited by a substate it is temporally dissective. In practice, most classes are temporally dissective, and one should just note those that are not, which usually have to do with some temporal property.

11.4 Space and Time

One thing to notice in Figure 11-3 is how time appears. A point in time goes across all of space, and a period of time is a spatio-temporal extent across all space—that is, across a possible world, bounded by two points in time. This is a rather different conception of time than you usually find, which is restricted to coordinate systems and scales for time (and space).

Figure 11-4 shows some key relationships objects have to time.[5] Note that the black pieces are in fact one object that is discontinuous in time, as happens sometimes.

Historical closure: the spatio-temporal extent that is all space (that is, everything going on at the same time) while the object exists

Pre-history: the spatio-temporal extent that is all space before the first point in time when the object existed

Post-history: the spatio-temporal extent that is all space after the point in time when the object has finally ceased to exist

[5]This is based on: J. G. Stell, M. West, A 4-Dimensionalist Mereotopology, in A.C. Varzi, L. Vieu, (Eds), Formal Ontology in Information Systems, IOS Press, 2004, 261–272.

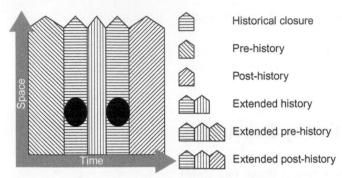

Figure 11-4 The relationship between an object and time.

Historical closure

Pre-history

Post-history

Extended history

Extended pre-history

Extended post-history

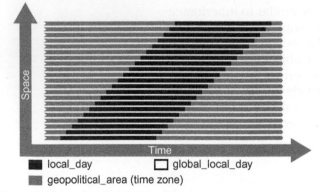

■ local_day   □ global_local_day

■ geopolitical_area (time zone)

Figure 11-5 Local and global local days.

Extended history: the spatio-temporal extent that is all space from the point in time that the object first existed, to the point in time after which it no longer ever exists

Extended pre-history: the spatio-temporal extent that is all space until the last point in time that the object exists

Extended post-history: the spatio-temporal extent that is all space after the first point in time that the object existed

Other useful operators are:

Historical connection: when the historical closures of two objects meet or overlap

Historical part: when the part falls within the historical closure of the whole

This at least is the case for pure time and pure periods. However, in business we might be interested in something slightly different. Imagine that you are running a business that works in lots of different time zones around the world, and that you need to keep global accounts of your sales on a daily basis. What then is your global day? Figure 11-5 illustrates how this looks as a spatio-temporal extent. Of course this is still relatively simple:

• There is summer time.
• Not all offsets are one hour.
• The start and end of the business day might be at different times (and not, say, midnight).

However, space-time maps and the 4D paradigm enable you to show these things in an intuitive way.

11.5 Ordinary Physical Objects

Ordinary physical objects such as rocks, people, neutrinos, equipment, and atoms correspond to a particular spatio-temporal pattern. Chapter 10 stated that the identity of a spatio-temporal extent is extensional, but what about change—in particular, if parts are removed or added? If something undergoes change, is it the same thing or not? How much change can something undergo and still be the same thing?

A simple but extreme example is a broom. A broom, as illustrated in Figure 11-6, can change parts or lose parts[6] over time without losing identity, but it cannot change all its parts at the same time.

Figure 11-6 shows the life of a broom. It starts off with handle A and head B. At some point in time handle A is replaced by handle C, and at a later time head B is replaced by head D. Thus, at the end of the period shown in Figure 11-6, none of the original parts of the broom are now part of the broom, but because not all the parts changed at once, we say it is the same broom. Organisms are similar in renewing themselves by gaining and losing parts.

Another question is whether or not ordinary objects must have continuous existence. The immediate expectation is that they do; however, this can be questioned. For example, when a car or watch is disassembled for repair or maintenance, is it still a car, or is it just a collection of parts? Is it the same car or watch when it is put back together?

I think the answer is that physical objects can go through periods of nonexistence when they are disassembled—you cannot use a watch or a car when it is disassembled—but on reassembly their life continues.

Notice I am not trying to define how things are, but to discover the pattern that is behind how we actually see things.

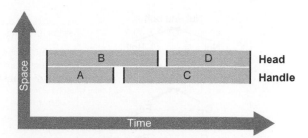

Figure 11-6 A broom, with various heads and handles.

11.6 Levels of Reality

Something to note from the example of the broom is that the broom has a handle and a head as parts: the handle is made from wood (say); the wood is made from cells, and so on. In each case the whole is not merely the sum of the parts, but something more than that in virtue of the relationships between the parts. This is a pattern that we can see in all things from microscopic to cosmological and these different levels at which things exist are sometimes referred to as levels of reality. It is for

---

[6]The diagram has been simplified: only the states of the heads and handles that are parts of the broom are shown.

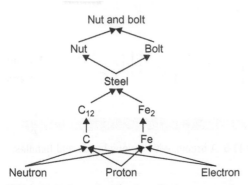

Figure 11-7 Some levels of reality in a nut and bolt.

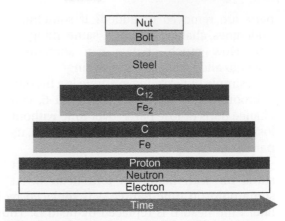

Figure 11-8 The levels as potentially distinct objects.

this kind of aggregation, when the whole is more than the sum of the parts, that I use the term composition.

A problem that arises here is exactly how many objects are there? Since the whole is coincident with what it is made out of, perhaps what things are made out of is all there is? After all, we have said that identity for individuals is defined by its extent. Four-dimensionalism can help to explain this apparent coincidence of different objects. An example is presented in Figure 11-7.

The problem arises when, because of the way that parts are arranged, the whole has emergent properties that are not present in the simple aggregate of the parts. So in this case

- When the nut and bolt are screwed together, they act as a fastener.
- When the steel they consist of is formed into the shape required, they have the properties of a nut and bolt, respectively.
- When iron and carbon are mixed and arranged appropriately, they make steel.
- Carbon and iron molecules are arrangements of carbon and iron atoms, respectively.
- A carbon or iron atom is an arrangement of particular numbers of protons, neutrons, and electrons.

Now at a point in time, each of these is coincident. However, when you look over time, you can see that the spatio-temporal extents for each level are different, as illustrated in Figure 11-8, so there are different objects at each level.

Notice here that although the nut and the bolt are individuals, they are also states of the steel they consist of, which in turn is a state of the carbon and iron it consists of, and so on.

In Chapter 10 I introduced a problem case that is often used in the philosophical literature of the two pieces of clay that are brought together to form a vase, which at some later time is broken into a number of pieces (see Figure 11-9).

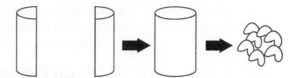

Figure 11-9 The example of the coincident piece of clay and vase.

Neither the clay nor the pot exists as one piece before the two parts are brought together or after the vase is smashed. So there is one object that is both the vase and the piece of clay it is made from. The consequence of this for an extensionalist is that the same individual can belong to classes at different levels of reality.[7]

Figure 11-10 shows the levels of reality that are implicit in the data model of ISO 15926-2. The arrows show the direction of composition with the *whole* at the head of the arrow. It should be noted that, because any *whole* that has emergent properties because of the arrangement of its parts is a new level, there are an arbitrary number of levels, and those shown are only some that have been found to be

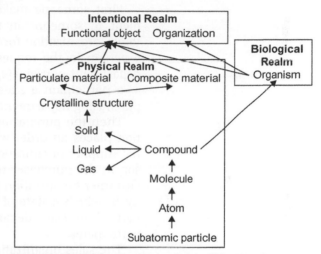

Figure 11-10 Levels of reality implicit in ISO 15926-2.

useful. The three realms are significant. The physical and biological realms are, I hope, obvious. However, the intentional realm consists of things that exist as a matter of will or intention and includes things that we make and things that exist by agreement, such as money and organizations. I will return to intentionally constructed objects later.

11.7 Activities and Events

Another key pattern is activity. You might think that it is difficult to determine the spatio-temporal extent of an activity; however, this becomes much easier when you think about the participants in the activity and the roles they play.

A participant is a state of an individual that is a part of (taking part in) an activity. The role is a kind of participant—for

---

[7]As an alternative approach, some nonextensionalists say that there is necessarily a different object at each level of reality, as a result of this rule; on some occasions two objects (in this case the clay and the vase) can be coincident.

example, customer, supplier, inspector—that may be a member of role, or a subtype of participant. The activity itself consists of its participants.

11.7.1 An Example of Participants and Activities

Figure 11-11 illustrates an example of the way that individuals participate in an activity. This example is for the replacement of a pump impeller.

First someone makes a request in the engineering department to someone in the purchasing department of the customer organization for a new impeller. More formally, a state of a person in the requestor role that is part of the engineering department participates in a requisition activity, which also has as a participant a state of a person in a purchaser role in the purchasing department of the same organization.

Then the purchasing department of the customer organization places an order with someone in the sales department of the supplier organization. Again, more formally, a state of a person in the purchaser role in the purchasing department of the customer organization participates in an order placement activity, in which a state of a person in the sales receipt role that is part of the sales department of the supplier organization also participates.

The sales organization then requests delivery of the impeller to the customer organization by their delivery department, who executes the delivery, which is received by the customer organization. More formally, a state of a person in a sales fulfillment role participates in a delivery activity and a state of a person in a goods receipt role in the customer organization also participates in this activity.

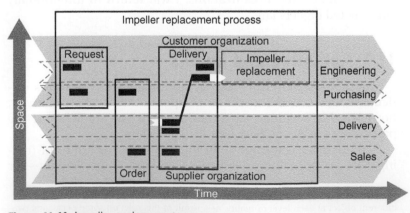

Figure 11-11 Impeller replacement process.

The impeller is then installed (details not shown).

The participants in the activity are the states of the individuals while they are participating. The activity consists of these participants, where each participant is a member of the role in which it is participating.

Notice how similar this diagram is to a swim-lane diagram.

11.7.2 Events

I introduced events in Chapter 10 as the temporal boundaries of spatio-temporal extents. An example of this is the life of a broom from Figure 11-6 shown again in Figure 11-12 where the temporal boundaries of the state of the handle and head while they are parts of the broom are events. Change is brought about by an activity; that is, an event is caused by an activity. In fact it is necessary that an activity brings about some change for it to be an activity.

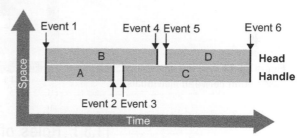

Figure 11-12 Events in the life of a broom.

11.7.3 References

An activity can have other kinds of relationship. One of these is reference. For example, it is quite possible for me to talk about Winston Churchill, but he is not a participant in the conversation. I am making a reference to him. I could also make reference to a class.

11.7.4 Discovery, Observation, Deeming, Measurement

An important type of activity is one that finds things out, or decides, or measures. These are the activities that determine the state of affairs represented by members of other entity types in the model. This gives rise to a relationship between an activity and the thing it determines.

11.8 Associations

An *association* is a state of affairs that exists for a period of time between at least two individuals and consists of the participant states of those individuals. An exception is whole-part, because the whole already includes any of its parts, so this is just a simple relationship.

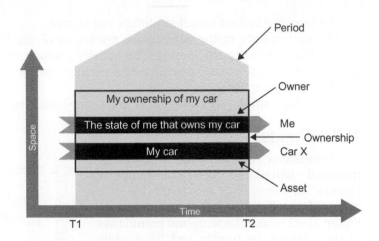

Figure 11-13 A space-time map for an association between individuals.

11.8.1 Roles of Individuals in Associations

I shall start with a space-time diagram of ownership as an example association of participants (see Figure 11-13).

The figure illustrates the ownership of my car by me. The grey chevrons represent me for the whole of my life and car X for the whole of its life; the chevrons indicate that the start and end are beyond the limits of this diagram. The black rectangles represent the state of me that owns my car and the state of car X (my car) the asset owned by me, respectively, and the empty black box contains the aggregation of those states that together constitute the ownership association that is my ownership of my car. Thus the association is itself a spatio-temporal extent. The arrows show a classification of each state by the appropriate class; in the case of the black rectangles these are kinds of participant, that is, roles.

In 4D, a period in time is all of the space between two points in time. So it goes up the page indefinitely. The light grey vertical chevron in Figure 11-13 represents a period. This is the period during which the association holds. The participants in the association, and indeed the whole association, are a spatial part of this period of time.

The consequence is that rather than a somewhat complex temporal relationship, we have some states of particular kinds, bound together by whole-part relationships. This occurs three times in Figure 11-13, as the asset and owner roles are parts of the ownership association, and in turn the ownership association is part of the period that the ownership occurs in, and finally the owner and owned participants are temporal parts of me and Car X.

This pattern is very similar to the pattern for activity; states of individuals play roles in the association, just as they do with the activity. There are two important differences:

1. An activity causes one or more events; an association does not (not actively at least).
2. The roles in an association are necessarily parts of the same period of time; whereas for an activity, the roles may be parts of different periods of time.

11.9 A Data Model for Individuals

Figure 11-14 shows a high level data model of the key elements from this chapter extending the data model from Figure 11-3. Picking up from there, **period_of_time** *is a* **state** that is a **possible_world** or a *temporal_part_of* a **possible_world**. A **period_of_time** may be a *temporal_part_of* one or more **possible_worlds**.

A **state_of_physical_object** *is a* **state** that is a **physical_object**[8] or a *temporal_part_of* a **physical_object**. A **physical_object** *is a* **state_of_physical_object** and an **individual** that is a distribution of matter or energy. A **state_of_physical_object** may be a *temporal_part_of* one or more **physical_objects**.

A **state_of_ordinary_physical_object** *is a* **state_of_physical_object** that is an **ordinary_physical_object** or a *temporal_part_of* an **ordinary_physical_object**. An **ordinary_physical_object** *is a* **state_of_ordinary_physical_object** and a **physical_object** that does not change all its parts at once.

A **state_of_biological_object** *is a* **state_of_physical_object** that is a **biological_object** or a *temporal_part_of* a **biological_object**. A **biological_object** *is a* **physical_object** that sustains itself and reproduces.

A **state_of_intentionally_constructed_object** *is an* **intentionally_constructed_object** or a *temporal_part_of* an **intentionally_constructed_object**. An **intentionally_constructed_object** *is an* **individual** that is what it is in part at least as an act of will.

A **participant** *is a* **state** that is a *temporal_part_of* an **individual** that is a *participant_in* an **activity** or an **association**.[9] An **activity** *is an* **individual** that *causes* one or more **events**. An **association** *is a* **state** that consists of two or more **participants**

---

[8]Earlier in this chapter I introduced ordinary physical objects; in later chapters, I will introduce other kinds of physical object as well as those here.

[9]The highlighted box in Figure 11-13 is an EXPRESS SELECT. It is used when a relationship can be with one of two or more entity types. It is equivalent to an exclusive arc used in some other notations.

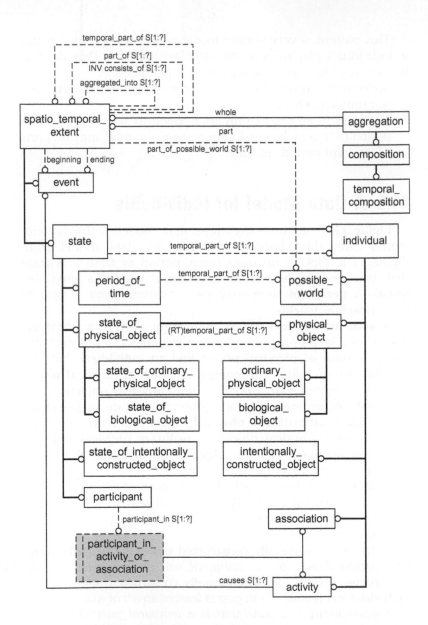

Figure 11-14 High level data model for individuals.

that are a *temporal_part_of* the **individuals** that participate in the **association**.

I have provided the basic framework, but there are details I have mentioned that are not included here, for example, the *determines* and *references* relationship types for **activity**. A more complete model can be found in Chapter 17.

12

CLASSES

In this chapter I look at classes as sets in a general way and relate this to their use in data modeling as both entity types and data.

12.1 What Is a Set?

You will recall that a *set* is a thing that has members, and its identity is defined by its membership (the null set is the set that has no members). That is, if two sets have the same members, they are the same set; if two sets have different members, they are different sets. In saying this, it is important to note that although its members define the identity of a set, it may be that at any point in time, not all the members of a set may be known.

12.1.1 Classification and Specialization

There are two key relationships that it is important to distinguish: classification, where a thing is a member of a set, and

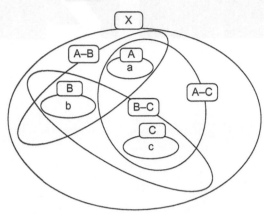

Figure 12-1 Classification and specialization.

specialization (or subtype/supertype), where all the members of the subtype are members of the supertype.

Figure 12-1 shows a Venn diagram for three instances, a,b,c, and all the possible sets that can be made from them using the classification (membership) relationship:

- A: a, B: b, C: c—the singleton sets
- A-B: a,b, A-C: a,c, B-C: b,c
- X: a,b,c

Now the specialization relationships are between the classes and are when all the members of the subtype are also members of the supertype; that is, when one ellipse that represents a set is wholly inside another. So showing Y subtype of Z as Y< Z gives you the following:

- C<B-C, C<A-C, C<X
- B<A-B, B< B-C, B<X
- A<A-B, A<A-C, A<X
- A-B<X, B-C<X, A-C<X

It is very easy to confuse classification and specialization, but they are rather different. Specialization is transitive—that is, if A is a subtype of A-B, and A-B is a subtype of X, then A is necessarily a subtype of X. For example, a hatchback is a car, and car is a vehicle, therefore a hatchback is a vehicle.

Now let's try an example of the classification relationship. My car is a car, and car is a vehicle type. However, my car is not a vehicle type, so classification is not transitive.

Confusion often arises because we use "is a" as the usual words for both types of relationship. However, the meaning is quite different. In natural language, the difference is in the use of the indefinite article "a." In the subtype relationship, we say "*a* hatchback is *a* car", whereas in the classification, it is just "car is a vehicle type"; that is, it is car itself, rather than a member of car, that is a member.

12.2 Sets and Four-Dimensionalism

You will also recall that an advantage of four-dimensionalism is that because it is spatio-temporal extents that are members of a class, the members of a class do not change over time—viewed from any point in time that state of the car is red. Also, because I am using possible worlds, you can have sets across possible worlds that allow you to talk about unicorns, fusion power stations, and the like. This means that we do not need anything other than set theory, whereas others need both a set theory and a type theory that is not extensional.

12.3 Some Different Kinds of Set Theory

I am not going to give a formal description of set theory; you can find this in many standard text books on mathematics. However, I am going to describe several levels of set theory so that you can recognize them when you see them and also so you will not be fooled into thinking you have to live within someone else's limitations.

12.3.1 Single Level Sets

Single level sets allow sets to have members, but these sets cannot themselves be members of other sets. Entity-relationship models are an example of this. Instances are members of entity types, but the entity types themselves cannot be members of anything else. This is illustrated in Figure 12-2, where boxes indicate sets, ellipses indicate objects that are base instances, and arrows indicate that the thing at the head of an arrow is a member of the set at the foot of the arrow. Note: these diagrams only show set membership relationships, and not specialization relationships.

In some cases, it is not allowed to be a member of more than one set; that is, the sets are disjointed.

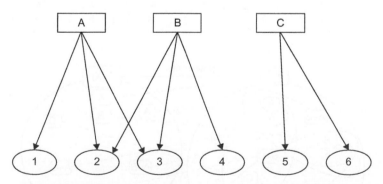

Figure 12-2 Single level sets.

12.3.2 Hierarchical Sets

With hierarchical sets, sets at one level may be members of sets at the level above, but there is no crossing of levels. So sets can only have members in the level below. Figure 12-3 illustrates this. Note that the relationship between levels is membership, and not specialization. So 1, 2, and 3 are members of A, and A is a member of N, but 1, 2, and 3 are not members of N.

Hierarchical sets occur naturally and this is a useful pattern to look for (but not to force). It should be noted that hierarchical sets include single level sets as a subset. An example of hierarchical sets in use is in data model, metamodel, and meta-metamodel approaches.

A limiting case in the relationship between levels in hierarchical sets is the powerset. A *powerset* is the set of all possible subsets of a set (including itself). An illustration of a powerset is given in Figure 12-4. The representation is based on the Venn diagram; however, a set may be represented both as a set

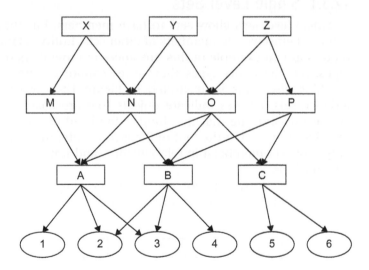

Figure 12-3 An example of hierarchical sets.

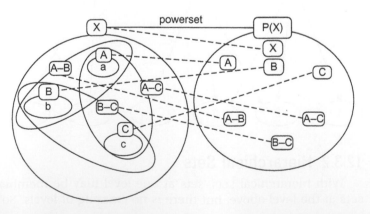

Figure 12-4 An example of a powerset.

container, as an ellipse, and as an instance of a set as a rounded rectangle. A straight line links the two representations.

The left hand side of Figure 12-4 is the same as in Figure 12-1. What is added is the right hand side where the sets that are ellipses on the left hand side become instances themselves of P(X), the powerset of X.

In ISO 15926-2 this pattern can be found, for example, in the relationship between the entity types **possible_individual**, **class_of_individual**, and **class_of_class_of_individual**, where **class_of_individual** is any member of the powerset of **possible_individual**, and **class_of_class_of_individual** is any member of the powerset of **class_of_individual**. Although we are not necessarily interested in all the members of the powerset, it is still useful to know that any member of the powerset you are interested in is a valid member.

12.3.3 Well-Founded Sets

Well-founded sets are the sets of "standard" set theories such as the Zermelo-Fraenkel (ZF) set theory and the von Neumann, Bernays, Gödel (NBG) set theory that can be found in standard texts. Well-founded sets can take members from any level below their own, but are not allowed membership loops (for example, a set being a member of itself). This is illustrated in Figure 12-5.

This form of set theory was largely developed as a reaction (perhaps even an overreaction) to Russell's Paradox. An early version of set theory developed by Gottlob Frege allowed that

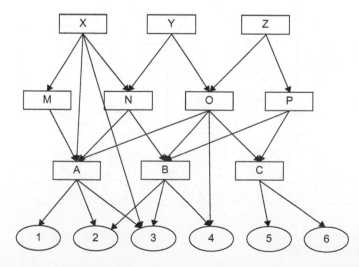

Figure 12-5 An example of well-founded sets.

for any intensional definition, there was a set that corresponded to that intensional definition. Bertrand Russell gave an example of such an intensional set that gave rise to a contradiction: the set of all sets that do not contain themselves. Either the resulting set is a member of itself (in which case it should not be) or it is not a member of itself (in which case it should be). Those working on set theory at the time felt that the best way to solve this problem was to disallow sets that had themselves as members (or other membership loops) and retain the property that any intensional definition (that did not involve a self reference or loop) would result in a set. However, this leaves some untidiness; for example, how does one say that a set is a set?[1]

It should be noted that well-founded sets include hierarchical sets as a subset.

12.3.4 Non-Well-Founded Set Theory

The essence of non-well-founded sets (also known as hypersets) is to allow sets to be members of themselves, where the membership graphs can be constructed. This is illustrated in Figure 12-6.

In this case, Russell's Paradox is avoided by requiring that all sets be constructed out of their members, so it is not assumed that there is a set that corresponds to any intensional definition. So for example, the set of all sets that do not include themselves

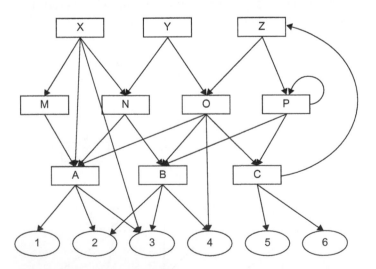

Figure 12-6 An example of non-well-founded sets.

would simply not refer to any set—it would be literally non-sense. Using non-well-founded sets allows useful things to be said that well-founded sets prevent, like "class is a class," "thing is a member of class," and "class is a member of thing."

It should be noted that non-well-founded sets include well-founded sets as a subset, and indeed almost all the sets/classes we are interested in are well-founded, so non-well-founded sets effectively give us a framework within which standard sets reside.

12.4 A High Level Data Model for Classes

Figure 12-7 presents a high level data model for classes. A **class** is a set whose identity is defined by its membership and is at least non-well-founded. A **specialization** *is a* **relationship** where each member of the *subclass* is a member of the *super-class*. A **specialization** has exactly one *subclass* that is a **class**, and exactly one *superclass* that is a **class**.

Class_of_class is the powerset of class; that is, its members are **class** and any of its possible subtypes. A **class** may be a *member_of* one or more **class_of_class**.

A **spatio_temporal_extent** may be a *member_of* one or more **class_of_spatio_temporal_extent**.

Class_of_spatio_temporal_extent is the powerset of **spatio_temporal_extent**; that is, it may have **spatio_temporal_extent** and any of its possible subtypes as a member. Similarly, **class_of_class_of_spatio_temporal_extent** may have **class_of_spatio_temporal_extent** and any of its possible subtypes as members. A **class_of_spatio_temporal_extent** may be a *member_of* one or more **class_of_class_of_spatio_temporal_extent**.

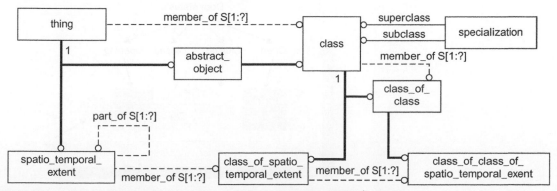

Figure 12-7 A high level data model for **class** and **class_of_spatio_temporal_extent**.

There are three consequences of this:

1. You can choose whether or not to show subtypes as entity types and have any you choose not to show as data. This may be very useful when there are large numbers of subtypes, as for example with subtypes of equipment.
2. If you have forgotten a subtype in your data model, you have a get-out-of-jail-free card, because you can create it as data.
3. The pattern presented above can be repeated for any subtype of **spatio_temporal_extent**.
4. Notice that this blurs the traditional distinction between data and data model.

The **specialization** relationship between classes allows the thick black subtype lines of the data model to be represented as data.

12.5 Properties and Quantities

One way in which the powerset pattern is used is in physical properties and physical quantities.

A physical property is something like a status of a door, such as open and closed; some of these are physical quantities, like particular degrees of hotness such as 20°C, or a particular mass such as 5 kg.

With the case of the door, a number of physical properties could apply. Let us suppose that it is an automatic door, so the door is open, closing, closed, or opening, as illustrated in Figure 12-8. These values are physical properties, and for a particular door, states can be classified by these physical properties, so physical properties are classes of spatio-temporal extent.

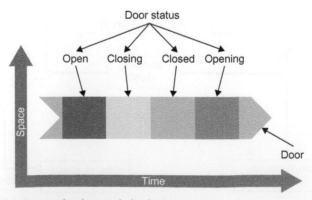

Figure 12-8 States of a door and physical properties.

So far so good; however, these physical properties are mixed up with all the other hundreds and thousands of other physical properties doors and other things can have. What we want is a way to group just the door status properties. There are three things we can do:

1. We can add a door status subtype to **physical_property**; then the values can be found as members of this entity type.
2. We can add door status as an instance of **kind_of_physical_property**, and classify the door status values.
3. We can add an attribute to the door entity type (if we have one in the data model) with a domain that has the four values.

For an integration data model, the second option is likely to be preferred. It is a more general and portable solution, and you can add new kinds of physical property and property values as data, rather than having to change the data model.

Figure 12-9 presents a data model for this case with the important entity types highlighted. A **state** may be a *member_of* one or more **classes_of_state**. A **physical_property** *is a* **class_of_state** that is a set of **state** that shares a characteristic. A **class_of_physical_property** *is a* **class_of_class_of_spatio_temporal_extent**. A **kind_of_physical_property** *is a* **class_of_physical_property** all of whose members are comparable.

A **physical_property** may be a *member_of* one or more **classes_of_physical_property**. A **physical_property** must be a *member_of* exactly one **kind_of_physical_property**.

Figure 12-10 shows a data model for physical quantities such as temperatures and pressures, building on the data model

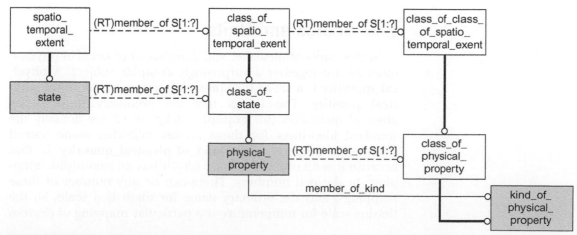

Figure 12-9 A data model for physical properties.

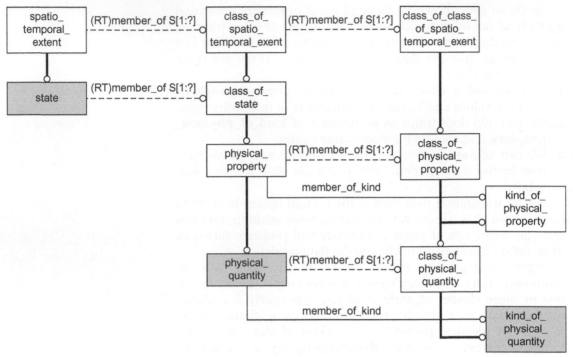

Figure 12-10 A data model for physical quantity.

from Figure 12-9. A **physical_quantity** *is a* **physical_property** where the set of **physical_quantity** of the same **kind_of_physical_quantity** can be ordered by a greater than function.

12.6 Scales and Units

Scales, units of measure, and dimensions of kinds of physical quantity are together a surprisingly complex subject. A **physical_quantity** is a set of the **states** that are members of the **physical_quantity**. The things that we ordinarily think of as physical quantities (for example, 30 kg, 20°C) are actually the standard identifiers for these classes following some agreed scheme. A property of a **kind_of_physical_quantity** is that because it is an ordered infinite set—it has an isomorphic mapping[2] to the real numbers. There can be any number of these mappings, and the ordinary name for them is a scale. So the Celsius scale for temperature is a particular mapping of degrees

---

[2]*Isomorphic* means that it is a one-to-one mapping.

of hotness to real numbers. This is a scale where adding one degree Celsius anywhere along the scale means the same thing. Therefore there is a unit of measure, the degree Celsius. Now different scales can use the same unit of measure. For example, the maximum allowable working temperature is a **kind_of_ physical_quantity** that has a mapping to the real numbers, and we will naturally choose that this scale will use the same unit of measure as one of our temperature scales.

The data model in Figure 12-11 is a simplified data model for identifying a **physical_quantity** by a **scale** and *value*. A **scale** is an isomorphic functional[3] mapping from **physical_quantity_ kind** to a number space, for example, the positive reals for mass. I have not shown number space in this simplified data model, only number representations (REAL).

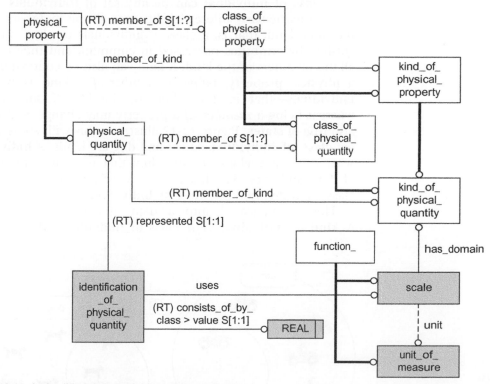

Figure 12-11 A simplified data model for scales and units.

---

[3]A function is used in its mathematical sense of a one-to-many relationship. Being isomorphic makes it one-to-one.

A **physical_quantity** has a quantification mapping to a number that is a *member_of* a particular **scale**, and that number has an **identification** by, for example, some data type such as a **REAL**. I have combined the quantification, number, and identification into **identification_of_physical_quantity**. A **scale** may have not more than one **unit_of_measure**. An **identification_of_physical_quantity** *represents* exactly one **physical_quantity**. An **identification_of_physical_quantity** is an **identification** that *uses* exactly one **scale** and has exactly one *value* that is a **REAL**. The *value* relationship type is a renaming of the *consists_of_by_class* relationship type. Section 13.9 in the following chapter will deal with representation in more detail.

12.7 Kinds

A **class_of_individual** can be any set of **individuals**. Some sets are particularly interesting because all the members are of the same kind; that is, a class of individuals or objects distinguished by attributes possessed in common, and they contain all the members of the kind. A kind can also be contrasted with a **physical_property**, being a *member_of* a kind is true for **individuals**—that is, the whole of the life of something—whereas being a *member_of* a property may change, and this is also true of **states**. Figure 12-12 illustrates this with some different **class_of_individual**, so car and dog are kinds of **individual**, whereas **???** is a **class_of_individual** that is some combination of dogs and cars. So what we can see from this is that some **class_of_individual** is a **kind_of_individual**.

This is translated into a data model in Figure 12-13. A **kind_of_individual** *is a* **class_of_individual** where all the

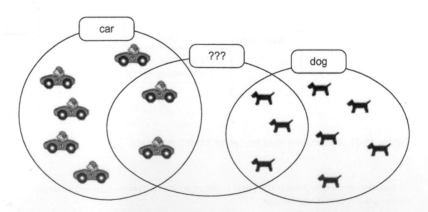

Figure 12-12 A Venn diagram illustrating kinds vs. sets.

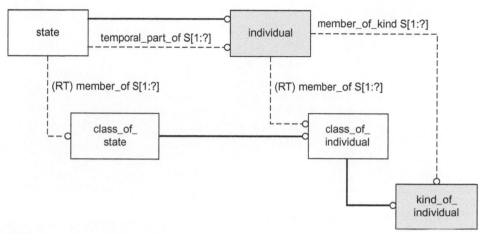

Figure 12-13 A data model for kind of individual.

members possess attributes in common. An **individual** may be a *member_of* one or **more kind_of_individual**.

12.8 Concluding Remarks

I have taken the lid off classes in this chapter. I have taken advantage of the fact that when using a four-dimensional approach to individuals with possible worlds, set theory is sufficient. I have looked at the different restrictions on set theory that you may find in different environments and have shown you how to recognize them. I have also noted the utility of powersets in the context of hierarchical sets, which commonly occur. Finally, I have presented a data model fragment that shows how the pattern derived from powersets can be applied to give flexibility to a data model, and I have illustrated this by considering how this applies to physical properties and kinds of individual.

13

INTENTIONALLY CONSTRUCTED OBJECTS

13.1 Introduction

Many of the objects in the world around us only exist because we are here: products, money, companies, agreements, and so on. In Chapter 11, we briefly noted that some objects are what they are because we say so (that is, they are intentionally constructed). In this chapter, I more thoroughly explore some of the different kinds of intentionally constructed objects. The idea is to give you an insight into the world of intentional objects and to show you how to recognize, analyze, and model them. The view I have taken in this case follows the work of John Searle.[1]

An important thing to remember about intentional objects that distinguishes them from natural objects is that they are what they are because we say so. With natural objects you are trying to discover what something is by observing its

---

[1]Much of this chapter is based on J. R. Searle, The Construction of Social Reality, Penguin Books, 1996.

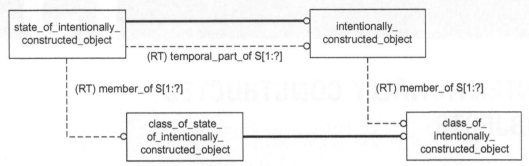

Figure 13-1 A data model for an intentionally constructed object.

characteristics; with intentional objects you are trying to discover the rules for the object and where the authoritative source for them lies. Sometimes this may be obscure or vague.

Figure 13-1 starts with **state_of_intentionally_constructed_object** and **intentionally_constructed_object** from Figure 11-14. As with **state** and **individual**, an **intentionally_constructed_object** *is a* **state_of_intentionally_constructed_object**, because it is just a special **state** where the period is the whole of its life. On the other hand, a **state_of_intentionally_constructed_object** *is an* **intentionally_constructed_object**, or a *temporal_part_of* an **intentionally_constructed_object**, and may be a *temporal_part_of* more than one.

13.2 Functional Objects

The simplest type of intentional object is a functional object. This is where an object is created in order to perform a function or role[2] or where a role is imposed on an object.

Typical functional objects are those that are part of the man-made world around us: cars, houses, offices, tools, computers, and so on. They are made to perform a function, and it is that function that defines them. So, although we may use a screwdriver to open a tin of paint, it does not thereby become a paint-tin-opener, it remains a screwdriver because that is its intended purpose. Equally, if a screwdriver is never actually used to drive screws, it is still a screwdriver.

It is always interesting to consider marginal cases. So let us consider for a moment a person walking along the beach who sees a smooth stone and decides that it will make a nice

---

[2]These are sometimes also known as artifacts.

paperweight. So he or she picks it up, takes it home, and uses it as such. At what point did it stop being simply a stone on a beach and become a paperweight? That is, when did the paperweight, which is a state of the stone, start? In this case it is actually the act of deciding it was a paperweight that made it one. So a state of a stone is a paperweight because someone (anyone) said so, and while they said so. There are, however, limits to the power of will. If I decide that the Empire State Building would make a nice paperweight, it does not become one simply by my act of will, so the object needs to be fit for purpose as well.

Although the stone becoming a paperweight is a simple act of will, most functional objects acquire their function by being made or at least shaped to provide features to meet their intended purpose. Simple tools may consist of just a single component, but more complex ones (systems) have multiple components. However, in both cases it is the arrangement of the parts that provides the function. So a bag of pump parts is not a pump until they are correctly assembled. You will recall that in Chapter 11 we called this type of aggregation composition. Assembly is the intentional composition of objects, as opposed to the natural composition of objects (of molecules from atoms, for example).

One of the possibilities with functional objects is to make multiple ones that are sufficiently similar as to be interchangeable. Today we take such things for granted, but it is worth remembering that before Joseph Whitworth and the Whitworth thread, nuts and bolts were made individually as a pair and that there was no expectation that a nut that would fit on one bolt would fit on another bolt of the same size. It was the genius of Whitworth that worked out what tolerances the nuts and bolts had to be made to so that any nut of a certain size would fit any bolt of the same size. This was a huge breakthrough in engineering both for mass production and maintenance, since it allowed parts to be replaced. Systems and system components like this are a major topic in their own right, so I will return to them in the next chapter.

Figure 13-2 shows a basic data model for functional objects as just described. A **functional_object** *is an* **intentionally_ constructed_object**, a **physical_object**, and a **state_of_functional_ object** that has a **role** as an *intended_role*, where **role** is the usual term used for kind of **participant**. A **kind_of_functional_ object** *is a* **class_of_functional_object** where all of the members are of the same kind. A **functional_object** may be a *member_of* one or more **kind_of_functional_object**. A **functional_object** has an *intended_role* that is *part_of_by_class* a **class_of_activity**

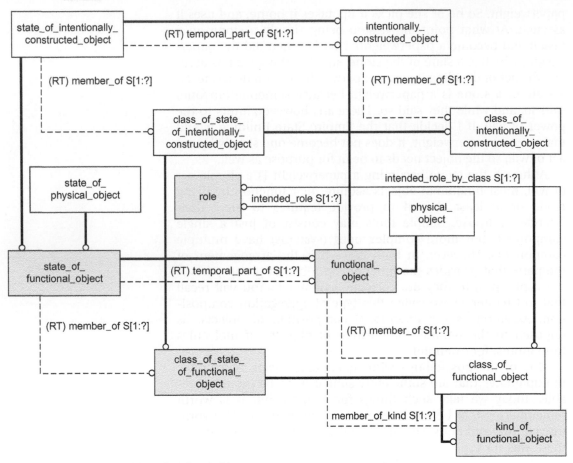

Figure 13-2 A data model for a functional object.

or **class_of_association**. This does not mean that the **functional_ object** is always playing this **role** as a **participant**; it means that it is intended that some **state_of_functional_object** should play this **role**.

Similarly, at a class level, a **kind_of_functional_object** has an *intended_role_by_class*, meaning that each instance of the **kind_ of_functional_object** has that **role** as an *intended_role*.

13.3 Socially Constructed Objects

Socially constructed objects require the agreement of a social community (at least two people) to exist: contracts, companies, money, and so on. For example, money requires not only the authority of the issuer, but the acceptance of the populace who use it as money. A key aspect of socially constructed objects is that they need a process to manage their life, since they do not come into existence except by human will.

Since it is the basis for many socially constructed objects, I will start with ownership.

13.4 Ownership

Ownership is one of the things that is deeply ingrained in our society. Much of trade is based on ownership so that we can exchange what we own but do not need for things that we want that others own. Although ownership can be simply asserted by a party, this has to be acquiesced to by others. Ownership is an association that consists of an asset state of a thing, an asset, and the owner state of a party in the ownership of that thing. Ownership can be transferred between parties. Figure 13-3 illustrates this with a space-time map.

This space-time map shows a gift. The top bar is a physical object. There are two states of this that are assets, one before the transfer of ownership, and one after. There are also two owner states shown. These are for the owner of the first asset state and the owner of the second asset state. There are two ownership associations consisting of the first asset and owner states, and the second asset and owner states (shown by the unshaded box containing them). The transfer of ownership causes the termination of the first ownership association, and its constituent participants, and the beginning of the second ownership association and its constituent participants. Usually, there is an exchange with a transfer of money in the opposite direction to the transfer of goods.

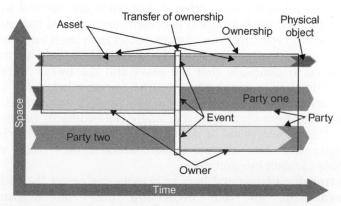

Figure 13-3 A space-time map for ownership and transfer of ownership.

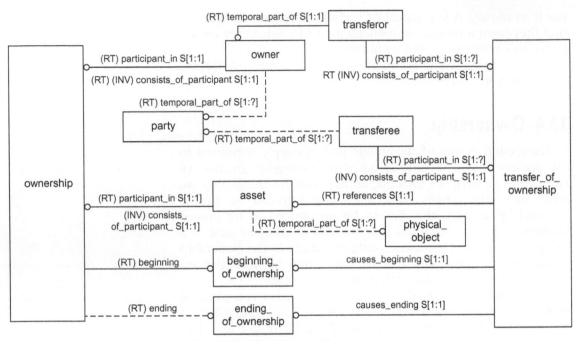

Figure 13-4 A data model for ownership and transfer of ownership.

Figure 13-4 presents a data model for ownership and transfer of ownership. I have left out the supertypes of the various entity types on this occasion to keep the diagram clearer, but you can find them in the version in Chapter 17.

An **ownership** *is an* **association** that *consists_of* exactly one **owner** and exactly one **asset**. An **owner** is a *temporal_part_of* a **party** and an **asset** is a *temporal_part_of* a **physical_object**, where a **party** may be a person or an organization.

These two one-to-one relationship types are unusual in traditional data models where it is sometimes assumed that such a relationship type indicates that the objects at each end are the same thing. Clearly that is not the case here, or else we would be forced to conclude that the **asset** and the **owner** were the same thing, since they both have one-to-one relationship types to **ownership**. What is true is that this kind of ontological data modeling throws up objects that might not ordinarily be considered. This greater level of detail is one of the things that helps to make the data models stable, which makes them more suitable for data integration.

A **transfer_of_ownership** *is an* **activity** that *causes* the **ending_of_ownership** for one **ownership** and the **beginning_of_ownership** for another. A **transferor** and a **transferee** is a *participant_in* a **transfer_of_ownership** where the **transferor** is also a *temporal_part_of* the **owner** of the **asset** they are transferring ownership of. The **transferee** is a *temporal_part_of* the **party** that is taking ownership of the **physical_object**. It is not a *temporal_part_of* an **owner** of the object transferred.

One of the things you can see with this model is that when you get to the level of business terminology that there are appropriate entity types for the terms that are used.

An important thing about ownership is that it confers rights and obligations on the owner. The owner has the right to enjoy the things he owns, and to dispose of them as he sees fit. However, there may also be obligations. For example, when you own a car, you not only have the right to drive the car, but you can also authorize others to drive it and eventually sell it. You also have the obligation to keep it in a roadworthy condition and to insure it. These rights and obligations are classes of activity that we may or are obliged to perform.

13.5 Agreements

An *agreement* is two or more people determining a course of action. There are actually three things here:

1. Reaching agreement
2. Executing the agreement
3. The agreement process that is the two of these together

A space-time map for an agreement process is shown in Figure 13-5.

What is agreed to is the agreement execution. This one is very simple, but they can be complex and deal with what will happen in different possible worlds with different outcomes, such as one of the parties failing to meet their obligations. Notice that both reaching agreement and agreement execution activities may have multiple activities as parts.

Figure 13-6 shows a data model for agreements. All agreement related activities are instances of **intentional_ activity**. An **agreement_process** *consists_of* exactly one **reaching_agreement** and *consists_of* exactly one **agreement_execution** part. Similarly, an **agreement_execution** and a

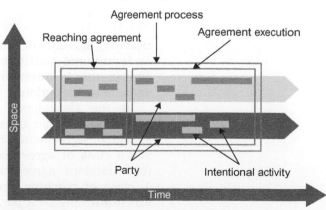

Figure 13-5 A space-time map for a simple agreement.

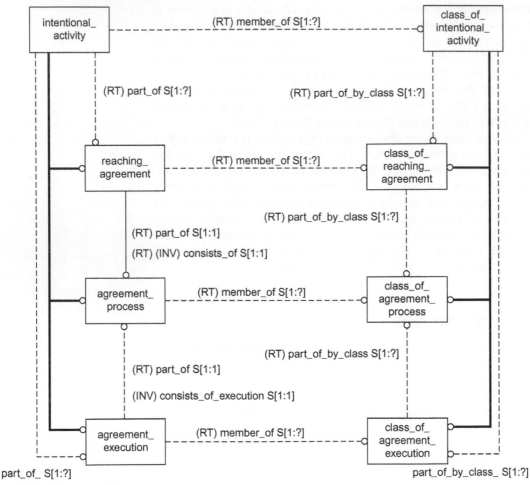

Figure 13-6 A data model for agreements.

reaching_agreement must be *part_of* an **agreement_process**. An **intentional_activity** may be a *part_of* one or more **reaching_agreements**. An **intentional_activity** may be *part_of* one or more **agreement_executions**.

At the class level, an **agreement_process**, a **reaching_agreement**, and an **agreement_execution** may be a *member_of* a **class_of_agreement_process**, a **class_of_reaching_agreement**, and a **class_of_agreement_execution**, respectively. This means that standard agreements and processes can be captured. A **class_of_reaching_agreement** and a **class_of_agreement_execution** may be a *part_of_by_class* of a **class_of_agreement_process**.

13.6 Contracts

An important kind of agreement is a contract. A contract is an arrangement of mutual obligations, usually an exchange of a good or service for money (but barter is also included) when one party to the exchange makes an offer, and the other accepts it. The contract is made when the offer is accepted. It should be noted that it is not necessarily the first offer that is accepted. On Saturday, I sold my Wayfarer sailing dinghy. I had advertised it for sale at £2500 (my opening offer). A person interested in the dinghy came along and after looking it over, he offered £2000. I rejected the offer and said that the least I would accept was £2250. He offered £2100. I rejected the offer. He accepted my offer of £2250. The contract was made. Either party might have made the final offer or accepted it.

Figure 13-7 illustrates this exchange in a space-time map. I have simplified the representation of the transfers of ownership compared to Figure 13-3 and omitted the ownership associations.

A simpler version of this happens in a supermarket or at a gas station. The supermarket offers to sell a certain good at a certain price. It is generally understood that they will not accept counter-offers. You accept the offer by taking the article to the check-out to pay. That you have accepted their offer by taking the product to the check-out is why, when a supermarket has mispriced an item for some reason, they are obliged to sell it to

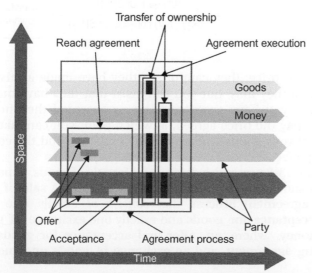

Figure 13-7 A space-time map for an exchange of goods for money.

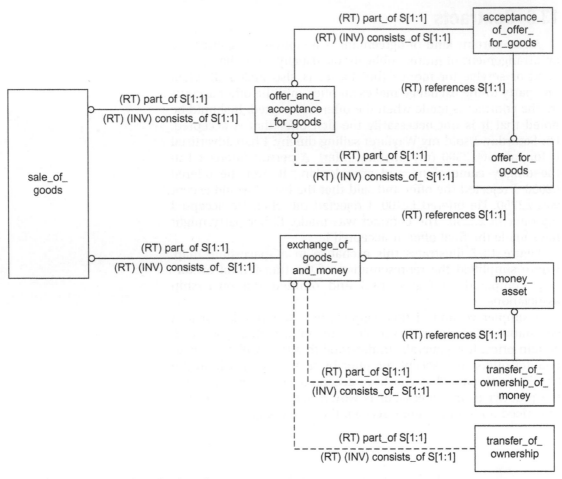

Figure 13-8 A data model for sale of goods.

you at that price; they cannot say they have made a mistake—or at least they may, but you can insist that they have made an offer that you have accepted.[3] Having accepted the offer, you need to pay the price agreed, at which point you can take ownership of your goods whereupon the exchange and the contract is completed.

Figure 13-8 presents a data model for sale of goods. Supertypes are not shown to keep the diagram uncluttered. A **sale_of_goods** *is an* **agreement_process** that *consists_of* exactly one **offer_and_acceptance_for_goods** and exactly one **exchange_of_goods_and_money**, where an **offer_and_acceptance_for_goods** *is a* **reaching_agreement**, and an **exchange_of_goods_and_money** *is*

[3]This, at least, is the case under English law.

an **agreement_execution**. An **offer_and_acceptance_for_goods** *consists_of* exactly one **offer_for_goods**, which *references* the **exchange_of_goods_and_money** that is the subject of the offer, and exactly one **acceptance_of_offer_for_goods** that *references* the **offer_for_goods** accepted. An **exchange_of_goods_and_money** *consists_of* exactly one **transfer_of_ownership** and exactly one **transfer_of_ownership_of_money**. A **transfer_of_ownership_of_money** *is a* **transfer_of_ownership** that *references* a **money_asset** as the **asset** that is transferred.

You should refer back to Figure 13-4 for other relationship types of **transfer_of_ownership** such as the **transferor** and **transferee** and the **asset** involved.

13.7 Organizations

What an organization is precisely is surprisingly difficult to answer. What is clear is that an organization is brought into existence by the agreement of some people who want to form the organization for some common purpose. However, is an organization the following?
1. The agreement execution that is the pursuit of that common purpose
2. What is established by the agreement execution
3. A system
4. Those who contribute to the organization's purpose as directors, employees, or members while they are in that role
5. What the directors, employees, or members of an organization do
6. What is owned by the organization
7. Some combination of the above

A spatio-temporal analysis requires that an organization, as an individual and non-abstract object, is a spatio-temporal extent of some kind, and that must be based in some way on the spatio-temporal extents of the people who are its directors, employees, or members. Perhaps the key question is whether— let's say for an employee—it is the state of them from when their employment contract starts until their employment is terminated, or the person while they are actually working, say from 9 to 5, Monday to Friday.

Therefore an organization is a system, because it has a purpose, and it consists of the participants acting for it and is established as the result of an agreement process.

Figure 13-9 shows a space-time map for establishing an organization. The agreement process consists of reaching an agreement to establish an organization and then the agreement

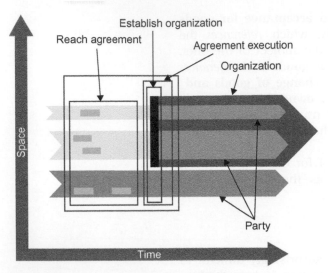

Figure 13-9 A space-time map for establishing an organization.

execution is establishing the organization. It would be expected that the organization would consist of some of the parties to the agreement. However, not all parties necessarily become part of the organization. For example, a registration authority would participate in the establishment of the organization but would not be a part of it.

Generally, an organization is considered as a legal person, in which case what is owned by an organization is not part of the organization any more than what is owned by a person is part of a person. However, I am told that there are countries where what is owned by particular types of organization is part of that organization, and there is no reason why that cannot be, given that organizations are socially constructed and the legal framework for that construction can specify what it wishes.

This example illustrates the process of social construction, but it is not particularly interesting to create a separate data model for this when the general data model for agreement can be applied.

A key association between a party and a person is employment, where a person is employed by a party. This is illustrated in Figure 13-10. Here you can see that there is an agreement process that consists of a reach agreement, and an employment as the result of an agreement execution. The employment consists of an association between an employer and an employee. Notice in particular that the employee is a state of a person (and not a person). Of course, the employment association includes a number of activities as parts, including the work the employee does for the organization, and the payment that the employer makes to the employee.

This is also shown in Figure 13-11. An **employer** and an **employee** are the *participants_in* exactly one **employment** where an **employee** *is a* **state_of_person** and a **participant** that is a *temporal_part_of* a **person**. An **employer** *is a* **state_of_party** and a **participant** that is a *temporal_part_of* a **party**.

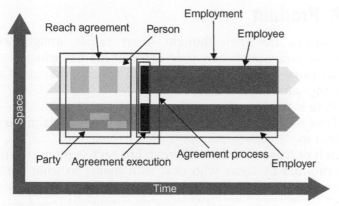

Figure 13-10 A space-time diagram for employment.

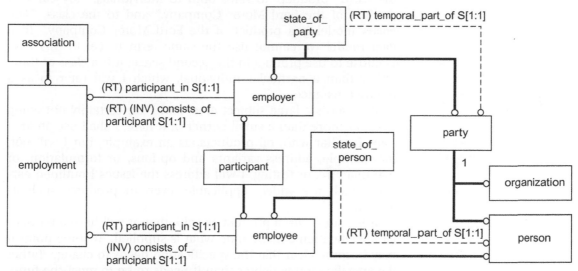

Figure 13-11 A data model for employment.

Notice that **employee** is a subtype of **participant** and **state_of_person** and not **person**. This is quite clear in a four-dimensional analysis, though it is a common error in data modeling to consider **employee** to be a subtype of **person,** and indeed other roles to be subtypes of the entity type playing the role.

In *Data Modeling Essentials* Simsion and Witt also notice that **employee** is not a subtype of **person**: they find that it is not a 1:1 relationship type; however, they are not able to offer an explanation as to why that should be. Four-dimensional analysis is able to supply that explanation.

13.8 Product

Products are often thought of as rather straightforward things in data models. However, consider the following:

- The price of the same product will vary from store to store in the same supermarket chain.
- There is the brand name the product is sold as.
- There is usually a specification that a product claims to conform to.

Each of these is clearly different, but each is often referred to as a product by those who deal with them. So what are they, how are they distinguished, and how do they relate to each other?

In addition to this, there is the issue of ambiguity. We use the word "product" to refer both to individuals, "My car is a product of the Ford Motor Company," and to the class, "The Focus model is a product of the Ford Motor Company." In a data model we cannot use the same term twice. In this case I choose to use product in the second sense: it is a class of thing rather than a particular individual, which I will refer to as a product instance.

Product is a large subject area, and I am certainly not going to cover more than a small corner of it here. I shall use an area I am familiar with, oil products, as an example, but I will not, for example, address variants and options, or formulation, or manufacture, or testing. I will address the issues I outlined earlier, which are widely applicable, even to products such as aircraft.

If we start with a product as sold, then it will have a particular specification constraining what is supplied. At some point it may become clear that the specification needs to change. Either the specification is tighter than it needs to be to meet the functional requirements, or a different way has been found to meet the same requirements, or you wish to offer enhanced functionality. Under these circumstances you consider it to be the same product, but a different version. It is the version that carries the detailed specification. This is illustrated in the Venn diagram of Figure 13-12.

The dots correspond to individual product instances that are manufactured and supplied for sale; I will call these a sales product. I will call the different versions sold as the sales product the sales product version. The usual distinction between a version and a variant is that variants are available for sale at the same time, so some of their differences are apparent to the buyer, whereas versions are available for sale sequentially at a

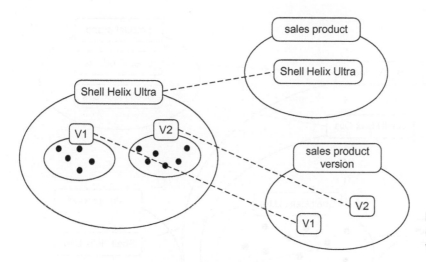

Figure 13-12 A Venn diagram of sales product and product versions.

place and differences are not apparent to the buyer. Notice the different levels of abstraction in the Venn diagram. I have illustrated this example with some products taken from Shell's public website. At one level Shell Helix Ultra is a set with oil product instances, shown by the black dots; at the next level it is an instance of sales product. What you can also see is that the V1 and V2 of the Shell Helix Ultra are subsets of it.

Now when you look at the name for this product it is clear that there are several elements that have to do with how it is sold. Ultra is a premium brand (as opposed to Plus and various other brandings). These brand elements in turn fall under the Helix brand used to promote lubricants for vehicles apart from motorbikes (as opposed to marine or machinery applications). This in turn falls under the Shell brand (as opposed to the Royal Dutch Shell Company). This is illustrated in Figure 13-13. Notice that Shell Helix and Shell Products are superclasses of the various sales products.

You can see that a product brand is a supertype of products as sold, and that there can be many levels of supertype. On the right hand side of the diagram, you can see that a distinction is made between levels at which there is a sales product; that is, something you can buy and get something specific, and product brands, which are groupings for marketing purposes.

A data model that reflects this is shown in Figure 13-14. Notice that although the data model is mostly about classes, it is still rooted in individuals, with **state_of_sales_product_instance** and **sales_product_instance**, and similarly **class_of_state_of_sales_product_instance** and **class_of_sales_product_instance**.

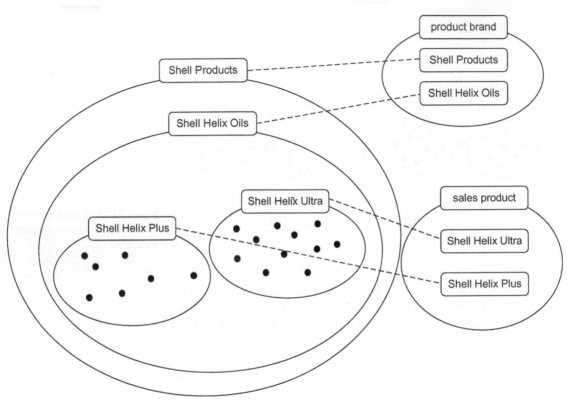

Figure 13-13 A Venn diagram for some of Shell's products and brands as presented on their website.

These rather formal entity types provide the framework for those that are really of interest **product_brand**, **sales_product**, and **sales_product_version**, which are kinds of **sales_product_instance**.

Now I will turn to how the product is actually sold, with a price, at a point of sale. We have actually already dealt with this when we looked at the sale of goods example. What happened here is that there was an offer and an acceptance of offer. Figure 13-15 illustrates this in a Venn diagram. So placing a sales product on the shelf and putting a price on it is making an offer. Interestingly, this is an activity rather than a physical object. A product does not generally have a single price wherever and whenever it is sold, but for this sales product in this place and time, it is offered at this price. This is a class of offer that I will call a *product offering*. Now the product offering at a price can be specific to a point of sale, to a sales channel, or globally, and is for a period of time.

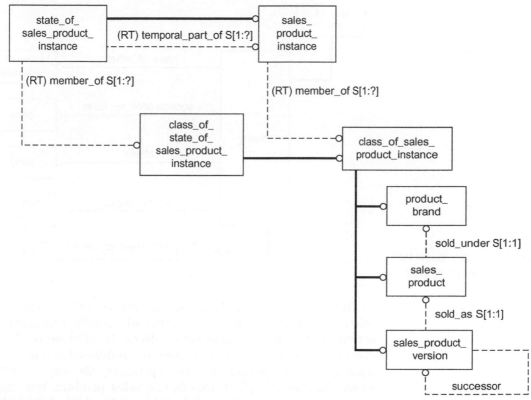

Figure 13-14 A data model for sales product.

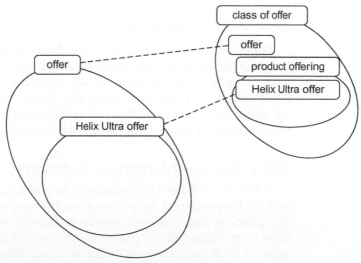

Figure 13-15 A Venn diagram for product offering.

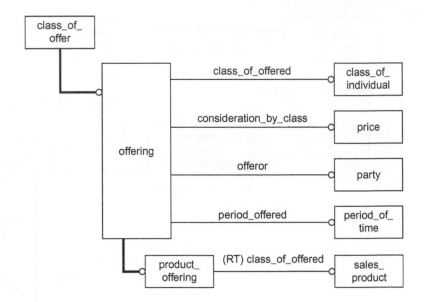

Figure 13-16 A data model for offering and product offering.

Figure 13-16 shows a data model for class of offer and product offering. A **class_of_offer** *is a* **class_of_socially_constructed_activity** that is any possible set of **offers**. An **offering** is all and every **offer** for an instance of a **class_of_individual** at a **price**, by a **party**, and for a **period_of_time**. A **product_offering** *is an* **offer** where the *class_of_offer* is exactly one **sales_product**. You might also want to add something about where it is sold to the mix, but I have assumed a universal price for simplicity in this example.

13.9 Representation

Representation is a matter of one thing standing for another. In principle, anything can stand for anything else, if we agree to that. So in a game of chess, a salt shaker may stand for the white queen, and waving a hand may mean hello or goodbye if we agree that. However, most of our interest is in information representing the real-world things that it stands for.

13.9.1 Signs—Information Instances

It is easy to think of information as abstract, but it is important to be grounded in physical reality and work from there. The physical reality of information is usually marks on physical objects, perhaps ink on paper, or magnetic flux on a disc, and so on. I shall refer to such things as *signs*. They are generally a state of some physical object, or an activity. However, many

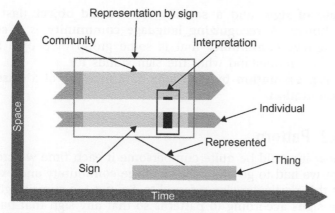

Figure 13-17 Usage of sign to represent some thing.

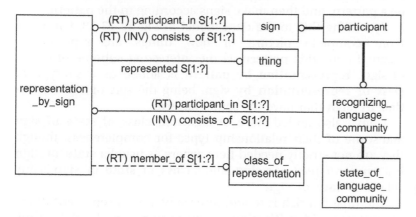

Figure 13-18 A data model for representation by sign.

signs, like this book, are intentionally constructed to be particular signs. Here a community represents some thing by a sign. The thing represented may be abstract, or it may not be contemporaneous with the sign that represents it, so it is not a participant in the representation, it is just referenced by it as the thing represented. This is illustrated in Figure 13-17, where I have chosen an individual to be the thing represented for convenience.

At some point a member of the community may come along and interpret the sign, like you reading this book. I have shown an example of this in the figure, but we do not normally record interpretations and it is straightforward, so I will not take that further.

Figure 13-18 is a data model for representation by sign. A **representation_by_sign** *is an* **association** of a **sign** and a **recognizing_language_community**. A **sign** *is a* **participant**, a **state_of_sign**, and a **socially_constructed_object** (last two not shown). A **recognizing_language_community** *is a* **state_of_language_community** that is some group of people for a time that understand what the sign stands for.

A **representation_by_sign** may be a member of a **class_of_representation**.

13.9.2 Pattern

Now it would be quite cumbersome if each time we created a sign we had to go around a language community and explain what this particular sign referred to. So, not too surprisingly, we make signs according to patterns so that any sign that has the same pattern represents the same thing. This is illustrated in Figure 13-19. This is the general way that we do things: we agree on a pattern, and then make signs according to the pattern.

By adding this to the data model in Figure 13-18, you get a more complete picture of how things are represented. Figure 13-20 adds **pattern** as the interesting subtype of **class_of_sign**. **representation_by_pattern** is added as a subtype of **class_of_representation_by_sign**, being the sets of **representation_by_sign** that have the same **pattern**.

I have also added **state_of_sign** and **class_of_state_of_sign** and some of their relationship types for completeness, though they are not strictly needed here, where as usual a **state_of_sign** is a *temporal_part_of* a **sign**, and a **class_of_state_of_sign** is any subset of **state_of_sign**.

The final flourish is to add three subtypes to **representation_by_pattern**: **identification**, **description**, and **definition**. An **identification** is where the **pattern** is a surrogate for the

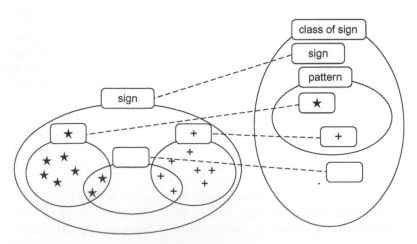

Figure 13-19 A Venn diagram showing the relationship between signs and patterns.

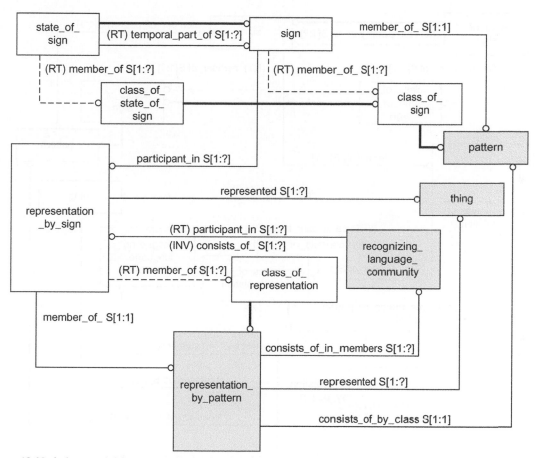

Figure 13-20 A data model for representation by sign and representation by pattern.

thing represented. A **description** is where the **pattern** describes the **thing** represented. Finally, a **definition** is where the **pattern** defines the members of the **class** that is represented. Note that it only makes sense to define classes; individuals are what they are and can only be described. **identification_of_physical_quantity** is shown as a subtype of **identification**. You will recall that it was first defined when I looked at **physical_quantity**. These subtypes are added in Figure 13-21.

This is certainly not everything there is to say about representation—I have not covered things like formats and document definitions, for instance—but it is a good start to being able to deal with multiple identifiers by different communities for the same thing, a problem frequently found in data integration.

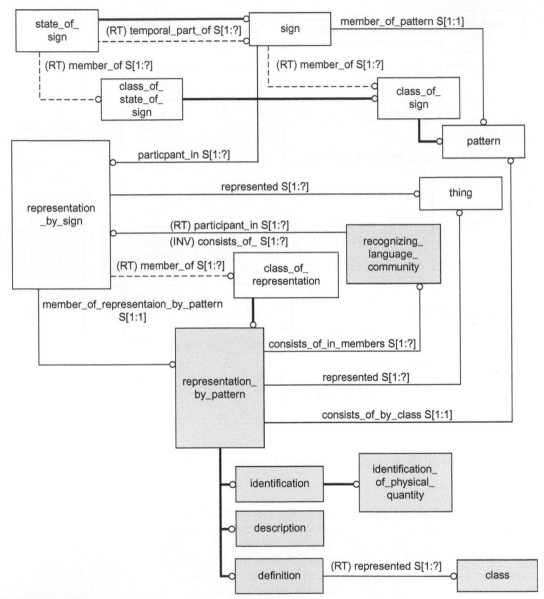

Figure 13-21 Adding identification, description, and definition.

13.10 Concluding Remarks

I have taken a look at intentionally constructed objects. The essence of them is that they are what they are because we say so. In some ways this makes them easy—you just have to understand how they are defined. In other ways this makes them more difficult, because they can be very varied and different people can define things that could be the same but are not in arbitrary ways. They are also the things that are involved in much of our daily life.

One of the central intentionally constructed objects is agreements. Many intentionally constructed objects either are agreements or are the result of agreements. Another key intentionally constructed object for information management is the sign. It is the root of all that we do with information, yet it arises from conventional use.

I have also finally looked at some of the things that are commonly found in data models, in particular, organizations and people. Here, we were not only able to conclude that employee is not a subtype of person, as I have sometimes seen it modeled, but I have been able to explain why it is not through four-dimensional analysis; even though others who have been able to discern this have not been able to explain it.

14

SYSTEMS AND SYSTEM COMPONENTS

This chapter looks at systems and a surprising kind of physical object that can survive all its parts being replaced simultaneously—a system component. System components are found in certain circumstances when the same role (in some sense) in a system is played by a succession of objects. It is easy to confuse system components with other types of object, and you need to take care to distinguish system components from ordinary physical objects, classes of activity, and classes of physical object.

14.1 What Are Systems and System Components?

A *system* is a complex physical object that consists of many components that play a role in how the system functions. Systems may be either naturally occurring, or intentionally constructed.

System components arise in systems, in particular in complex artifacts. In this case, they are part of how we make things

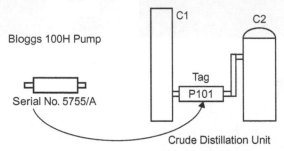

Figure 14-1 Tag and serial number.

maintainable, and they arise by design. For example, with a system component, when a part of the system fails, instead of needing to replace the whole, you can replace the part with one that is identical, and thus you can restore the whole to use. Examples are an engine on an aircraft, a pump in a process plant, and a blade in a rack mounted server farm.

Something to notice about these examples is that the system components are themselves high-value objects that will have serial numbers that identify them, independently of where they are installed. This is not always the case. Many system components are disposable, such as oil filters, spark plugs, nuts, and bolts. As a result, the parts that are replaced will not have serial numbers, will not be tracked, except perhaps as part of a batch or stock level.

In the process industry it is custom and practice to design process plants with system components, and it is well understood that the system components have tag identifiers, and that these would appear on the drawing for the plant, as shown in Figure 14-1.

During construction, for example, a particular pump with its own serial number is installed in the tag position. The maintainence technicians may need to remove the pump periodically in order to perform maintenance in the workshop; they might install another pump in its place. The plant operators talk in terms of the tag, starting up the equipment and shutting it down in those terms. The maintenance technicians talk about the equipment item using the serial number. That is what they maintain.

A similar example comes from air travel. A twin-engine jet has a port and a starboard engine. In each position a particular engine with a serial number is installed. The pilot thinks in terms of operating the port and starboard engine, and the maintenance engineer is concerned with the particular engine installed, its running hours, and its maintenance schedule. A point to note from this example is that when the plane is finally disassembled, the engines may well survive this activity and go on to be installed on another plane, but the port and starboard engine necessarily cease to exist with the plane.

The important point that arises from this is that a system component is existence-dependent on the system it is a system component of and does not have a separate existence from it. It is therefore important to know what system a system component is a component of. In the case of P101 in Figure 14-1, it is a system component of the Crude Distillation Unit. When that is demolished, P101 no longer exists, even though the pump with a serial number that last stood there was probably removed and sold.

A complicating factor is hierarchies of system components. The plane has an engine as a system component, and the engine has a fuel pump as a system component, which is therefore also a part of the plane. How does this work?

What is clear is that if the engine is removed, then the fuel pump is removed with it. So if the fuel pump needed to be replaced, you would want to know which fuel pump relative to the engine, which might itself have been removed from the aircraft. This means that you at least need to have the system component as part of the next higher assembly. However, there is also the operational perspective. Normally you would expect that the system component would hide its details from higher levels, but it is possible that operationally you would need to be able to refer to the port engine fuel pump and to consider it also to be a system component of the aircraft as a whole. This creates an additional system component, which will itself coincide with the system component of the installed engine when it is installed, as well as with the fuel pump with serial number installed in the particular engine. Notice that what distinguishes the two system components is what they are system components of. A brief thought experiment will also confirm that they have potentially different spatio-temporal extents.

From these two examples, you should note that a system component can go through periods of nonexistence, when nothing is installed. This is consistent with our experience. When there is no port engine installed, the pilot will not think that it exists and that he can start it.

An example from human affairs is The President of the United States; from time to time, the person acting as the President changes completely. At one time it is George W. Bush, and at another time it is Barack Obama. The office survives these changes. I already covered this example in Chapter 10.

14.2 The Nature of System Components

From the earlier examples, a number of points arise:
- Three objects are involved: the system, the system component, and the item that is installed.
- The system component can be completely replaced in a material sense and its identity survives.
- The system component can survive periods when no item is installed; that is, its existence is not necessarily continuous.

- The system component is coincident with the item installed while it is installed.
- The system component does not survive the destruction of the object it is a part of, though an item installed may survive.
- Where there are multiple levels of assembly, there may be a system component for each level where each is existence-dependent on the level it is part of.

One thing is clear: These system components are different from "ordinary" physical objects, which at least do not survive simultaneous complete replacement of all their parts, and are not dependent on the existence of some other object. The question is: what are they?

Two approaches I have come across that I disagree with are as follows (I mentioned them in Chapter 10 when talking about The President of the United States):

1. The system components are "logical" rather than physical objects.

   This recognizes two kinds of individual but denies the system component physicality. This does not match well with intuition. Pilots think they are starting a physical engine when they start the port engine. Another problem is that it means admitting that things exist in space-time that are abstract. This would add to our commitments, which is also not attractive if there is an alternative.

2. The system components are role classes whose members are the states of the physical objects that play the role. So The President of the United States is a class, and a state of Barack Obama is a member of that class.

   The first thing to say is that there is such a class. You can have any class that you can construct, and you can certainly construct this class. The question is whether it is what you really mean. A consequence of treating the President of the United States as a class is that you would have to say that it is nonsense to claim that you have shaken the hand of the President because you cannot shake the hand of a class. I would not wish to have to maintain this.

So what does a four-dimensional analysis bring?

Figure 14-2 shows a space-time map for a system component. Here, tag P101, the system component, undergoes but survives complete replacement. What you can see is that the system component consists of the temporal parts of the ordinary physical objects that are installed.

The only question is how tag P101 is constituted from the temporal parts of Pump 1 and Pump 2. There are two possibilities:

1. Tag P101 is the set of temporal parts that stand in this place.

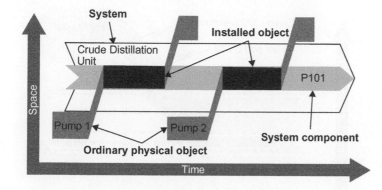

Figure 14-2 A space-time map for a system component.

2. Tag P101 is the composition of the states of the pumps that stand in this place.

The first thing to say is that both of these are valid objects. The question is which is indicated in this case.

As mentioned earlier, the set of temporal parts is an abstract object, and so it does not sit well with a tag being something that is operated.

The composition of the temporal parts is itself a spatio-temporal extent. Thus it matches well the intuition that it can be operated. However, it is not an ordinary physical object, because it changes all its parts at once and can have periods of nonexistence. It is important to note this as a distinguishing feature. This also matches with common sense. You cannot operate a system component during a period of nonexistence. Nor would one expect this to be the case.[1]

Another consequence of this is the coincidence of system component and the ordinary physical objects installed: a temporal part of the former is also a temporal part of the latter, which is called installed object.

All system components are existent dependent on an ordinary physical object that they are part of, and these are not themselves system components (though they may be installed as a system component).

Figure 14-3 illustrates both this and system components existing at different levels. Aircraft 684 has a port engine as a system component. Whatever physical engine is installed there, it is Aircraft 684 port engine. Now Aircraft 684 has a port engine

---

[1]It is important here to distinguish between being able to use something and being able to refer to it. You can refer to things that do not exist at the time they are referred to. We can refer to historical figures that no longer exist like Winston Churchill, and we can refer to things that will (or may) exist in the future but do not now.

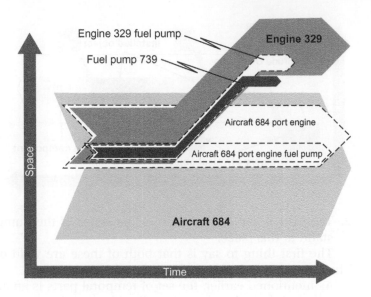

Figure 14-3 A space-time map for system components at more than one level.

fuel pump as a component. This is Aircraft 684 port engine fuel pump. It is also existence dependent on Aircraft 684. Engine 329 is initially installed as Aircraft 684 port engine. It has as a system component a fuel pump, Engine 329 fuel pump. Engine 329 fuel pump is existence-dependent on Engine 329, and not on Aircraft 684. You can see that Engine 329 fuel pump and Aircraft 684 port engine fuel pump are not the same thing when Engine 329 is removed as the port engine. Although these two components started as coincident, once the engine is removed, they no longer are. Finally, fuel pump 739 was originally installed as both Aircraft 684 port engine fuel pump and Engine 329 fuel pump. When the engine is removed, it is no longer coincident with Aircraft 684 port engine fuel pump and when it is later removed from Engine 329 fuel pump, it can be seen as an independent physical object.

14.3 Another Example: A Football[2] Match

Figure 14-4 shows a space-time map (simplified) for a football match. A football team has 11 players. These are independent of both the number on the player's back, and the role (goalkeeper, forward, defense) to which a player is allocated. Furthermore, one player may be substituted for another.

[2]Since I am English, this means Association Football, sometimes referred to as soccer in the US and not American football, though similar principles apply.

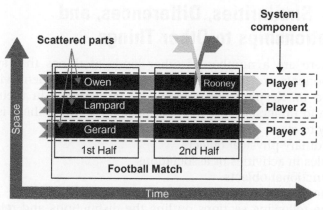

Figure 14-4 A football match showing players as system components of a team and of the football match itself.

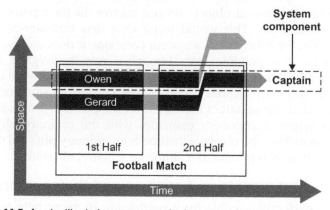

Figure 14-5 A role, like being team captain, is a type of system component.

Figure 14-4 shows Rooney is substituted for Owen in the middle of the second half of the game.

A key thing to note here is that all the parts of player 1 have been substituted at the same time, something that with ordinary physical objects would mean you had a new object. So this pattern again illustrates the distinctive pattern of system components.

Some system components can be roles. This is illustrated in Figure 14-5. This is another view of the same game, but here we see that Owen was captain while he was on the field, but when he left, the captaincy was given to Gerard. Notice that while Owen's numerical replacement was Rooney that did not mean that Rooney took over the role of captain. These can be seen as distinct, because they have different spatio-temporal extents.

14.4 Similarities, Differences, and Relationships to Other Things

There are a number of other kinds of things that system components are sometimes confused with, coincident with, or related to. Keeping the different kinds of things in their own box, and understanding the relationships between them is necessary to avoid making mistakes. They are

- Ordinary physical objects
- Roles in activities or associations
- Functional objects
- The class of activity performed by a functional object

The following sections outline the distinctions and relationships between each of these and system components.

14.4.1 Ordinary Functional Objects

Ordinary physical objects do not survive all their parts being changed at once. This would result in a new ordinary physical object. On the other hand, a system component does survive such a change. It is possible that although a part is designed to be replaceable, it actually does not get replaced during the life of the thing it is a part of, and the part was created in situ and was destroyed in situ as part of the whole. So it is possible (but unlikely) that a system component coincides with the ordinary physical object installed. The object is then both an ordinary physical object and a system component, but simply as a matter of accident.

14.4.2 Participants in Activities and Associations

It is perfectly possible for a participant in an activity to be a system component. The earlier football example illustrates this. The eleven players are participants in the activity. However, they are also system components, because the person filling the position of one or more of the eleven players can be replaced.

However, this does not mean that all system components are participants in activities or associations. So for example, P101 performs a pumping operation in normal operation. However, when the Crude Distillation Unit is shut down, P101 is not performing a pumping activity. However, it is still a system component of the Crude Distillation Unit.

14.4.3 Functional Objects

A *functional object* is something that is intended to perform a function (class of activity). It is common for a system component to also be a functional object. For example, the pump P101 is a functional object as well as a system component. However, that does not mean that all system components are functional objects or that all functional objects are system components.

14.4.4 The Class of Activity Performed by a Functional Object

In the design process for a process plant, the first thing that you do is set out the processes that are to be performed to determine the inputs and outputs (mass and energy) and to decompose the process and sequence the steps to such a level that you can identify the functional objects that will perform the process steps. These process steps are classes of activity (rather than being a process execution). Some have suggested that these are what the tags of a process plant are all about. You cannot start up a class, however, and you can start up P101 (or at least that is what plant operators think they are doing). So tags are the system components that are going to perform the class of activity, not the class of activity itself.

14.5 Do I Need a Separate Set of Classes for System Components?

One of the consequences of introducing systems components is that we now seem to have two kinds of pumps: a system component pump and an ordinary physical object pump. Do we really need both of these?

You may recall that we talked about some properties being temporally *dissective*; that is, if the property applies to the whole, then it applies to any temporal part of it. Being a pump is temporally dissective, but being a whole life pump is not. So if we look at a system component pump, we find that each of its existent states is a state of an ordinary physical object pump. There is no state of existence that is not also a state of an ordinary physical object pump—though not necessarily a state of the same ordinary physical object pump. So we can say quite happily that a system component pump is a pump, and that an ordinary physical object pump is a pump, so we do not need a separate class for each. Of course if we want those pumps that are ordinary physical objects, or those pumps that are system components, then we can construct those classes with ease.

14.6 Extending the Framework for System and System Component

Figure 14-6 shows a data model that reflects the preceding analysis. The key entity types are highlighted.

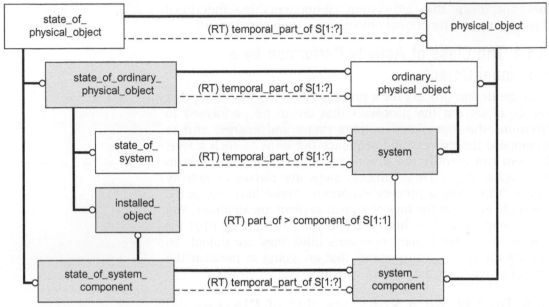

Figure 14-6 Data model for system and system component.

Reading through the diagram, a **system** *is an* **ordinary_ physical_object** that has a number of **system_components** as parts. A **system_component** *is a* **physical_object** that can be replaced, and that can go through periods of nonexistence. An **installed_object** *is a* **state_of_system_component** that is also the **state_of_ordinary_physical_object** of the **ordinary_physical_ object** installed, for the whole period of its installation.

This basic pattern can be specialized for particular circumstances. For example, complex artifacts are usually systems and can be modeled with a direct specialization of the basic pattern for systems and system components as shown in Figure 14-7. The key entity types are highlighted. Note that some relationship types from the basic pattern are not shown.

The pattern also applies to the **person_in_position** of a **person** to a **position** in an **organization**, but this time the specialization is not quite so straightforward, as Figure 14-8 shows.

A **position** *is an* **organization_component** that *is part_of* an **organization**. A **person_in_position** *is a* **state_of_person** that is also a **state_of_position** for the whole time a **person** holds that **position**.

Some people model **person_in_position** as a relationship type between **person** and **position**. The question then arises as

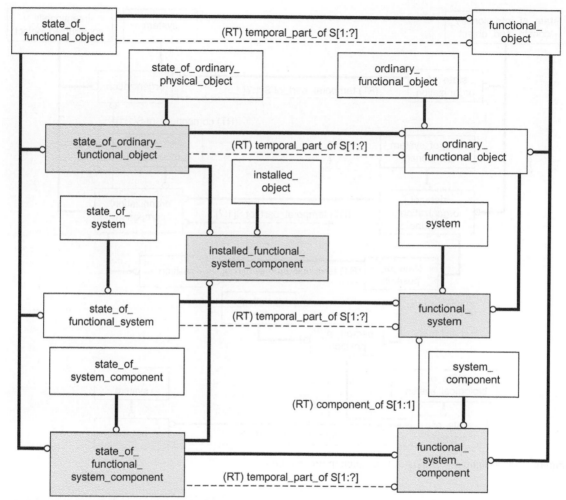

Figure 14-7 Systems that are complex artifacts.

to whether it was the **position** or the **person** who performed some **activity**. In this model, you can see that it is the **person_ in_position** that performs the **activity**, which means that *both* the **position** and the **person** performed it.

You might also be asking right now whether you really need this entire data model just to assign a person to a position. The answer is no. What I have done here is show all the working. You need to have the detail there in the background, but that does not mean you have to show it to your customers. An example of what you might show your customers is illustrated in Figure 14-9.

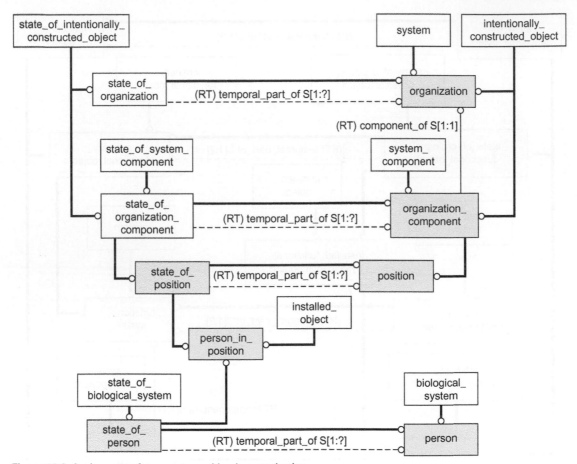

Figure 14-8 Assignment of person to position in organization.

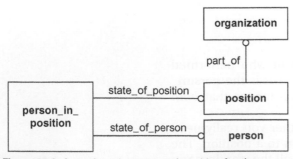

Figure 14-9 A version of person and position for the customer.

14.7 Concluding Remarks

In this chapter, I have taken an extended look at a particular data model pattern, that of the system and system component. I have shown how a 4D analysis clarifies what sorts of things system components are, and I have shown how this pattern turns up in a number of different contexts.

15

REQUIREMENTS SPECIFICATION

In previous chapters I have been looking at some of the elements of a procurement process. In this chapter I will start by considering the procurement process as a whole and then focus on the final key element of a procurement process, the requirements specification.

15.1 A Process for Procurement

Figure 15-1 shows a very general high level procurement process that covers a wide range of procurement situations, though I am certainly not trying to suggest that it is the last word in procurement processes.

At this level it looks as if one process fits all needs, but this is not the case. Figure 15-2 shows a number of different cases that will cause variations in the process, and information, required. The graph shows purchase processes for different areas of an Item Volume, Item Value map.

The scales on the axes will vary depending on the size of the organization, and the place where the lines are drawn may vary for different product categories.

15.1.1 Card Purchase

Card purchases are those low-value purchases where the person who has the card has the requirement and the authority to make the purchase of that value for that product category, but stock of the product is not held. Examples include most of what is often thought of as incidental expenses such as meals, books, and travel costs. However, for some categories standard products may be specified. These are the characteristics of this type of procurement:

- Low value
- Low volume—not worth keeping a stock
- End user, purchaser, and authorizer are the same
  - May be through a standard supplier or for standard products
  - Payment before delivery

15.1.2 Purchase on Demand

Purchase on demand is a process for relatively low volume and medium value items where the person with the requirement does not have the financial authority to make the purchase. He has to submit the requirement and the proposed solution for authorization of the expenditure.

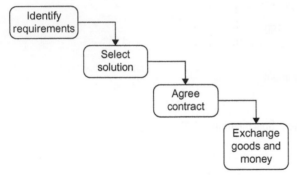

Figure 15-1 An example procurement process.

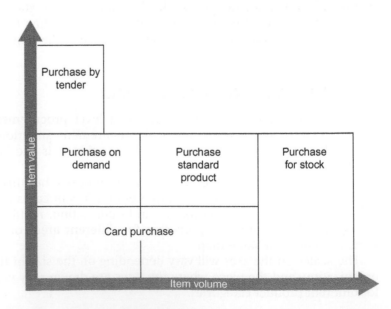

Figure 15-2 Different types of procurement.

The overhead of identifying and managing standard products is not worth the value of business this represents. These are the characteristics of this type of procurement:
- Medium value items
- Volume low, and not worth having a standard product
- Authorizer not the same as purchaser or end user
- Purchase by order and payment on receipt of invoice

15.1.3 Purchase Standard Product

The value of business in this area is sufficient, or compatibility in use is important enough that standard products in various product categories are chosen and volume discounts are agreed upon. However, purchases follow identification of requirements, rather than for being purchased for stock, and then issue from stock. Examples include computer hardware, mobile phones, and industrial equipment. The characteristics of this type of purchase are as follows:
- Medium value, medium volume items
- Compatibility of items of the same type may be important
- Purchase agreements with suppliers may be in place
- Payment occurs on receipt of invoice
- Authorizer is not the end user

15.1.4 Purchase for Stock

High volume items, of low and medium value, often consumables, are often held as stock by an organization and then issued from stores to those who need them. Standard products will be supplied from suppliers with whom long-term contracts are in place that take maximum advantage of the volume of business represented. Authorization comes in the selection of suppliers and the agreement of the supply contracts. These are the characteristics of this type of procurement:
- High volume, low to medium value products
- Volume purchase agreements with suppliers with agreed delivery times
- Stock management
- Issue from stores
- Payment by account
- Authorizer not the same as the end user

15.1.5 Purchase by Tender

High-value, usually one-off items are often purchased using a competitive tender process. These high-value items represent a significant investment and so there will be several stages of authorization. At the requirements level there will be a number of parties bidding, followed by a selection process among the bidders. There will then be a contract agreement phase, which will perhaps include provision for stage payments and penalty clauses. The characteristics of this type of procurement are:

- Low-volume, high-value items
- Multiple authorizations at different stages
- A requirements development stage with separate authorization
- A tender process to select the supplier
- A complex contract perhaps with penalty clauses and stage payments

15.1.6 Comparison of Tender and Card Processes

What you can see from the earlier descriptions is that although all these types of procurement follow the same basic pattern, the details may be different, both in the process followed and the information required. To make this point, Table 15-1 compares the two extremes, Purchase by Tender and Card Purchase.

Notice that there is no point of contact between these two extremes.

Although you can see from Table 15-1 that recording the requirements specification is not necessary for a card purchase, it is needed for all the other sorts of procurement. So in the rest

Table 15-1 Comparison of Tender and Card Procurements

	Purchase by Tender	Card Purchase
Identify Requirements	Detailed processes and requirements documentation with formal authorization process.	Cursory process with no information recorded
Select Solution	Detailed process with price/performance analysis of alternate tenders.	Cursory process with no information recorded
Agree Contract	Non-standard, one-off contract for the particular procurement. May have penalty clauses.	Standard retail purchase governed by Sale of Goods legislation
Exchange Goods and Money	Payment may be staged, with final payment withheld until the performance of the product is confirmed.	Payment before delivery

of this chapter I will look at what a requirements specification is and describe a supporting data model.

15.2 Requirements Specification

15.2.1 Overview

A requirement is about something that you want to exist in the future, as opposed to something in the present or the past. "Possible worlds" is the way I deal with this kind of situation. Since the requirement is a spatio-temporal extent, we can talk about it existing whether it is in the past, the present, or the future. A requirement is one in the future, and since we therefore cannot be certain if it is part of the possible world that we are part of, then it is part of some possible world in which our plan for it does come to pass.

A requirement will also be of some other type, and although a requirement can in principle be for any spatio-temporal extent, in practice it is most often for a functional object, a thing that has an intended role in an activity, and in particular for a system or a system component. I'm going to use a car as an example of a requirement that is a system and a pump as a component of a process plant to demonstrate an example of a requirement that is a system component. Pumps are common pieces of equipment used across a wide range of industries, and depending on the type and the industry, an organization might either purchase them on demand, or have determined standard products that they will purchase for higher volume applications—for example, inclusion as a component in another product.

I want to start by reviewing what we do when we buy something like this.

A requirement will usually be for a **state_of_functional_object**—something that has an intended role. Most likely it will be for a **state_of_functional_system** or a **state_of_functional_system_component**. I'd just like to look at these two for a moment.

The procurement of a car is an example of meeting a **requirement** for a whole system. Figure 15-3 illustrates this case for a car. Notice that the **requirement** is not the same thing as the whole life of the thing procured, but it is an **asset**, that is, an owned state of a **physical_object**. It exists owned by its manufacturer before it meets your **requirement**, and it may be sold or otherwise disposed of before the **requirement** ends, or indeed it may outlast the **requirement**.

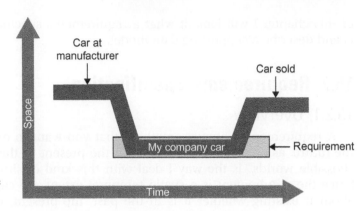

Figure 15-3 Requirement that is a state of a functional system.

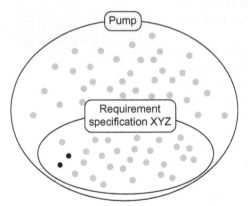

Figure 15-4 What are the required pumps?

Another possibility is that the requirement is for a **functional_system_component**. This happens, for example, when you are constructing a complex system, such as an assembly line or a process plant. What is required is something to play a particular role in the overall system, which will be assembled on site.

When I used to design process plants for Shell, I often found that I needed a pump; either liquid needed to be moved from one place to another, or it needed to be moved from a lower pressure environment to a higher pressure environment, or both. The question is: what is this? It is not an actual pump here and now, because I cannot kick it, but at some point in the future there may be (there will be, if my plans work out) a pump that I can kick that does the job that I am specifying. So we have a pump whose life will start at some point in the future that is part of a possible world that may be our actual world if our plans come to fruition.

Figure 15-4 illustrates the situation. The large ellipse is the set of all the pumps (the small circles) that are part of any possible world. The smaller ellipse is the set of those pumps that meet our requirement specification—say requirement specification XYZ—and the two solid circles are the ones that are our requirement.

Now the two pumps that are our requirement are members of a product of another organization. I looked at products in Chapter 13. Since we are looking at a specification-based view of the product from a customer perspective, then we are

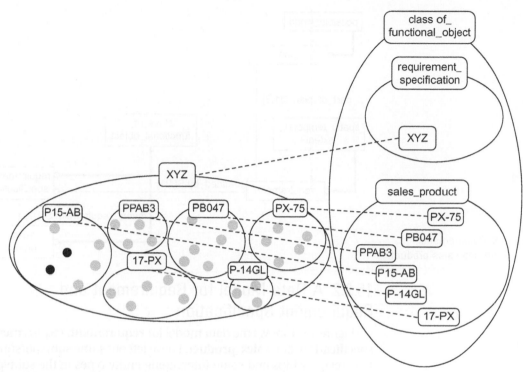

Figure 15-5 Pump product selection.

interested in members of **sales_product**. Different versions of a **sales_product** are improved ways of meeting the same specification as seen by the purchaser.

Figure 15-5 illustrates this. The **sales_product** we have chosen (and we could have chosen from any of the **sales_products** in this diagram, since I have only shown those that meet our requirements) is P15-AB. The diagram also shows that **sales_product** is a subset of **class_of_functional_object**, and that our requirement specification **XYZ** is a member of **requirement_specification** that is also a subset of **class_of_functional_object**.

At this point I would just like to distinguish between our **requirement**, and our **requirement_specification**. Our **requirement** is for two pumps, that is, two spatio-temporal extents. Our **requirement_specification** defines the properties that these two pumps must have in order to be suitable; its members are all those pumps that are suitable, not just the pumps we end up with.

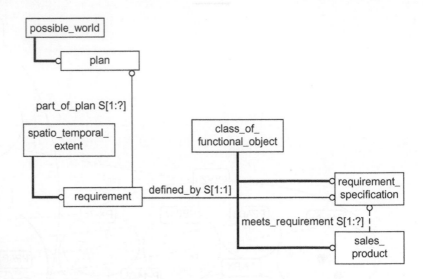

Figure 15-6 Requirements specification and sales product.

15.2.2 A Data Model for Requirement and Requirement Specification

Figure 15-6 shows the data model for **requirement**, **requirement_specification**, and **sales_product**. I have left out some subtype/supertype relationships and some intervening entity types in the subtype/supertype network.

A **plan** is a **possible_world** that some **party** would like to bring about.

A **requirement** is a **spatio_temporal_extent** that is *part_of_plan* of at least one **plan** and is *defined_by* exactly one **requirement_specification**, where the *part_of_plan* relationship type is a subtype of the *part_of* relationship type and the *defined_by* relationship type is a subtype of the *member_of* relationship type.

A **requirement_specification** is a **class_of_functional_object** that is the set of possible **functional_objects** that meet the specification.

15.2.3 Requirement Specifications

In the preceding overview, I said that there was a **requirement_specification** that any possible **functional_object** that met the specification was a member of, but that did not say much about what the specification was. I will cover this here.

A specification is a collection of individual elements, each of which is a class that each object that meets the specification is a member of. So the specification itself is the intersection of these

Table 15-2 Excerpt from API 676 Pump Data Sheet

Operating Conditions		
Parameter	*Maximum*	*Minimum*
Discharge Pressure (kPa)	10000	5000
Differential Pressure (kPa)	3000	2000
NPSH[1] available (m)	5	
CONSTRUCTION		
Pump Type	○ Internal Gear ○ Twin Screw ● Vane	
	○ External Gear ○ Three Screw ○ Progressing Cavity	

[1]NPSH stands for Net Positive Suction Head, the difference between the actual pressure of a liquid in a pipe and its vapor pressure at a given temperature.

classes that are elements of the specification. To illustrate this I take some examples from the American Petroleum Institute's standard pump data sheet, API 676, shown in Table 15-2.

Notice that the first two parameters have a maximum and minimum value; that is, they specify a range. This is quite normal as it would be difficult for any pump to have an exact discharge pressure. You will notice that NPSH is shown as a single value; however, if you understand pumps, you will know that this is actually a minimum value but that there is no particular upper limit. Some parameters are single valued though; take, for example, the pump type, which can be one of the six types listed (in this case).

Figure 15-7 shows a Venn diagram for the elements from Table 15-2 of the XYZ **requirement_specification**.

One particular thing to note here is the ranges of **kind_of_ physical_quantity**. In Chapter 12, I developed a data model for physical quantities, but this did not cover ranges. A range of physical quantities is simply the superclass of all the physical quantities that are in the range. It is not generally useful to note

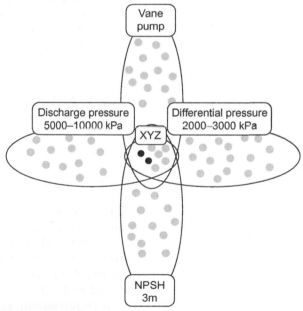

Figure 15-7 Building up the requirement specification from the elements.

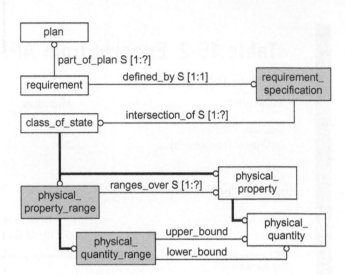

Figure 15-8 A data model that shows the elements of a requirements specification.

all the subclasses of a range; noting the largest and the smallest is sufficient to define the membership. Ranges of **kind_of_ physical_property** are also possible, of course, though less commonly encountered.

15.2.4 A Data Model for Elements of a Requirement Specification

Figure 15-8 is a data model that shows the elements of a requirements specification. A **physical_property_range** is a **class_of_state** that *ranges_over* (is a superset of) one or more **physical_property** of the same **kind_of_physical_property**. A **state** is a *member_of* a **property_range** when its value for the **kind_of_physical_property** falls within the range.

A **physical_quantity_range** is a **physical_property_range** where the **kind_of_physical_property** is a **kind_of_physical_ quantity** and where the **physical_quantity_range** has an *upper_ bound* and a *lower_bound* that are a **physical_quantity**.

A **requirement_specification** is a **class_of_spatio_temporal_ extent** that is the *intersection_of* one or more **class_of_state**.

16

CONCLUDING REMARKS

In this part I have presented a data model that
- Provides a framework for analyzing business requirements
- Provides a data model of some detailed areas that shows how business terms can be incorporated into a data model
- Is easily extensible, either by adding entity types or reference data

This makes it particularly suitable as an integration model.

As I have developed this framework, I have spread data model fragments over several chapters, so it may not be obvious that there is a cohesive whole. I have therefore put the whole model in Chapter 17. From this it can clearly be seen that the model is coherent and cohesive, as well as extensible in a regular way; all desirable properties in a changing world. Chapter 17 also makes a handy reference.

One pattern is particularly important and is shown in Figure 16-1.

If we are interested in Xs where an **X** is a kind of **individual**, then in addition to an entity type **X** there will be **state_of_X**, of which **X** is a subtype. **state_of_X** may have subtypes that are the roles Xs play as **participant**s in an **activity** or **association**; examples shown here are **X_in_role_Y** and **X_in_role_Z**.

A **class_of_X** is a **class** that necessarily applies to an **X** for the whole of its life. The most interesting of these I call **kind_of_X**, which is a class of Xs of the same kind—that have properties in common—excluding the random sets that **class_of_X** allows. Other subtypes may be interesting where particular rules apply.

When a **state_of_X** is not a **participant**, it is usually interesting because it has a **property_of_X**. I have dealt with properties that apply widely to individuals, but there can also be properties that are specific to a particular **kind_of_individual**.

Constructing your data model using a template like this is like showing your working when you are solving a problem in mathematics. You do it to make sure you have the right answer. But having worked the answer out, it is up to you whether you

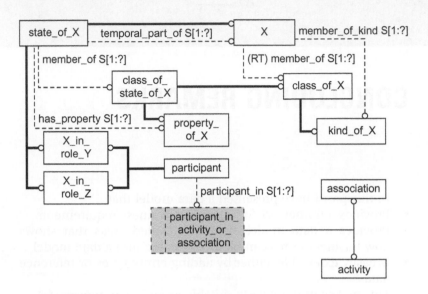

Figure 16-1 A basic data model template.

show the working or not. For example, it will not be helpful for people who do not understand the method you have used, but it would be convincing for those who do.

Another question is whether it is worth showing your working at all; there are some extra boxes involved, surely it would be quicker without them? The answer is the same as in mathematics. Working things out properly is actually the fastest way to the right answer, plus it helps to assure that you have the right answer. In data modeling, it is not the time it takes to produce a model that determines the effort it takes, but how many times you have to redo the model before you get it right.

The result overall is improved consistency, especially when you have a team of data modelers, and a reduction in errors and rework. All of which leads to high quality data models that meet the information requirements of the business.

THE HQDM FRAMEWORK SCHEMA

This part provides the full data model that I have been working through in this book as an EXPRESS schema including both the EXPRESS-G diagrams and the lexical EXPRESS that is computer interpretable, descriptions of the diagrams, and definitions of the entity types and relationship types on each diagram. It is intended as a reference document and an extension to the data model fragments that I introduced in Part 3.

This schema was developed using Jotne EPM Technology's EDMVisualExpress data modeling tool. This part covers one way in which a data model may be published by VisualEXPRESS. It may also be published as a website. I intend to publish this schema as a web resource. You should be able to find it by searching the web for the schema name.

The data model presented here is broadly compatible with ISO 15926-2, but there are four key differences.

1. The first is that the metamodel for **relationship** takes a different approach. The approach in ISO 15926-2 is a little cumbersome, in particular in the way that n-ary **relationship**s are represented. This has little significance since the implementation environment will determine the way that

the metamodel will be implemented; what is presented here is a statement of requirements.

2. The second area of difference is in the way that representation is modeled. In ISO 15926-2, the involvement of those who interpret the **sign** or **pattern** was optional. This is clearly a weakness, and I have remedied this.

3. The third area is in the **classes** that are represented as entity types. ISO 15926's **possible_individual** is equivalent to **spatio_temporal_extent** in the model presented here, and **whole_life_individual** is equivalent to **individual** here. If **X** is a subtype of **possible_individual**, then **X** is equivalent to **state_of_X** in this model, and **class_of_X** is equivalent to **class_of_state_of_X**. ISO 15926-2 does not make explicit the subtypes of **whole_life_individual** as I have done here. Although this made the ISO 15926-2 data model smaller, I think it also made it a lot less easy to see how it should be used.

4. The fourth area of difference is in the use of **association** in this data model. An **association** *is a* **state** that *consists_of* its **participants**. In ISO 15926-2, these are modeled as **relationships** between the **states**, rather than as an **association** that *consists_of* the **states**.

A mapping of the key entity types in the schema presented here to ISO 15926-2 is presented in Appendix A.

17

HQDM_FRAMEWORK

The HQDM_FRAMEWORK schema starts here.

EXPRESS specification:

```
*)
SCHEMA HQDM_FRAMEWORK;
(*
```

17.1 Thing and Abstract Object

Figure 17-1 shows **thing** and **abstract_object**. A **thing** is anything that exists and is the ultimate supertype of all the other entity types in the schema. The immediate subtypes of **thing** are **individual** and **abstract_object**. The "1" on the subtype graph means that these two entity types are mutually exclusive. A **spatio_temporal_extent** exists in space and time, while an **abstract_object** exists in neither space nor time. A **thing** may be a *member_of* a **class**. An **abstract_object** may be either a **class** or a **relationship**, but a **relationship** may not also be a **class**.

One **thing** to notice in this diagram is the use of off-page connectors—the lozenges. I described their use in Chapter 2, but this is their first use, so here is a brief summary.

Home page connector: In a set of EXPRESS-G diagrams each entity type has a home page, where it appears as a rectangle. On its home page, it may have a lozenge attached that numbers the connector and provides a list of the diagram numbers where the entity type appears in a relationship type. An example of this is the lozenge attached to **thing** (1,1 (2,14,45)). This means that **thing** appears in diagrams 2, 14, and 45.

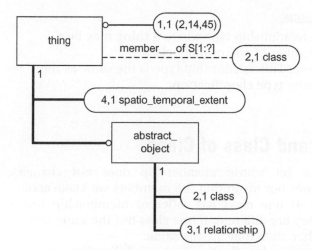

Figure 17-1 HQDM_FRAMEWORK EXPRESS-G diagram 1 of 46.

Other page connectors: On the diagram referred to there is another lozenge on the other end of the relationship type with the number of its home diagram, the connector number on that diagram, and the name of the entity type. So if you look on diagram 2 you will see a lozenge (1,1 thing). Together these act as a very effective cross reference between the diagrams.

17.1.1 Abstract_object

A **thing** that does not exist in space or time.

EXPRESS specification:

```
*)
  ENTITY abstract_object
    SUPERTYPE OF (ONEOF(class, relationship))
    SUBTYPE OF(thing);
  END_ENTITY;
(*
```

17.1.2 Thing

Anything that exists, real or imagined.

EXPRESS specification:

```
*)
  ENTITY thing
    SUPERTYPE OF (ONEOF(spatio_temporal_extent, abstract_object));
    member__of                :OPTIONAL SET [1:?] OF class;
  END_ENTITY;
(*
```

Attribute definitions:

member__of A relationship type where a **thing** may be a member of one or more **class.**
Note: This relationship type is the same as the entity type **classification.**

17.2 Class and Class of Class

A **class** is a set whose membership does not change. However, this does not mean that the members we *know* about do not change. If one **class** has different membership from another, then they are different. If one class has the same membership as another, then they are the same.

I have shown the **classification** and **specialization** relationships in Figure 17-2 as entity types. **classification** is also shown in Figure 17-1 as the relationship type *member__of* and **specialization** is also shown as the relationship type *has_superclass* in Figure 17-2. The only difference is that when represented by an entity type, the **relationship** can itself have attributes and **relationships.** A **classification** relationship has a **thing** as *member* and a **class** as *classifier.* A **specialization** relationship has a *superclass* and a *subclass*, where each *member__of* the *subclass* is a *member__of* the *superclass.* This relationship has the same meaning as the thick black lines on the diagram. The difference is that this relationship holds between members of entity types instead of the entity types themselves. As such, it is part of the metamodel that supports extensibility in data of what might otherwise be presented in the data model.

An **enumerated_class** is a **class** where the total membership is known. This is useful if you actually wish to perform set operations, since they will only be valid for such a **class.** The other subtype tree shows **class_of_spatio_temporal_extent** and **class_of_abstract_object** as the immediate subtypes of **class.** It also shows them as mutually exclusive. In turn **class_of_class** and **class_of_relationship** are subtypes of **class_of_class.** A **class** may be a *member_of* a **class_of_class.**

17.2.1 Class

An **abstract_object** that has members and whose identity is defined by its membership.

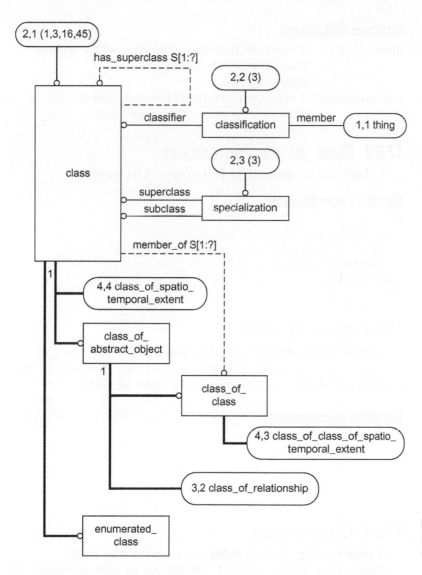

Figure 17-2 HQDM_
FRAMEWORK EXPRESS-G
diagram 2 of 46.

EXPRESS specification:

```
*)
  ENTITY class
    SUPERTYPE OF (ONEOF(class_of_spatio_temporal_extent,
             class_of_abstract_object) ANDOR enumerated_class)
    SUBTYPE OF(abstract_object);
    member_of          :OPTIONAL SET [1:?] OF class_of_class;
    has_superclass     :OPTIONAL SET [1:?] OF class;
  END_ENTITY;
(*
```

Attribute definitions:

member_of   A *member_of* relationship type where a **class** may be a *member_of* one or more **class_of_class.**

has_superclass   A relationship type where each *member_of* the **class** is a *member_of* the *superclass.*

17.2.2 Class_of_abstract_object

A **class** that is **abstract_object** or any of its subsets.

EXPRESS specification:

```
*)
 ENTITY class_of_abstract_object
   SUPERTYPE OF (ONEOF(class_of_relationship, class_of_class))
   SUBTYPE OF(class);
 END_ENTITY;
(*
```

17.2.3 Class_of_class

A **class** that is **class** or any of its subsets.

Note: More formally this means that any *member_of* the powerset of **class** is a valid *member_of* **class_of_class.**

EXPRESS specification:

```
*)
 ENTITY class_of_class
   SUBTYPE OF(class_of_abstract_object);
 END_ENTITY;
(*
```

17.2.4 Classification

A **relationship** where a **thing** is a *member* of a **class.**

Note: This entity type is replicated as the *member__of* relationship type.

EXPRESS specification:

```
*)
 ENTITY classification
   SUBTYPE OF(relationship);
   classifier      :class;
   member          :thing;
 END_ENTITY;
(*
```

Attribute definitions:

classifier   A relationship type where a **classification** has exactly one classifier.

member   A relationship type where a **classification** has exactly one member.

17.2.5 Enumerated_class

A **class** where each *member__of* the **class** is known.

EXPRESS specification:

```
*)
 ENTITY enumerated_class
  SUBTYPE OF(class);
 END_ENTITY;
(*
```

17.2.6 Specialization

A **relationship** where each *member__of* the *subclass* is a *member__of* the *superclass*.

EXPRESS specification:

```
*)
 ENTITY specialization
  SUBTYPE OF(relationship);
  superclass      :class;
  subclass        :class;
 END_ENTITY;
(*
```

Attribute definitions:

superclass   A relationship type where each **specialization** has exactly one **class** as superclass.

subclass   A relationship type where each **specialization** has exactly one **class** as subclass.

17.3 Relationship and Class of Relationship

Figure 17-3 shows the data model for **relationship** and **class_of_relationship**. It is part of the metamodel for the HQDM Framework supporting the addition of types of **relationships** and their instances through data.

relationship is an abstract entity type, so its members must belong to one of its subtypes. There are two possibilities, either it is an explicit subtype with roles defined, such as **classification**

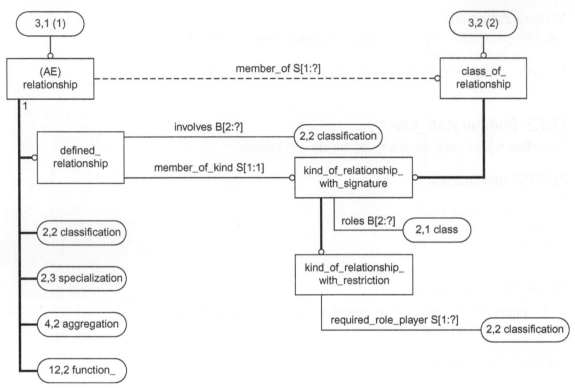

Figure 17-3 HQDM_FRAMEWORK EXPRESS-G diagram 3 of 46.

and **aggregation**, or it is a **defined_relationship**. A **defined_relationship** *involves* at least two **things** with each in a particular role. These turn out to be **classifications** where the *member* is the **thing** playing the role, and the *classifier* is the role played. Notice the B[2:?] on the involves relationship type. This means that rather than a set of **classifications**, it is a bag of **classifications**, where in a bag the same element may appear more than once. This allows relationships that are reflexive and symmetric to be supported. A **defined_relationship** is a *member_of* exactly one **kind_of_relationship_with_signature** that provides the definition of the **defined_relationship**. A **kind_of_relationship_with_signature** has a bag of two or more **class** that are the *roles* played by the related objects where the **class** here is also the **class** in a **classification** that is involved in the **defined_relationship**.

A **kind_of_relationship_with_restriction** is a **class_of_relationship** where one of the **classifications** is fixed for all members of the **class_of_relationship**. The fixed *member* is the **classification** that is the *required_role_player*.

17.3.1 Class_of_relationship

A **class** that is **relationship** or any of its subsets.

EXPRESS specification:

```
*)
  ENTITY class_of_relationship
    SUBTYPE OF(class_of_abstract_object);
  END_ENTITY;
(*
```

17.3.2 Defined_relationship

A **relationship** that is defined by a **kind_of_relationship_with_signature**.

EXPRESS specification:

```
*)
  ENTITY defined_relationship
    SUBTYPE OF(relationship);
    member_of_kind    :SET [1:1] OF
                        kind_of_relationship_with_signature;
    involves          :BAG [2:?] OF classification;
  END_ENTITY;
(*
```

Attribute definitions:

member_of   A *member_of* relationship type where each **defined_relationship** is a *member_of* exactly one **kind_of_relationship_with_signature**.

involves   A meta-relationship type where the **classification** of some **thing** in a role is involved in a **relationship**.

17.3.3 Kind_of_relationship_with_restriction

A **kind_of_relationship_with_signature** where one or more *roles* have fixed players.

EXPRESS specification:

```
*)
  ENTITY kind_of_relationship_with_restriction
    SUBTYPE OF(kind_of_relationship_with_signature);
    required_role_player    :SET [1:?] OF classification;
  END_ENTITY;
(*
```

<u>Attribute definitions:</u>

required_role_player A relationship type where the
classification is of a required role player
for the members of a
kind_of_relationship_with_restriction.

17.3.4 Kind_of_relationship_with_signature

A **class_of_relationship** that is a subset of **defined_relationship**
where the **classifications** involved in each **defined_relationship**
have as *classifier*s the *roles* specified by the **kind_of_
relationship_with_signature**.

<u>EXPRESS specification:</u>

```
*)
  ENTITY kind_of_relationship_with_signature
    SUBTYPE OF(class_of_relationship);
    roles        :BAG [2:?] OF class;
  END_ENTITY;
(*
```

<u>Attribute definitions:</u>

roles   The roles that must be filled by members of a
kind_of_relationship_with_signature.

17.3.5 Relationship

An **abstract_object** that is what one **thing** has to do with one
or more others.

<u>EXPRESS specification:</u>

```
*)
  ENTITY relationship
    ABSTRACT
    SUPERTYPE OF (ONEOF(classification, aggregation,
                 specialization, defined_relationship, function_))
    SUBTYPE OF(abstract_object);
    member_of        :OPTIONAL SET [1:?] OF class_of_relationship;
  END_ENTITY;
(*
```

<u>Attribute definitions:</u>

member_of A *member_of* relationship type where a **relationship**
is a *member_of* a **class_of_relationship**.

17.4 Spatio-Temporal Extent and Class of Spatio-Temporal Extent

Figure 17-4 presents a data model for **spatio_temporal_extent** and **class_of_spatio_temporal_extent**. A **spatio_temporal_extent** is some arbitrary piece of space-time that is not necessarily contiguous and is *part_of* at least one **possible_world**. A **spatio_temporal_extent** may have a *beginning* **event** and an *ending* **event** (it will necessarily have both, but you will not necessarily know them).

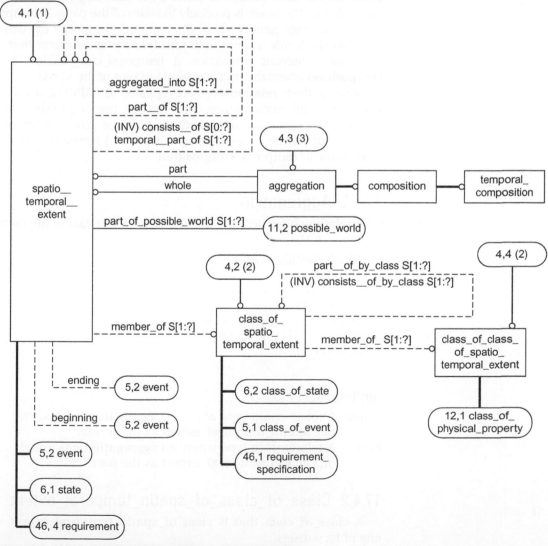

Figure 17-4 HQDM_FRAMEWORK EXPRESS-G diagram 4 of 46.

A **spatio_temporal_extent** may be a *member_of* one or more **class_of_spatio_temporal_extent**, which in turn may be a *member_of* one or more **class_of_class_of_spatio_temporal_extent**. In later diagrams I do not make explicit subtypes of **class_of_class_of_spatio_temporal_extent**, but this diagram makes them available. A **class_of_spatio_temporal_extent** may have one or more *part__of_by_class* relationships to another **class_of_spatio_temporal_extent** where a *member_of* one has a *member_of* the other as a part.

Aggregation is a **relationship** between one **spatio_temporal_extent** and another where the *whole* is the mereological sum of the parts; that is, the *whole* is precisely the sum of the parts. A **composition** is an **aggregation** where the parts are composed in such a way that the *whole* is more than just the sum of the *parts; that is,* there are emergent properties. A **temporal_composition** is a **composition** where the *part* is a temporal part of the *whole*.

Some of these **relationship**s are repeated as EXPRESS relationship types for convenience and further use: *aggregated_into* means the same as **aggregation**, *part__of* and its inverse *consists__of* are the same as **composition**, and *temporal__part_of* is the same as **temporal_composition**.

17.4.1 Aggregation

A **relationship** where the *whole* is at least the sum of the *parts*.

EXPRESS specification:
```
*)
  ENTITY aggregation
    SUBTYPE OF(relationship);
    whole        :spatio_temporal_extent;
    part         :spatio_temporal_extent:
  END_ENTITY;
(*
```

Attribute definitions:

whole A relationship type where an **aggregation** has exactly one **spatio_temporal_extent** as the whole.

part A relationship type where an **aggregation** has exactly one **spatio_temporal_extent** as the part.

17.4.2 Class_of_class_of_spatio_temporal_extent

A **class_of_class** that is **class_of_spatio_temporal_extent** or any of its subsets.

EXPRESS specification:
```
*)
  ENTITY class_of_class_of_spatio_temporal_extent
    SUBTYPE OF(class_of_class);
  END_ENTITY;
(*
```

17.4.3 Class_of_spatio_temporal_extent

A **class** that is **spatio_temporal_extent** or any of its subsets.

EXPRESS specification:
```
*)
  ENTITY class_of_spatio_temporal_extent
    SUBTYPE OF(class);
    member_of_              :OPTIONAL SET [1:?] OF class_of_class_
                             of_spatio_temporal_extent;
    part__of_by_class       :OPTIONAL SET [1:?] OF class_of_spatio_
                             temporal_extent;
  INVERSE
    consists__of_by_class :SET [1:?] OF class_of_spatio_
                             temporal_extent FOR
                             part_of_by_class;
  END_ENTITY;
(*
```

Attribute definitions:

*member_of_*	A *member_of* relationship type where a **class_of_spatio_temporal_extent** may be a *member_of* one or more **class_of_class_of_spatio_temporal_extent**.
part__of_by_class	A relationship type where a *member_of* a **class_of_spatio_temporal_extent** is *part_of* a *member_of* some **class_of_spatio_temporal_extent**.
consists__of_by_class	An inverse *part__of_by_class* relationship type where a *member_of* one **class_of_spatio_temporal_extent** *consists_of* another *member_of* a **class_of_spatio_temporal_extent**.

17.4.4 Composition

An **aggregation** where the *whole* is an arrangement of the parts that results in emergent properties.

EXPRESS specification:

```
*)
  ENTITY composition
    SUBTYPE OF(aggregation);
  END_ENTITY;
(*
```

17.4.5 Spatio_temporal_extent

A **thing** that exists in time and space.

EXPRESS specification:

```
*)
  ENTITY spatio_temporal_extent
    SUBTYPE OF(thing);
    part__of                    :OPTIONAL SET [1:?] OF spatio_
                                 temporal_extent;
    beginning                   :OPTIONAL event;
    ending                      :OPTIONAL event;
    part_of_possible_world      :SET [1:?] OF possible_world;
    member_of                   :OPTIONAL SET [1:?] OF class_of_
                                 spatio_temporal_extent;
    temporal__part_of           :OPTIONAL SET [1:?] OF spatio_
                                 temporal_extent;
    aggregated_into             :OPTIONAL SET [1:?] OF spatio_
                                 temporal_extent;
  INVERSE
    consists__of                 :SET OF spatio_temporal_extent FOR
                                 part__of;
  END_ENTITY;
(*
```

Attribute definitions:

part__of	An *aggregated_into* relationship type where a **spatio_temporal_extent** may be part of another and the whole has emergent properties and is more than just the sum of its parts. Note: This relationship type has the same meaning but is a different representation of the **composition** entity type.
beginning	A *part_of* relationship type where a **spatio_temporal_extent** has exactly one **event** that is its beginning.

ending	A *part_of* relationship type where a **spatio_temporal_extent** has exactly one **event** that is its ending.
part_of_possible_world	A *part_of* relationship type where a **spatio_temporal_extent** may be *part_of* one or more **possible_world**. Note: The relationship type is optional because a **possible_world** is not *part_of* any other **spatio_temporal_extent**.
member_of	A *member_of* relationship type where a **spatio_temporal_extent** is a *member_of* a **class_of_spatio_temporal_extent**.
temporal__part_of	A *part_of* relationship type where a **spatio_temporal_extent** may be a temporal part of one or more other **spatio_temporal_extent**. Note: this is **temporal_composition** represented as a relationship type instead of an entity type.
aggregated_into	A relationship type where a **spatio_temporal_extent** may be aggregated into one or more others. Note: This has the same meaning as, but different representation to, the **aggregation** entity type.
consists__of	A relationship type where a **spatio_temporal_extent** may consist of one or more others. Note: This is the inverse of *part__of*.

17.4.6 Temporal_composition

A **composition** where the part is the entire *whole* spatially, but part of the *whole* temporally.

<u>EXPRESS specification:</u>

```
*)
  ENTITY temporal_composition
    SUBTYPE OF(composition);
  END_ENTITY;
(*
```

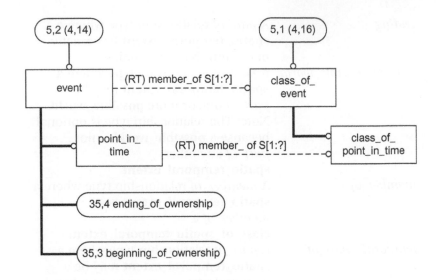

Figure 17-5 HQDM_
FRAMEWORK EXPRESS-G
diagram 5 of 46.

17.5 Event, Class of Event, and Point in Time

Figure 17-5 provides the EXPRESS-G for **event** and **class_of_event**. An **event** is a **spatio_temporal_extent** with zero thickness in time. An **event** temporally bounds one or more **spatio_temporal_extents**. An **event** may be a *member_of* one or more **class_of_event**.

A **point_in_time** is an **event** across all of space. A **point_in_time** may be a *member_of* a **class_of_point_in_time**.

17.5.1 Class_of_event

A **class_of_spatio_temporal_extent** that is **event** or any of its subsets.

<u>EXPRESS specification:</u>
```
*)
  ENTITY class_of_event
    SUBTYPE OF(class_of_spatio_temporal_extent);
  END_ENTITY;
(*
```

17.5.2 Class_of_point_in_time

A **class_of_event** that is **point_in_time** or any of its subsets.

EXPRESS specification:

```
*)
  ENTITY class_of_point_in_time
    SUBTYPE OF(class_of_event);
  END_ENTITY;
(*
```

17.5.3 Event

A **spatio_temporal_extent** that has zero temporal thickness and may bound some **spatio_temporal_extent**.

EXPRESS specification:

```
*)
  ENTITY event
    SUBTYPE OF(spatio_temporal_extent);
    SELF\spatio_temporal_
        extent.member_of        :OPTIONAL SET [1:?] OF
                                  class_of_event;
  END_ENTITY;
(*
```

Attribute definitions:

member_of A *member_of* relationship type where an **event** may be a *member_of* one or more **class_of_event**.

17.5.4 Point_in_time

An **event** that is all of space at an instant from some viewpoint.

EXPRESS specification:

```
*)
  ENTITY point_in_time
    SUBTYPE OF(event);
    SELF\event.member_of        :OPTIONAL SET [1:?] OF
                                  class_of_point_in_time;
  END_ENTITY;
(*
```

Attribute definitions:

member_of A *member_of* relationship type where a **point_in_time** may be a *member_of* one or more **class_of_point_in_time**.

17.6 State and Individual

Figure 17-6 shows the data model for **state** and **individual**. A **state** is a **spatio_temporal_extent** that is an **individual**, or a *temporal_part_of* an **individual**. A **state** may be a *temporal_part_of* one or more **individuals** and may be a *member_of* one or more **class_of_state**. An **individual** is a **state** that is a *member_of* a **kind_of_individual** for the whole of its life. An **individual** may be a *member_of* one or more **class_of_individual**, and a *member_of* one or more **kind_of_individual**.

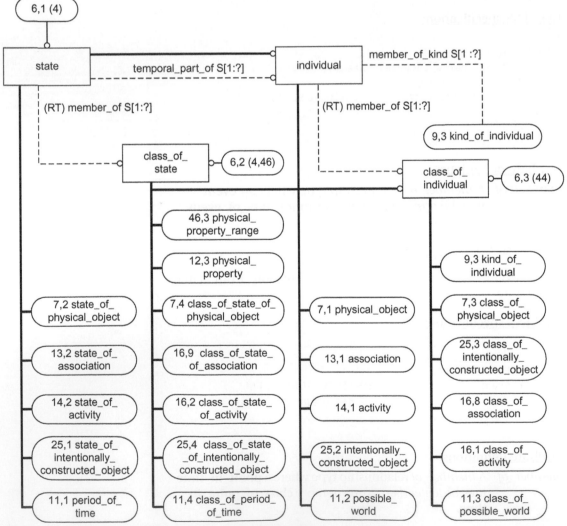

Figure 17-6 HQDM_FRAMEWORK EXPRESS-G diagram 6 of 46.

There are many subtypes of these entity types.

17.6.1 Class_of_individual

A **class_of_state** that is **individual** or any of its subsets.

Note: Only a **class** that necessarily applies to an **individual** for the whole of its life is a valid member. Others are members of **class_of_state** and apply to the **state** that is the **individual** for the period of time that the **class** applies for.

<u>EXPRESS specification:</u>

```
*)
  ENTITY class_of_individual
    SUBTYPE OF(class_of_state);
  END_ENTITY;
(*
```

17.6.2 Class_of_state

A **class_of_spatio_temporal_extent** that is **state** or any of its subsets.

<u>EXPRESS specification:</u>

```
*)
  ENTITY class_of_state
    SUBTYPE OF(class_of_spatio_temporal_extent);
  END_ENTITY;
(*
```

17.6.3 Individual

A **spatio_temporal_extent** that is not a proper *temporal_part_of* any other **individual** of the same kind.

Note: In standard mereology, a **spatio_temporal_extent** is a part of itself. Parts of an **individual** excluding itself are called *proper parts*.

<u>EXPRESS specification:</u>

```
*)
  ENTITY individual
    SUBTYPE OF(state);
    SELF\state.member_of  :OPTIONAL SET [1:?] OF class_of_
                              individual;
    member_of_kind        :OPTIONAL SET [1:?] OF kind_of_
                              individual;
  END_ENTITY;
(*
```

Attribute definitions:

member_of	A *member_of* relationship type where an **individual** may be a *member_of* one or more **class_of_individual**.
member_of_kind	A *member_of* relationship type where an **individual** may be a *member_of* one or more **kind_of_individual**.

17.6.4 State

A **spatio_temporal_extent** that is an **individual** or a *temporal_part_of* some **individual**.

EXPRESS specification:

```
*)
  ENTITY state
    SUBTYPE OF(spatio_temporal_extent);
    temporal_part_of      :OPTIONAL SET [1:?] OF individual;
    SELF\spatio_temporal_
        extent.member_of   :OPTIONAL SET [1:?] OF class_of_state;
  END_ENTITY;
(*
```

Attribute definitions:

temporal_part_of	A *temporal_part_of* relationship type where a **state** may be a *temporal_part_of* one or more **individual**. Note: The relationship type is optional because an **individual** is not necessarily a *temporal_part_of* another **individual**, yet is a *member_of* **state** as well as **individual**. This applies to all subtypes of *temporal_part_of* that are between a **state_of_X** and **X**.
member_of	A *member_of* relationship type where a **state** may be a *member_of* one or more **class_of_state**.

17.7 Physical Object

Figure 17-7 shows the data model for **physical_object**. The data model follows the same **pattern** as that for **state** and **individual**.

A **state_of_physical_object** is a **state** that is a **physical_object** or a *temporal_part_of* a **physical_object**, where a **physical_object** is an **individual** that is distribution of matter, or energy, or both. A **physical_object** may be a *member_of* one or more

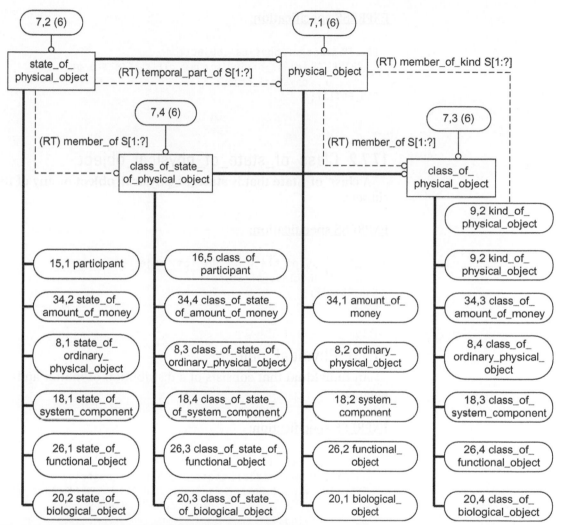

Figure 17-7 HQDM_FRAMEWORK EXPRESS-G diagram 7 of 46.

kind_of_physical_object, and one or more **class_of_physical_object**. A **state_of_physical_object** may be a *member_of* one or more **class_of_state_of_physical_object**.

17.7.1 Class_of_physical_object

A **class_of_individual** that is also a **class_of_state_of_physical_object** that is **physical_object** or any of its subsets.

<u>EXPRESS specification:</u>

```
*)
  ENTITY class_of_physical_object
    SUBTYPE OF (class_of_individual, class_of_state_of_
              physical_object);
  END_ENTITY;
(*
```

17.7.2 Class_of_state_of_physical_object

A **class_of_state** that is **state_of_physical_object** or any of its subsets.

<u>EXPRESS specification:</u>

```
*)
  ENTITY class_of_state_of_physical_object
    SUBTYPE OF(class_of_state);
  END_ENTITY;
(*
```

17.7.3 Physical_object

An **individual** that consists of a distribution of matter and/or energy.

<u>EXPRESS specification:</u>

```
*)
  ENTITY physical_object
    SUBTYPE OF(individual, state_of_physical_object);
    SELF\individual.member_of  :OPTIONAL SET [1:?] OF class_of_
                                  physical_object;
    SELF\individual.
        member_of_kind          :OPTIONAL SET [1:?] OF
                                  kind_of_physical_object;
  END_ENTITY;
(*
```

<u>Attribute definitions:</u>

member_of	A *member_of* relationship type where a **physical_object** may be a *member_of* one or more **class_of_physical_object**.
member_of_kind	A *member_of* relationship type where a **physical_object** may be a *member_of* one or more **kind_of_physical_object**.

17.7.4 State_of_physical_object

A **state** that is a **physical_object** or a *temporal_part_of* a **physical_object**.

EXPRESS specification:

```
*)
  ENTITY state_of_physical_object
    SUBTYPE OF(state);
    SELF\state.
        temporal_part_of  :OPTIONAL SET [1:?] OF physical_
                              object;
    SELF\state.member_of  :OPTIONAL SET [1:?] OF class_of_
                              state_of_physical_object;
  END_ENTITY;
(*
```

Attribute definitions:

temporal_part_of	A *temporal_part_of* relationship type where a **state_of_physical_object** may be a *temporal_part_of* one or more **physical_object**.
member_of	A *member_of* relationship type where a **state_of_physical_object** may be a *member_of* one or more **class_of_state_of_physical_object**.

17.8 Ordinary Physical Object

Figure 17-8 shows the data model for **ordinary_physical_object**. An **ordinary_physical_object** is a **physical_object** that does not survive having all of its parts replaced simultaneously. A **state_of_ordinary_physical_object** is an **ordinary_physical_object** or a *temporal_part_of* one. A **state_of_ordinary_physical_object** may be a *temporal_part_of* one or more **ordinary_physical_object**.

A **state_of_ordinary_physical_object** may be a *member_of* one or more **class_of_state_of_ordinary_physical_object**, while an **ordinary_physical_object** may be a *member_of* one or more **class_of_ordinary_physical_object** and a *member_of* one or more **kind_of_ordinary_physical_object**.

17.8.1 Class_of_ordinary_physical_object

A **class_of_state_of_ordinary_physical_object** that is also a **class_of_physical_object** that is **ordinary_physical_object** or any of its subsets.

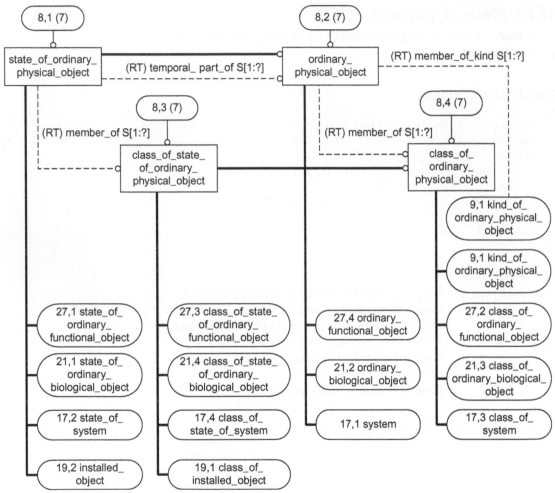

Figure 17-8 HQDM_FRAMEWORK EXPRESS-G diagram 8 of 46.

EXPRESS specification:
```
*)
  ENTITY class_of_ordinary_physical_object
    SUBTYPE OF(class_of_state_of_ordinary_physical_object,
              class_of_physical_object);
  END_ENTITY;
(*
```

17.8.2 Class_of_state_of_ordinary_physical_object

A **class_of_state_of_physical_object** that is **state_of_ordinary_physical_object** or any of its subsets.

<u>EXPRESS specification:</u>

```
*)
  ENTITY class_of_state_of_ordinary_physical_object
    SUBTYPE OF(class_of_state_of_physical_object);
  END_ENTITY;
(*
```

17.8.3 Ordinary_physical_object

A **physical_object** that does not survive changing all its parts at once.

<u>EXPRESS specification:</u>

```
*)
  ENTITY ordinary_physical_object
    SUBTYPE OF(physical_object, state_of_ordinary_physical_
              object);
    SELF\physical_object.
        member_of              :OPTIONAL SET [1:?] OF class_of_
                                ordinary_physical_object;
    SELF\physical_object.
        member_of_kind         :OPTIONAL SET [1:?] OF kind_of_
                                ordinary_physical_object;
  END_ENTITY;
(*
```

<u>Attribute definitions:</u>

member_of   A *member_of* relationship type where an **ordinary_physical_object** may be a *member_of* one or more **class_of_ordinary_physical_object**.

member_of_kind A *member_of_kind* relationship type where an **ordinary_physical_object** may be a *member_of* one or more **kind_of_ordinary_physical_object**.

17.8.4 State_of_ordinary_physical_object

A **state_of_physical_object** that is an **ordinary_physical_object** or a *temporal_part_of* one.

<u>EXPRESS specification:</u>

```
*)
  ENTITY state_of_ordinary_physical_object
    SUBTYPE OF(state_of_physical_object);
```

```
SELF\state_of_physical_object.
    temporal_part_of            :OPTIONAL SET [1:?] OF
                                 ordinary_physical_object;

SELF\state_of_physical_object.
    member_of                   :OPTIONAL SET [1:?] OF
                                 class_of_state_of_
                                 ordinary_physical_object;

END_ENTITY;
(*
```

Attribute definitions:

temporal_part_of   A *temporal_part_of* relationship type where a **state_of_ordinary_physical_object** may be a *temporal_part_of* one or more **ordinary_physical_object**.

member_of   A *member_of* relationship type where a **state_of_ordinary_physical_object** may be a *member_of* one or more **class_of_state_of_ordinary_physical_object**.

17.9 Kind of Individual and Subtypes

Figure 17-9, together with Figure 17-10, shows the subtype/supertype tree for **kind_of_individual** and many of its subtypes. **Individuals** are of the same kind if they share characteristics to a significant degree. The subtypes of **kind_of_individual** are **kind_of_physical_object** and **kind_of_intentionally_constructed_object**.

The subtypes of **kind_of_physical_object** are **kind_of_ordinary_physical_object**, **kind_of_functional_object**—which is also a subtype of **intentionally_constructed_object**—**kind_of_system_component**, and **kind_of_biological_object**.

The subtypes of **kind_of_ordinary_physical_object** are **kind_of_ordinary_functional_object**—which is also a subtype of **functional_object**—**kind_of_system**, and **kind_of_ordinary_biological_object**.

The subtypes of **intentionally_constructed_object** are **kind_of_socially_constructed_object**, **kind_of_organization**, and **kind_of_organization_component**.

17.9.1 Kind_of_biological_object

A **class_of_biological_object** that is also a **kind_of_physical_object** where each *member_of* a **kind_of_biological_object** is of the same kind.

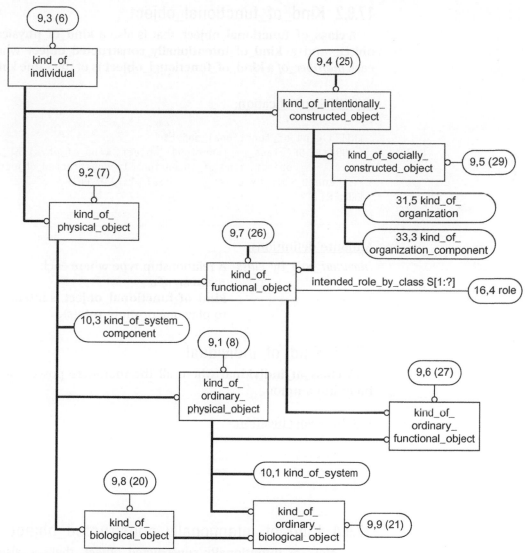

Figure 17-9 HQDM_FRAMEWORK EXPRESS-G diagram 9 of 46.

EXPRESS specification:

```
*)
  ENTITY kind_of_biological_object
    SUBTYPE OF(class_of_biological_object,
              kind_of_physical_object);
  END_ENTITY;
(*
```

17.9.2 Kind_of_functional_object

A **class_of_functional_object**, that is also a **kind_of_physical_object**, and a **kind_of_intentionally_constructed_object** where each *member_of* a **kind_of_functional_object** is of the same kind.

EXPRESS specification:

```
*)
  ENTITY kind_of_functional_object
    SUBTYPE OF(class_of_functional_object, kind_of_physical_
            object, kind_of_intentionally_constructed_object);
    intended_role_by_class        :SET [1:?] OF role;
  END_ENTITY;
(*
```

Attribute definitions:

intended_role_by_class   A relationship type where each *member_of* a **kind_of_functional_object** is intended to play one or more **role**(s).

17.9.3 Kind_of_individual

A **class_of_individual** where all the members possess attributes in common.

EXPRESS specification:

```
*)
  ENTITY kind_of_individual
    SUBTYPE OF(class_of_individual);
  END_ENTITY;
(*
```

17.9.4 Kind_of_intentionally_constructed_object

A **class_of_intentionally_constructed_object** that is also a **kind_of_individual** where each *member_of* a **kind_of_intentionally_constructed_object** is of the same kind.

EXPRESS specification:

```
*)
  ENTITY kind_of_intentionally_constructed_object
    SUBTYPE OF(class_of_intentionally_constructed_object,
            kind_of_individual);
    END_ENTITY;
(*
```

17.9.5 Kind_of_ordinary_biological_object

A **class_of_ordinary_biological_object**, that is also a **kind_of_ordinary_physical_object**, and a **kind_of_biological_object** where each *member_of* a **kind_of_ordinary_biological_object** is of the same kind.

EXPRESS specification:

```
*)
  ENTITY kind_of_ordinary_biological_object
    SUBTYPE OF(class_of_ordinary_biological_object, kind_of_
            biological_object, kind_of_ordinary_physical_
            object);
  END_ENTITY;
(*
```

17.9.6 Kind_of_ordinary_functional_object

A **class_of_ordinary_functional_object**, that is also a **kind_of_ordinary_physical_object**, and a **kind_of_functional_object** where each member_of a **kind_of_ordinary_functional_object** is of the same kind.

EXPRESS specification:

```
*)
  ENTITY kind_of_ordinary_functional_object
    SUBTYPE OF(class_of_ordinary_functional_object, kind_of_
            ordinary_physical_object, kind_of_functional_
            object);
  END_ENTITY;
(*
```

17.9.7 Kind_of_ordinary_physical_object

A **class_of_ordinary_physical_object** that is also a **kind_of_physical_object** where each **ordinary_physical_object** has members that are of the same kind.

EXPRESS specification:

```
*)
  ENTITY kind_of_ordinary_physical_object
    SUBTYPE OF(class_of_ordinary_physical_object,
            kind_of_physical_object);
  END_ENTITY;
(*
```

17.9.8 Kind_of_physical_object

A **class_of_physical_object** that is also a **kind_of_individual** where each **physical_object** has members that are of the same kind.

EXPRESS specification:

```
*)
  ENTITY kind_of_physical_object
    SUBTYPE OF(class_of_physical_object, kind_of_individual);
  END_ENTITY;
(*
```

17.9.9 Kind_of_socially_constructed_object

A **class_of_socially_constructed_object** that is also a **kind_of_intentionally_constructed_object** where each **kind_of_socially_constructed_object** has members that are of the same kind.

EXPRESS specification:

```
*)
  ENTITY kind_of_socially_constructed_object
    SUBTYPE OF(class_of_socially_contructed_object,
              kind_of_intentionally_constructed_object);
  END_ENTITY;
(*
```

17.10 Kind of System and System Component

Figure 17-10 shows some more subtypes of **kind_of_individual**. A **kind_of_system** is a **class_of_system** and **kind_of_ordinary_physical_object** that is a complex object that is a group of objects organized for a purpose. A **system** has one or more **system_components** that are wholly replaceable but do not survive the **system** itself. A **kind_of_system_component** is a **class_of_system_component** that is also a **kind_of_physical_object**.

Subtypes of **kind_of_system** are **kind_of_biological_system**, **kind_of_functional_system**, and **kind_of_party**. Similarly subtypes of **kind_of_system_component** are **kind_of_biological_system_component**, **kind_of_functional_system_component**, and **kind_of_organization_component**.

17.10.1 Kind_of_biological_system

A **class_of_biological_system** that is also a **kind_of_system** all of whose members have a natural **role** that they play.

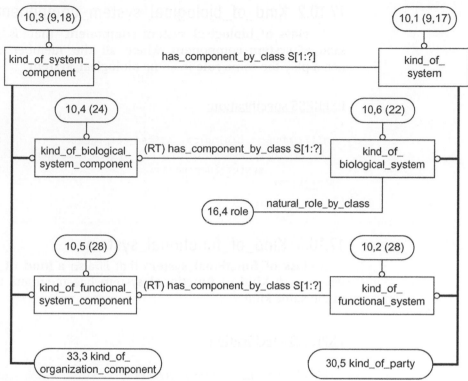

Figure 17-10 HQDM_FRAMEWORK EXPRESS-G diagram 10 of 46.

<u>EXPRESS specification:</u>

```
*)
  ENTITY kind_of_biological_system
    SUBTYPE OF(class_of_biological_system, kind_of_system);
    natural_role_by_class      :role;
    SELF\kind_of_system.has_
        component_by_class      :SET [1:?] OF kind_of_biological_
                                  system_component;
  END_ENTITY;
(*
```

<u>Attribute definitions:</u>

natural_role_by_class A relationship type where each
         member_of the **kind_of_biological_
         system** naturally participates in the **role**.

has_component_by_class A *has_component_by_class* relationship
         type where each *member_of* a **kind_
         of_biological_system** has a *member_of*
         one or more **kind_of_biological_
         system_component** as a component.

17.10.2 Kind_of_biological_system_component

A **class_of_biological_system_component** that is also a **kind_of_system_component** where all the member components play the same **role** in some **biological_system**.

EXPRESS specification:
```
*)
  ENTITY kind_of_biological_system_component
    SUBTYPE OF(class_of_biological_system_component, kind_of_
            system_component);
  END_ENTITY;
(*
```

17.10.3 Kind_of_functional_system

A **class_of_functional_system** that is also a **kind_of_system** where each **kind_of_functional_system** has members that are of the same kind.

EXPRESS specification:
```
*)
  ENTITY kind_of_functional_system
    SUBTYPE OF(class_of_functional_system, kind_of_system);
    SELF\kind_of_system.
        has_component_by_class  :SET [1:?] OF kind_of_
                                    functional_system_component;

  END_ENTITY;
(*
```

Attribute definitions:

has_component_by_class   A *has_component_by_class* relationship type where each *member_of* the **kind_of_functional_system** has a *member_of* one or more **kind_of_functional_system_component** as a component.

17.10.4 Kind_of_functional_system_component

A **class_of_functional_system_component** that is also a **kind_of_system_component** where each *member_of* a **kind_of_functional_system_component** is of the same kind.

<u>EXPRESS specification:</u>

```
*)
  ENTITY kind_of_functional_system_component
    SUBTYPE OF(class_of_functional_system_component,
            kind_of_system_component);
  END_ENTITY;
(*
```

17.10.5 Kind_of_system

A **class_of_system** that is also a **kind_of_ordinary_physical_ object** where each *member_of* a **kind_of_system** is of the same kind.

<u>EXPRESS specification:</u>

```
*)
  ENTITY kind_of_system
    SUBTYPE OF(class_of_system,
            kind_of_ordinary_physical_object);
    has_component_by_class        :SET [1:?] OF
                            kind_of_system_component;
  END_ENTITY;
(*
```

<u>Attribute definitions:</u>

has_component_by_class   A *consists_of_by_class* relationship type where each *member_of* a **kind_of_system** has a *member_of* one or more **kind_of_system_ component** as a component.

17.10.6 Kind_of_system_component

A **class_of_system_component** that is also a **kind_of_ physical_object** where all the members are of the same kind.

<u>EXPRESS specification:</u>

```
*)
  ENTITY kind_of_system_component
    SUBTYPE OF(class_of_system_component,
            kind_of_physical_object);
(*END_ENTITY;
```

17.11 Period of Time and Possible Worlds

Figure 17-11 shows the data model for **period_of_time** and **possible_world**. A **period_of_time** is all of space between one

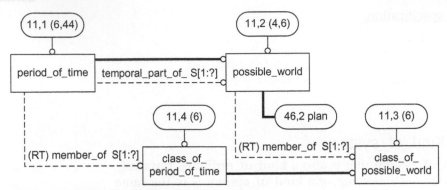

Figure 17-11 HQDM_FRAMEWORK EXPRESS-G diagram 11 of 46.

point_in_time and another, and so it is a *temporal_part_of* a **possible_world** (possible world should probably be called possible universe, but the convention is to call it a possible world).

A **period_of_time** may be a *member_of* one or more **class_of_period_of_time** and a **possible_world** may be a *member_of* one or more **class_of_possible_world**.

17.11.1 Class_of_period_of_time

A **class_of_state** that is **period_of_time** or any of its subsets.

EXPRESS specification:

```
*)
  ENTITY class_of_period_of_time
    SUBTYPE OF(class_of_state);
  END_ENTITY;
(*
```

17.11.2 Class_of_possible_world

A **class_of_individual** that is also a **class_of_period_of_time** that is **possible_world** or any of its subsets.

EXPRESS specification:

```
*)
  ENTITY class_of_possible_world
    SUBTYPE OF(class_of_individual, class_of_period_of_time);
  END_ENTITY;
(*
```

17.11.3 Period_of_time

A **state** that is a *temporal_part_of* some **possible_world**.

EXPRESS specification:

```
*)
  ENTITY period_of_time
    SUBTYPE OF(state);
    temporal_part_of_        :OPTIONAL SET [1:?] OF possible_world;
    SELF\state.member_of     :OPTIONAL SET [1:?] OF class_of_
                              period_of_time;
  END_ENTITY;
(*
```

Attribute definitions:

temporal_part_of	A *temporal_part_of* relationship type where a **period_of_time** may be a *temporal_part_of* one or more **possible_world**.
member_of	A *member_of* relationship type where a **period_of_time** may be a *member_of* one or more **class_of_period_of_time**.

17.11.4 Possible_world

An **individual** that is a complete spatio-temporal history of some possible world.

EXPRESS specification:

```
*)
  ENTITY possible_world
    SUBTYPE OF(individual, period_of_time);
    SELF\individual.member_of    :OPTIONAL SET [1:?] OF
                                  class_of_possible_world;
  END_ENTITY;
(*
```

Attribute definitions:

member_of	A *member_of* relationship type where a **possible_world** may be a *member_of* one or more **class_of_possible_world**.

17.12 Physical Properties and Physical Quantities

Figure 17-12 shows a basic data model of physical properties and physical quantities.

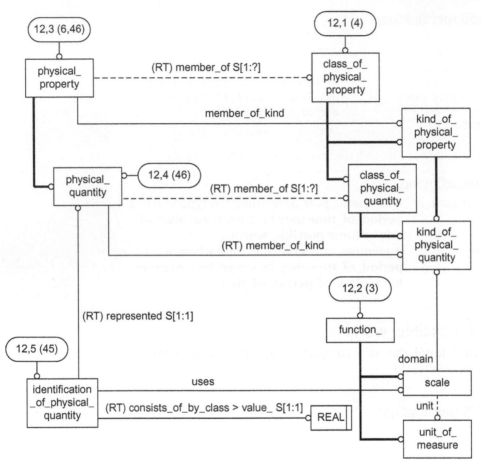

Figure 17-12 HQDM_FRAMEWORK EXPRESS-G diagram 12 of 46.

A **physical_property** is a **class_of_state** that is a *member_of* a **kind_of_physical_property** that a **state** can be a *member_of* (or more colloquially, possess). For example, red is a color that a **state** of a **physical_object** can possess.

A **physical_quantity** is a *member_of* an ordered set that is the **kind_of_physical_quantity** it is a *member_of*. For example, 20 Celsius is a degree of hotness that is a *member_of* the set of temperatures. A **physical_quantity** may be a *member_of* one or more **class_of_physical_quantity** and is a *member_of_kind* of exactly one **kind_of_physical_quantity**.

A **kind_of_physical_quantity** has one or more **scales** that is a **function_** that is a functional mapping to a number space. Each **scale** has exactly one **kind_of_physical_quantity** as its *domain*. The number space is not shown in this data model.

A **function_** is a one-to-many **relationship** (which is its mathematical meaning). A **unit_of_measure** is a plus one **function_**. A **scale** may have just one **unit_of_measure** as *unit*.

An **identification_of_physical_quantity** is an **identification** that is of a **physical_quantity** that *uses* exactly one **scale** and has its *value_ represented* by exactly one **REAL**.

17.12.1 Class_of_physical_property

A **class_of_class_of_spatio_temporal_extent** that is **physical_property** or any of its subsets.

EXPRESS specification:
```
*)
  ENTITY class_of_physical_property
    SUBTYPE OF(class_of_class_of_spatio_temporal_extent);
  END_ENTITY;
(*
```

17.12.2 Class_of_physical_quantity

A **class_of_physical_property** that is **physical_quantity** or any of its subsets.

EXPRESS specification:
```
*)
  ENTITY class_of_physical_quantity
    SUBTYPE OF(class_of_physical_property);
  END_ENTITY;
(*
```

17.12.3 Function_

A one-to-many **relationship**.

EXPRESS specification:
```
*)
  ENTITY function_
    SUBTYPE OF(relationship);
  END_ENTITY;
(*
```

17.12.4 Identification_of_physical_quantity

An **identification** that identifies a **physical_quantity**. An **identification_of_physical_quantity** consists of a **REAL** that is a representation of the *value_* the physical quantity maps to on the **scale**.

<u>EXPRESS specification:</u>

```
*)
 ENTITY identification_of_physical_quantity
   SUBTYPE OF(identification);
   SELF\representation_by_
        pattern.represented    :SET [1:1] OF physical_quantity;
   SELF\representation_by_
        pattern.consists_of_by_
        class RENAMED value_    :SET [1:1] OF REAL;
     uses                       :scale;
 END_ENTITY;
(*
```

<u>Attribute definitions:</u>

represents_by_class	A relationship type where a *member_of* an **identification_of_physical_quantity** represents exactly one **physical_quantity**. Note: Represents by **class** means that each *member_of* an **identification_of_physical_quantity** represents the **physical_quantity**. For example any writing down of 20C represents that particular degree of hotness.
*value_*	A relationship type where an **identification_of_physical_quantity** consists of exactly one REAL as its value. Note 1: The members of the data type REAL provide an **identification** of a real number. Note 2: The relationship type name has been renamed from consists of by **class** to value.
uses	A relationship type where an **identification_of_physical_quantity** uses exactly one **scale**.

17.12.5 Kind_of_physical_property

A **class_of_physical_property** where each *member_of* a **kind_of_physical_property** is of the same kind.

Example: Color, with members including red, green, and blue.

<u>EXPRESS specification:</u>

```
*)
 ENTITY kind_of_physical_property
   SUBTYPE OF(class_of_physical_property);
 END_ENTITY;
(*
```

17.12.6 Kind_of_physical_quantity

A **class_of_physical_quantity** that is also a **kind_of_physical_ property** such that each *member_of* the same **kind_of_physical_ quantity** is comparable to the others.

Example: Temperature and pressure are members of **kind_of_physical_quantity**.

<u>EXPRESS specification:</u>

```
*)
  ENTITY kind_of_physical_quantity
    SUBTYPE OF(class_of_physical_quantity, kind_of_physical_
            property);
  END_ENTITY;
(*
```

17.12.7 Physical_property

A **class_of_state** that is some characteristic that is the same for each **state** that possesses it (is a *member_of* it).

Example: The color red is a **physical_property**.

<u>EXPRESS specification:</u>

```
*)
  ENTITY physical_property
    SUBTYPE OF(class_of_state);
    SELF\class_of_spatio_
        temporal_extent.member_of   :OPTIONAL SET [1:?] OF class_
                                      of_physical_property;
    member_of_kind                  :kind_of_physical_property;
  END_ENTITY;
(*
```

<u>Attribute definitions:</u>

member_of	A *member_of* relationship type where a **physical_property** may be a *member_of* one or more **class_of_physical_property**.
member_of_kind	A *member_of* relationship type where a **physical_property** is a *member_of* exactly one **kind_of_physical_property**.

17.12.8 Physical_quantity

A **physical_quantity** is a **physical_property** that is a measurable quantity of a **kind_of_physical_quantity**.

Example: The degree of hotness known as 20 Celsius is a **physical_quantity**.

<u>EXPRESS specification:</u>

```
*)
  ENTITY physical_quantity
    SUBTYPE OF(physical_property);
    SELF\physical_property.member_of    :OPTIONAL SET [1:?] OF
                                          class_of_
                                          physical_quantity;

    SELF\physical_property.
        member_of_kind                  :kind_of_physical_
                                          quantity;

  END_ENTITY;
(*
```

<u>Attribute definitions:</u>

member_of   A *member_of* relationship type where a **physical_quantity** may be a *member_of* one or more **class_of_physical_quantity**.

member_of_kind   A *member_of* relationship type where a **physical_quantity** is a *member_of* exactly one **kind_of_physical_quantity**.

17.12.9 Scale

A **scale** is a **function_** from **kind_of_physical_quantity** to the real numbers.

Example: The Celsius **scale** is a mapping from temperature to real number.

<u>EXPRESS specification:</u>

```
*)
  ENTITY scale
    SUBTYPE OF(function_);
    unit        :OPTIONAL unit_of_measure;
    domain      :kind_of_physical_quantity;
  END_ENTITY;
(*
```

<u>Attribute definitions:</u>

unit   A **scale** may have at most one **unit_of_measure**.
Note 1: A **unit_of_measure** may apply to more than one **scale**.
Note 2: A **scale** may not have a **unit_of_measure**. To have a **unit_of_measure** the points on the **scale** must be evenly placed so that adding one means the same

thing. This is not true for some **scale**s such as Rockwell Hardness where the points on the **scale** are an arbitrary distance apart. A **scale** will also not have a **unit_of_measure** when it is a dimensionless **scale**.

domain   A **scale** has exactly one **kind_of_physical_quantity** as its domain.

17.12.10 Unit_of_measure

A plus one **function_** for a **scale**.

EXPRESS specification:

```
*)
  ENTITY unit_of_measure
    SUBTYPE OF(function_);
  END_ENTITY;
(*
```

17.13 Association

Figure 17-13 shows the data model for **association**. An **association** consists of a *temporal_part_of* two or more **individuals** that are the **participants** in the **association**, where each **participant** plays a particular **role**. A **state_of_association** is an **association** or a *temporal_part_of* an **association**.

Each **association** is a *member_of* at least one **kind_of_association** (which may be a subtype of **association**). A **state_of_**

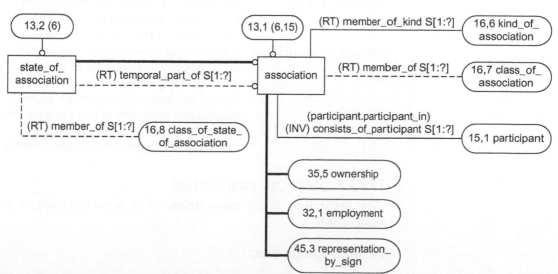

Figure 17-13 HQDM_FRAMEWORK EXPRESS-G diagram 13 of 46.

association may be a *member_of* one or more **class_of_state_of_association** and an **association** may be a *member_of* one or more **class_of_association**.

17.13.1 Association

An **individual** that *consists_of* the **participants** that are associated, and where the **participant**s are *part_of* the same **period_of_time**.

<u>EXPRESS specification:</u>

```
*)
  ENTITY association
    SUBTYPE OF(individual, state_of_association);
    SELF\individual.member_of        :OPTIONAL SET [1:?] OF
                                         class_of_association;
    SELF\individual.member_of_kind   :SET [1:?] OF
                                         kind_of_association;
  INVERSE
    consists_of_participant          :SET [1:?] OF participant
                                         FOR participant_in;
  END_ENTITY;
(*
```

<u>Attribute definitions:</u>

member_of	A *member_of* relationship type where an **association** may be a *member_of* one or more **class_of_association**.
member_of_kind	A *member_of_kind* relationship type where each **association** is a *member_of* one or more **kind_of_association**.
consists_of_participant	A *consists_of* relationship type where each **association** consists of two or more **participants**. Note: The cardinality constraint shows a minimum cardinality of one because this relationship type will be retyped for particular **participants** in an **association**.

17.13.2 State_of_association

A **state** that is an **association** or a *temporal_part_of* an **association**.

<u>EXPRESS specification:</u>

```
*)
  ENTITY state_of_association
```

```
   SUBTYPE OF(state);
   SELF\state.temporal_part_of    :OPTIONAL SET [1:?] OF
                                   association;
   SELF\state.member_of           :OPTIONAL SET [1:?] OF class_
                                   of_state_of_association;
 END_ENTITY;
(*
```

<u>Attribute definitions:</u>

temporal_part_of   A *temporal_part_of* relationship type where a **state_of_association** may be a *temporal_part_of* one or more **association**.

member_of   A *member_of* relationship type where a **state_of_association** may be a *member_of* one or more **class_of_state_of_association**.

17.14 Activity

Figure 17-14 shows the data model for **activity**. Like an **association**, an **activity** consists of its **participants**. It may also have parts in a more general sense. However, what distinguishes an **activity** from an **association** is that an **activity** *causes* at least

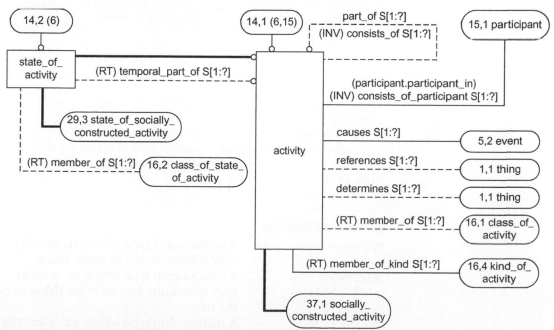

Figure 17-14 HQDM_FRAMEWORK EXPRESS-G diagram 14 of 46.

one **event**; that is, it brings about change in the world. An **activity** can also reference **things** that are not **participants**—for example, a conversation between two people may refer to Winston Churchill. An **activity** can also determine that something is the case, for example by taking a measurement, or validating the existence of some **individual**. Finally, an **activity** is a *member_of* at least one **kind_of_activity** and may be a *member_of* one or more **class_of_activity**.

A **state_of_activity** is an **activity** or a *temporal_part_of* an **activity**; for example, a football match has a first half and a second half. A **state_of_activity** may be a *member_of* a **class_of_state_of_activity**.

17.14.1 Activity

An **individual** that consists of its **participants** and *causes* some **event**.

<u>EXPRESS specification:</u>

```
*)
  ENTITY activity
    SUBTYPE OF(individual, state_of_activity);
    references              :OPTIONAL SET [1:?] OF thing;
    determines              :OPTIONAL SET [1:?] OF thing;
    causes                  :SET [1:?] OF event;
    SELF\individual.
        member_of           :OPTIONAL SET [1:?] OF
                             class_of_activity;
    part_of                 :OPTIONAL SET [1:?] OF activity;
    SELF\individual.
        member_of_kind      :SET [1:?] OF kind_of_activity;
  INVERSE
    consists_of             :SET OF activity FOR part_of;
    consists_of_participant :SET [1:?] OF participant FOR
                             participant_in;
  END_ENTITY;
(*
```

<u>Attribute definitions:</u>

references	A relationship type where an **activity** may reference one or more **thing**.
determines	A relationship type where an **activity** may determine one or more **thing** to be the case.
causes	A relationship type where each **activity** is the cause of one or more **event**.

member_of	A *member_of* relationship type where an **activity** may be a *member_of* one or more **class_of_activity**.
part_of	A *part_of* relationship type where one **activity** may be a *part_of* one or more others.
member_of_kind	A *member_of_kind* relationship type where each **activity** is a *member_of* one or more **kind_of_activity**.
consists_of	A *consists_of* relationship type where an **activity** may *consists_of* one or more other **activity**.
consists_of_participant	A *consists_of* relationship type where an **activity** *consists_of* one or more **participant**s.

17.14.2 State_of_activity

A **state** that is an **activity** or a *temporal_part_of* an **activity**.

<u>EXPRESS specification:</u>

```
*)
  ENTITY state_of_activity
    SUBTYPE OF(state);
    SELF\state.temporal_part_of     :OPTIONAL SET [1:?] OF
                                       activity;
    SELF\state.member_of            :OPTIONAL SET [1:?] OF class_
                                       of_state_of_activity;
  END_ENTITY;
(*
```

<u>Attribute definitions:</u>

temporal_part_of	A *temporal_part_of* relationship type where a **state_of_activity** may be a *temporal_part_of* one or more **activity**.
member_of	A *member_of* relationship type where a **state_of_activity** may be a *member_of* one or more **class_of_state_of_activity**.

17.15 Participant

Figure 17-15 is a data model of **participant**. A **participant** is a **state** that is a *participant_in* an **association** or an **activity**. The dashed box, **participant_in_activity_or_association,** is an EXPRESS

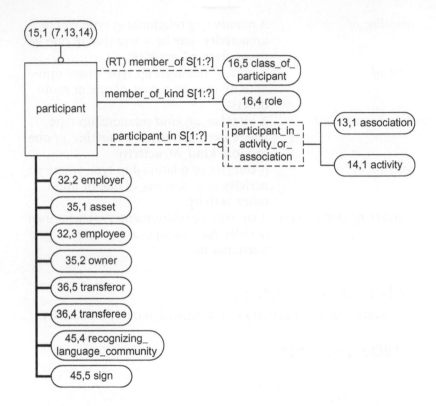

Figure 17-15 HQDM_FRAMEWORK EXPRESS-G diagram 15 of 46.

SELECT type that is the same as an exclusive arc in some other notations that allows the choice between an **activity** or an **association**. Many business terms find their proper place among the subtypes of **participant**, such as **employer**, **employee**, **asset**, and **owner**. A **participant** may be a *member_of* one or more **class_of_participant**, and each **participant** is a *member_of* one or more **roles**. You may notice that there is no kind of **participant**; that is because **role** is the term for kind of **participant**.

17.15.1 Participant_in_activity_or_association

A SELECT where a **participant** may be a *participant_in* an **activity** or an **association**.

EXPRESS specification:

```
*)
  TYPE participant_in_activity_or_association = SELECT
    (activity, association);
  END_TYPE;
(*
```

17.15.2 Participant

A **state** that is a *participant_in* an **activity** or **association**.

<u>EXPRESS specification:</u>

```
*)
  ENTITY participant
    SUBTYPE OF(state_of_physical_object);
    SELF\state_of_physical_
        object.member_of     :OPTIONAL SET [1:?] OF class_of_
                              participant;
    member_of_kind           :SET [1:?] OF role;
    participant_in           :OPTIONAL SET [1:?] OF participant_
                              in_activity_or_association;
  END_ENTITY;
(*
```

<u>Attribute definitions:</u>

member_of　　　　A *member_of* relationship type where a
　　　　　　　　　participant may be a *member_of* one or more
　　　　　　　　　class_of_participant.

member_of_kind　A *member_of_kind* relationship type where
　　　　　　　　　each **participant** is a *member_of* one or more
　　　　　　　　　role.

17.16 Role, Class of Activity, and Class of Association

Figure 17-16 shows a data model for **role**, **class_of_activity**, and **class_of_association**. A **role** is a **class_of_participant** where all the members are of the same kind and participate in the same way in an **association** or an **activity**. A *member_of* a **kind_of_activity** has a *member_of* a **role** as a **participant**; similarly, a *member_of* a **kind_of_association** has a *member_of* a **role** as a **participant**.

In addition, a *member_of* a **kind_of_activity** may cause a *member_of* a **class_of_event**, reference a *member_of* a **class**, or determine a *member_of* a **class.**

17.16.1 Class_of_activity

A **class_of_individual** that is also a **class_of_state_of_activity** that is **activity** or any of its subsets.

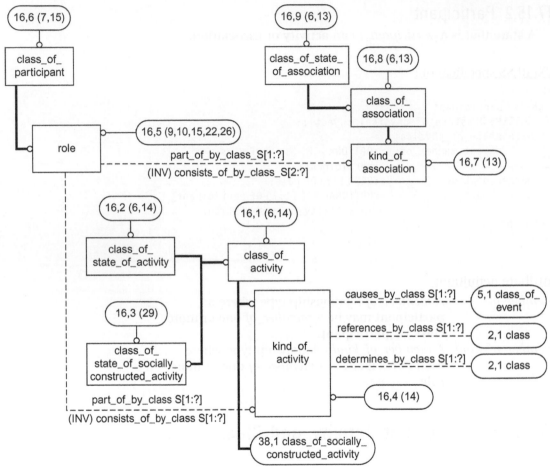

Figure 17-16 HQDM_FRAMEWORK EXPRESS-G diagram 16 of 46.

EXPRESS specification:

```
*)
  ENTITY class_of_activity
    SUBTYPE OF(class_of_individual,
               class_of_state_of_activity);
  END_ENTITY;
(*
```

17.16.2 Class_of_association

A **class_of_state_of_association** that is also a **class_of_individual** that is **association** or any of its subsets.

EXPRESS specification:

```
*)
  ENTITY class_of_association
    SUBTYPE OF(class_of_individual,
              class_of_state_of_association);
  END_ENTITY;
(*
```

17.16.3 Class_of_participant

A **class_of_state_of_physical_object** that is **participant** or any of its subsets.

EXPRESS specification:

```
*)
  ENTITY class_of_participant
    SUBTYPE OF(class_of_state_of_physical_object);
  END_ENTITY;
(*
```

17.16.4 Class_of_state_of_activity

A **class_of_state** that is **state_of_activity** or any of its subsets.

EXPRESS specification:

```
*)
  ENTITY class_of_state_of_activity
    SUBTYPE OF(class_of_state);
  END_ENTITY;
(*
```

17.16.5 Class_of_state_of_association

A **class_of_state** that is **state_of_association** or any of its subsets.

EXPRESS specification:

```
*)
  ENTITY class_of_state_of_association
    SUBTYPE OF(class_of_state);
  END_ENTITY;
(*
```

17.16.6 Class_of_state_of_socially_constructed_activity

A **class_of_state_of_socially_constructed_object** that is **state_of_socially_constructed_activity** or any of its subsets.

EXPRESS specification:

```
*)
  ENTITY class_of_state_of_socially_constructed_activity
    SUBTYPE OF(class_of_state_of_socially_constructed_object,
               class_of_state_of_activity);
  END_ENTITY;
(*
```

17.16.7 Kind_of_activity

A **class_of_activity** all of whose members are of the same kind.

EXPRESS specification:

```
*)
  ENTITY kind_of_activity
    SUBTYPE OF(class_of_activity);
    determines_by_class      :OPTIONAL SET [1:?] OF class;
    references_by_class       :OPTIONAL SET [1:?] OF class;
    causes_by_class          :OPTIONAL SET [1:?] OF class_of_event;
  INVERSE
    consists_of_by_class     :SET [1:?] OF role FOR part_of_by_class;
  END_ENTITY;
(*
```

Attribute definitions:

determines_by_class	A relationship type where a *member_of* the **kind_of_activity** *determines* a *member_of* the **class.**
references_by_class	A relationship type where a *member_of* the **kind_of_activity** *references* a *member_of* the **class.**
causes_by_class	A relationship type where a *member_of* the **kind_of_activity** *causes* a *member_of* the **class_of_event**.
consists_of_by_class	A *consists_of_by_class* relationship type where a *member_of* a **kind_of_activity** has a *member_of* a **role** as a **participant**.

17.16.8 Kind_of_association

A **class_of_association** where all the members are of the same kind.

EXPRESS specification:

```
*)
  ENTITY kind_of_association
    SUBTYPE OF(class_of_association);
```

```
INVERSE
  consists_of_by_class        :SET [2:?] OF role FOR part_of_
                               by_class_;
END_ENTITY;
(*
```

Attribute definitions:

consists_of_by_class   A *consists_of_by_class* relationship type where a *member_of* the **kind_of_association** has a *member_of* the **role** as a part.

17.16.9 Role

A **class_of_participant** where each member participates in the same way in an **activity** or **association**.

EXPRESS specification:

```
*)
  ENTITY role
    SUBTYPE OF(class_of_participant);
    part_of_by_class         :OPTIONAL SET [1:?] OF kind_of_
                              activity;
    part_of_by_class_        :OPTIONAL SET [1:?] OF kind_of_
                              association;
  END_ENTITY;
(*
```

Attribute definitions:

part_of_by_class   A *part_of_by_class* where a *member_of* a **role** is a **participant** in a *member_of* a **class_of_activity.**

*part_of_by_class_*   A *part_of_by_class* where a *member_of* a **role** is a *part_of* a *member_of* the **class.**

17.17 System

Figure 17-17 shows the data model for **system**. A **system** is a group of objects organized for some purpose. A **state_of_system** is a **system** or a *temporal_part_of* a **system**. A **state_of_system** may be a *temporal_part_of* a **system** and may be a *member_of* one or more **class_of_state_of_system**. A **system** may be a *member_of* one or more **class_of_system** and one or more **kind_of_system**.

17.17.1 Class_of_state_of_system

A **class_of_state_of_ordinary_physical_object** that is **state_of_system** or any of its subsets.

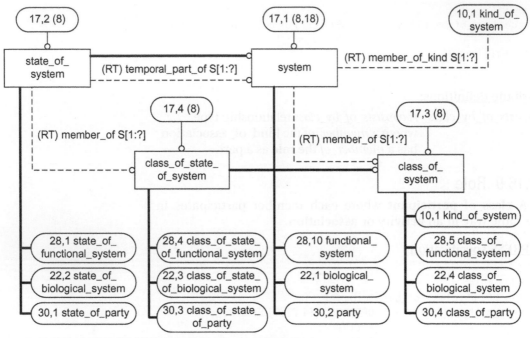

Figure 17-17 HQDM_FRAMEWORK EXPRESS-G diagram 17 of 46.

EXPRESS specification:

```
*)
  ENTITY class_of_state_of_system
    SUBTYPE OF(class_of_state_of_ordinary_physical_object);
  END_ENTITY;
(*
```

17.17.2 Class_of_system

A **class_of_state_of_system** that is also a **class_of_ ordinary_physical_object** that is **system** or any of its subsets.

EXPRESS specification:

```
*)
  ENTITY class_of_system
    SUBTYPE OF(class_of_state_of_system,
              class_of_ordinary_physical_object);
  END_ENTITY;
(*
```

17.17.3 State_of_system

A **state_of_ordinary_physical_object** that is a **system** or a *temporal_part_of* a **system**.

EXPRESS specification:

```
*)
  ENTITY state_of_system
    SUBTYPE OF(state_of_ordinary_physical_object);
    SELF\state_of_ordinary_
        physical_object.temporal_part_of  :OPTIONAL SET [1:?] OF
                                              system;
    SELF\state_of_ordinary_
        physical_object.member_of         :OPTIONAL SET [1:?] OF
                                              class_of_state_of_
                                              system;
  END_ENTITY;
(*
```

Attribute definitions:

temporal_part_of	A *temporal_part_of* relationship type where a **state_of_system** may be a *temporal_part_of* one or more **system**.
member_of	A *member_of* relationship type where a **state_of_system** may be a *member_of* one or more **class_of_state_of_system**.

17.17.4 System

An **ordinary_physical_object** that is an organized or connected group of **physical_object**.

EXPRESS specification:

```
*)
  ENTITY system
    SUBTYPE OF(state_of_system, ordinary_physical_object);
    SELF\state_of_system.member_of       :OPTIONAL SET [1:?] OF
                                              class_of_system;
    SELF\ordinary_physical_object.
        member_of_kind                   :OPTIONAL SET [1:?] OF
                                              kind_of_system;
  END_ENTITY;
(*
```

Attribute definitions:

member_of	A *member_of* relationship type where a **system** may be a *member_of* one or more **class_of_system**.
member_of_kind	A *member_of_kind* relationship type where a **system** may be a *member_of* one or more **kind_of_system**.

17.18 System Component

Figure 17-18 shows the data model for **system_component**. A **system_component** is a replaceable component of exactly one **system**. A **state_of_system_component** is a **system_component** or a *temporal_part_of* a **system_component**. A **state_of_system_component** may be a *member_of* one or more **class_of_state_of_system_component**, and a **system_component** may be a *member_of* one or more **class_of_system_component** and one or more **kind_of_system_component**.

17.18.1 Class_of_state_of_system_component

A **class_of_state_of_physical_object** that is **state_of_system_component** or any of its subsets.

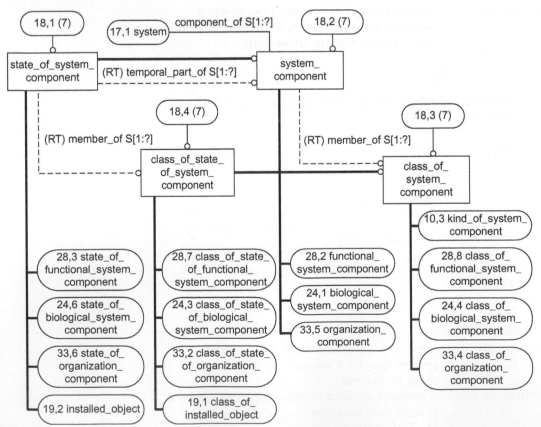

Figure 17-18 HQDM_FRAMEWORK EXPRESS-G diagram 18 of 46.

EXPRESS specification:

```
*)
  ENTITY class_of_state_of_system_component
    SUBTYPE OF(class_of_state_of_physical_object);
  END_ENTITY;
(*
```

17.18.2 Class_of_system_component

A **class_of_state_of_system_component** that is also a **class_of_ physical_object** that is **system_component** or any of its subsets.

EXPRESS specification:

```
*)
  ENTITY class_of_system_component
    SUBTYPE OF(class_of_state_of_system_component,
            class_of_physical_object);
  END_ENTITY;
(*
```

17.18.3 State_of_system_component

A **state_of_physical_object** that is a **system_component** or a *temporal_part_of* a **system_component**.

EXPRESS specification:

```
*)
  ENTITY state_of_system_component
    SUBTYPE OF(state_of_physical_object);
    SELF\state_of_physical_
        object.temporal_part_of    :OPTIONAL SET [1:?] OF
                                     system_component;
    SELF\state_of_physical_
        object.member_of           :OPTIONAL SET [1:?] OF class_
                                     of_state_of_system_
                                     component;
  END_ENTITY;
(*
```

Attribute definitions:

temporal_part_of	A *temporal_part_of* relationship type where a **state_of_system_component** may be a *temporal_part_of* one or more **system_ component**.
member_of	A *member_of* relationship type where a **state_of_system_component** may be a *member_of* one or more **class_of_state_of_ system_component**.

17.18.4 System_component

A **physical_object** that is a *component_of* a **system** and that can be completely replaced without losing identity.

Note: A **system_component** is existence dependent on the **system** it is a component of, unlike any **ordinary_physical_object** that may be installed as the component.

<u>EXPRESS specification:</u>

```
*)
  ENTITY system_component
    SUBTYPE OF(physical_object, state_of_system_component);
    component_of              :SET [1:1] OF system;
    SELF\physical_object.
        member_of             :OPTIONAL SET [1:?] OF class_of_
                               system_component;
  END_ENTITY;
(*
```

<u>Attribute definitions:</u>

component_of A *part_of* relationship type where each **system_component** is *part_of* exactly one **system**.

member_of A *member_of* relationship type where a **system_component** may be a *member_of* one or more **class_of_system_component**.

17.19 Installed Object

Figure 17-19 shows the data model for **installed_object**. An **installed_object** is a **state_of_ordinary_physical_object** that is

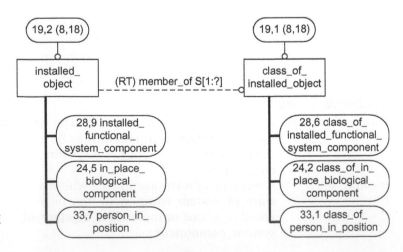

Figure 17-19 HQDM_FRAMEWORK EXPRESS-G diagram 19 of 46.

also a **state_of_system_component** from when the **ordinary_ physical_object** is installed as a **system_component** to when it is removed. An **installed_object** may be a *member_of* one or more **class_of_installed_object**.

17.19.1 Class_of_installed_object

A **class_of_state_of_system_component** that is also a **class_ of_state_of_ordinary_physical_object** that is **installed_object** or any of its subsets.

EXPRESS specification:

```
*)
  ENTITY class_of_installed_object
    SUBTYPE OF(class_of_state_of_system_component,
              class_of_state_of_ordinary_physical_object);
  END_ENTITY;
(*
```

17.19.2 Installed_object

A **state_of_ordinary_physical_object** that is also a **state_of_ system_component** that is a *temporal_part_of* an **ordinary_ physical_object** from when it is installed as a **system_component** to when it is removed.

EXPRESS specification:

```
*)
  ENTITY installed_object
    SUBTYPE OF(state_of_ordinary_physical_object,
              state_of_system_component);
    SELF\state_of_ordinary_
        physical_object.member_of     :OPTIONAL SET [1:?] OF
                                       class_of_installed_
                                       object;
  END_ENTITY;
(*
```

Attribute definitions:

member_of   A *member_of* relationship type where an
              installed_object may be a *member_of* one or more
              class_of_installed_object.

17.20 Biological Object

Figure 17-20 shows the data model for **biological_object**. A **biological_object** is a **physical_object** from the biological

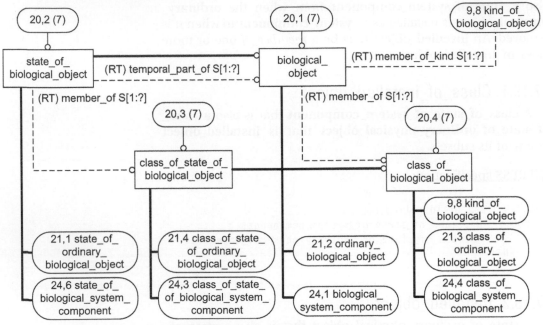

Figure 17-20 HQDM_FRAMEWORK EXPRESS-G diagram 20 of 46.

realm. A **state_of_biological_object** is a **biological_object** or a *temporal_part_of* a **biological_object**.

A **state_of_biological_object** may be a *member_of* one or more **class_of_state_of_biological_object** and a **biological_object** may be a *member_of* one or more **class_of_biological_object** and **kind_of_biological_object**.

17.20.1 Biological_object

A **state_of_biological_object** that is also a **physical_object** that sustains itself and reproduces.

EXPRESS specification:
```
*)
 ENTITY biological_object
  SUBTYPE OF(state_of_biological_object, physical_object);
  SELF\state_of_biological_
      object.member_of          :OPTIONAL SET [1:?] OF class_of_
                                   biological_object;
  SELF\physical_object.
      member_of_kind            :OPTIONAL SET [1:?] OF kind_of_
                                   biological_object;
 END_ENTITY;
(*
```

Attribute definitions:

member_of	A *member_of* relationship type where a **biological_object** may be a *member_of* one or more **class_of_biological_object**.
member_of_kind	A *member_of* relationship type where a **biological_object** may be a *member_of* one or more **kind_of_biological_object**.

17.20.2 Class_of_biological_object

A **class_of_state_of_biological_object** and **class_of_physical_object** that is **biological_object** or any of its subsets.

EXPRESS specification:

```
*)
  ENTITY class_of_biological_object
    SUBTYPE OF(class_of_state_of_biological_object,
           class_of_physical_object);
  END_ENTITY;
(*
```

17.20.3 Class_of_state_of_biological_object

A **class_of_state_of_physical_object** that is **state_of_biological_object** or any of its subsets.

EXPRESS specification:

```
*)
  ENTITY class_of_state_of_biological_object
    SUBTYPE OF(class_of_state_of_physical_object);
  END_ENTITY;
(*
```

17.20.4 State_of_biological_object

A **state_of_physical_object** that is a **biological_object** or a *temporal_part_of* a **biological_object**.

EXPRESS specification:

```
*)
  ENTITY state_of_biological_object
    SUBTYPE OF(state_of_physical_object);
    SELF\state_of_physical_
        object.temporal_part_of   :OPTIONAL SET [1:?] OF
                              biological_object;
```

```
    SELF\state_of_physical_
        object.member_of              :OPTIONAL SET [1:?] OF class_
                                      of_state_of_biological_
                                      object;

  END_ENTITY;
(*
```

Attribute definitions:

temporal_part_of	A *temporal_part_of* relationship type where a **state_of_biological_object** may be a *temporal_part_of* one or more **biological_object**.
member_of	A *member_of* relationship type where a **state_of_biological_object** may be a *member_of* one or more **class_of_biological_object**.

17.21 Ordinary Biological Object

Figure 17-21 shows the data model for **ordinary_biological_object**. An **ordinary_biological_object** is a **biological_object** that does not survive having all its parts changed at once. A **state_of_ordinary_biological_object** is an **ordinary_biological_object** or a *temporal_part_of* an **ordinary_biological_object**.

A **state_of_ordinary_biological_object** may be a *member_of* one or more **class_of_state_of_ordinary_biological_object**. An **ordinary_biological_object** may be a *member_of* one or more **class_of_biological_object** and **kind_of_biological_object**.

17.21.1 Class_of_ordinary_biological_object

A **class_of_biological_object**, **class_of_ordinary_physical_object** and **class_of_state_of_ordinary_biological_object** that is **ordinary_biological_object** or any of its subsets.

EXPRESS specification:

```
*)
  ENTITY class_of_ordinary_biological_object
    SUBTYPE OF(class_of_biological_object, class_of_state_of_
            ordinary_biological_object, class_of_ordinary_
            physical_object);
  END_ENTITY;
(*
```

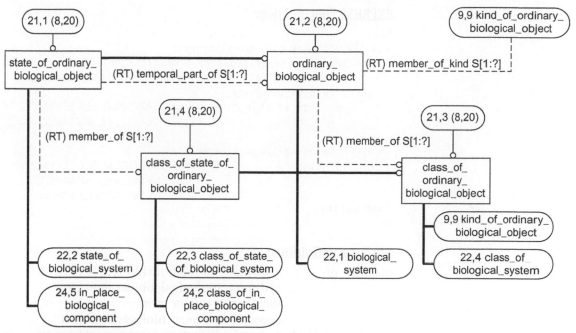

Figure 17-21 HQDM_FRAMEWORK EXPRESS-G diagram 21 of 46.

17.21.2 Class_of_state_of_ordinary_ biological_object

A **class_of_state_of_biological_object** that is also a **class_of_ state_of_ordinary_physical_object** that is **state_of_ordinary_ biological_object** or any of its subsets.

EXPRESS specification:

```
*)
  ENTITY class_of_state_of_ordinary_biological_object
    SUBTYPE OF(class_of_state_of_biological_object,
            class_of_state_of_ordinary_physical_object);
  END_ENTITY;
(*
```

17.21.3 Ordinary_biological_object

A **state_of_ordinary_biological_object**, a **biological_object**, and an **ordinary_physical_object** that is a **biological_object** that does not survive the replacement of all of its parts.

EXPRESS specification:

```
*)
  ENTITY ordinary_biological_object
    SUBTYPE OF(state_of_ordinary_biological_object,
              biological_object, ordinary_physical_object);
    SELF\state_of_ordinary_
        biological_object.member_of  :OPTIONAL SET [1:?] OF
                                              class_of_ordinary_
                                              biological_object;
    SELF\biological_object.member_
        of_kind                      :OPTIONAL SET [1:?] OF
                                              kind_of_ordinary_
                                              biological_object;

  END_ENTITY;
(*
```

Attribute definitions:

member_of   A *member_of* relationship type where an **ordinary_biological_object** may be a *member_of* one or more **class_of_ordinary_biological_object**.

member_of_kind A *member_of* relationship type where an **ordinary_biological_object** may be a *member_of* one or more **kind_of_ordinary_biological_object**.

17.21.4 State_of_ordinary_biological_object

A **state_of_biological_object** that is also a **state_of_ordinary_physical_object** that is an **ordinary_biological_object** or a *temporal_part_of* an **ordinary_biological_object**.

EXPRESS specification:

```
*)
  ENTITY state_of_ordinary_biological_object
    SUBTYPE OF(state_of_biological_object,
              state_of_ordinary_physical_object);
    SELF\state_of_biological_
        object.temporal_part_of   :OPTIONAL SET [1:?] OF
                                            ordinary_biological_
                                            object;
    SELF\state_of_biological_
        object.member_of          :OPTIONAL SET [1:?] OF class_
                                            of_state_of_ordinary_
                                            biological_object;
  END_ENTITY;
(*
```

Attribute definitions:

temporal_part_of	A *temporal_part_of* relationship type where a **state_of_ordinary_biological_object** may be a *temporal_part_of* one or more **ordinary_biological_object**.
member_of	A *member_of* relationship type where a **state_of_ordinary_biological_object** may be a *member_of* one or more **class_of_state_of_ordinary_biological_object**.

17.22 Biological System

Figure 17-22 shows the data model for **biological_system**. A **biological_system** is a **system** from the biological realm, including living things and ecosystems. A **state_of_biological_system** is a **biological_system** or a *temporal_part_of* a **biological_system**.

A **state_of_biological_system** may be a *member_of* one or more **class_of_state_of_biological_system**. A **biological_system** may be a *member_of* one or more **class_of_biological_system** and **kind_of_biological_system**.

17.22.1 Biological_system

Any **system** that is also an **ordinary_biological_object** and a **state of biological_system**.

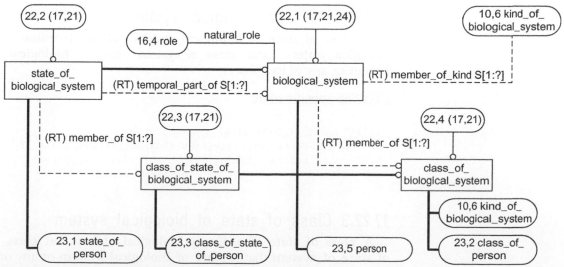

Figure 17-22 HQDM_FRAMEWORK EXPRESS-G diagram 22 of 46.

EXPRESS specification:

```
*)
  ENTITY biological_system
    SUBTYPE OF(ordinary_biological_object,
            state_of_biological_system, system);
    SELF\ordinary_biological_
        object.member_of        :OPTIONAL SET [1:?] OF class_
                                    of_biological_system;
      natural_role              :role;
    SELF\ordinary_biological_
        object.member_of_kind   :OPTIONAL SET [1:?] OF
                                    kind_of_biological_system;
  END_ENTITY;
(*
```

Attribute definitions:

member_of	A *member_of* relationship type where a **biological_system** may be a *member_of* one or more **class_of_biological_system**.
natural_role	A *member_of* relationship type where a **biological_system** has a natural **role** that it plays. Example: My circulatory system has the *natural_role* of circulating blood around the body.
member_of_kind	A *member_of_kind* relationship type where a **biological_system** may be a *member_of* one or more **kind_of_biological_system**.

17.22.2 Class_of_biological_system

A **class_of_state_of_biological_system**, **class_of_ordinary_biological_object**, and **class_of_system** that is **biological_system** or any of its subsets.

EXPRESS specification:

```
*)
  ENTITY class_of_biological_system
    SUBTYPE OF(class_of_state_of_biological_system, class_of_
            ordinary_biological_object, class_of_system);
  END_ENTITY;
(*
```

17.22.3 Class_of_state_of_biological_system

A **class_of_state_of_ordinary_biological_object** and **class_of_state_of_system** that is **state_of_biological_system** or any of its subsets.

<u>EXPRESS specification:</u>

```
*)
  ENTITY class_of_state_of_biological_system
    SUBTYPE OF(class_of_state_of_ordinary_biological_object,
             class_of_state_of_system);
  END_ENTITY;
(*
```

17.22.4 State_of_biological_system

A **state_of_ordinary_biological_object** and **state_of_system** that is **biological_system** or a *temporal_part_of* a **biological_system**.

<u>EXPRESS specification:</u>

```
*)
  ENTITY state_of_biological_system
    SUBTYPE OF(state_of_ordinary_biological_object,
             state_of_system);
    SELF\state_of_ordinary_biological_
        object.temporal_part_of        :OPTIONAL SET [1:?] OF
                                        biological_system;
    SELF\state_of_ordinary_biological_
        object.member_of               :OPTIONAL SET [1:?] OF
                                        class_of_state_of_
                                        biological_system;
  END_ENTITY;
(*
```

<u>Attribute definitions:</u>

temporal_part_of A *temporal_part_of* relationship type where a **state_of_biological_system** may be a *temporal_part_of* one or more **biological_system**.

member_of A *member_of* relationship type where a **state_of_biological_system** may be a *member_of* one or more **class_of_state_of_biological_system**.

17.23 Person

Figure 17-23 shows a data model for **person**. A **person** is a **biological_system** that is a human being. A **state_of_person** is a **person** or a *temporal_part_of* a **person**.

A **state_of_person** may be a *member_of* one or more **class_of_state_of_person**. A **person** may be a *member_of* one or more **class_of_person** and **kind_of_person**.

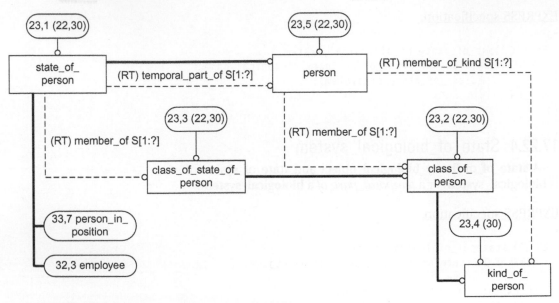

Figure 17-23 HQDM_FRAMEWORK EXPRESS-G diagram 23 of 46.

17.23.1 Class_of_person

A **class_of_biological_system, class_of_state_of_person,** and **class_of_party** that is **person** or any of its subsets.

EXPRESS specification:

```
*)
  ENTITY class_of_person
    SUBTYPE OF(class_of_biological_system,
               class_of_state_of_person, class_of_party);
  END_ENTITY;
(*
```

17.23.2 Class_of_state_of_person

A **class_of_state_of_biological_system** and **class_of_state_of_party** that is **state_of_person** or any of its subsets.

EXPRESS specification:

```
*)
  ENTITY class_of_state_of_person
    SUBTYPE OF(class_of_state_of_biological_system,
               class_of_state_of_party);
  END_ENTITY;
(*
```

17.23.3 Kind_of_person

A **class_of_person** that is also a **kind_of_party** whose members are all of the same kind.

EXPRESS specification:
```
*)
  ENTITY kind_of_person
    SUBTYPE OF(kind_of_party, class_of_person);
  END_ENTITY;
(*
```

17.23.4 Person

A **biological_system** that is also, a **state_of_person,** and a **party** that is a human being.

EXPRESS specification:
```
*)
  ENTITY person
    SUBTYPE OF(biological_system, state_of_person, party);
    SELF\biological_system.member_of      :OPTIONAL SET [1:?] OF
                                           class_of_person;
    SELF\biological_system.
       member_of_kind                     :OPTIONAL SET [1:?] OF
                                           kind_of_person;
  END_ENTITY;
(*
```

Attribute definitions:

member_of	A *member_of* relationship type where a **person** may be a *member_of* one or more **class_of_person**.
member_of_kind	A *member_of_kind* relationship type where a **person** may be a *member_of* one or more **kind_of_person**.

17.23.5 State_of_person

A **state_of_biological_system** and **state_of_party** that is a **person** or a *temporal_part_of* a **person**.

EXPRESS specification:
```
*)
  ENTITY state_of_person
    SUBTYPE OF(state_of_biological_system, state_of_party);
```

```
         SELF\state_of_biological_
              system.temporal_part_of    :OPTIONAL SET [1:?] OF person;
         SELF\state_of_biological_
              system.member_of           :OPTIONAL SET [1:?] OF
                                          class_of_state_of_person;

     END_ENTITY;
(*
```

Attribute definitions:

temporal_part_of A *temporal_part_of* relationship type where a
state_of_person may be a *temporal_part_of*
one or more **person**.

member_of A *member_of* relationship type where a
state_of_person may be a *member_of* one or
more **class_of_state_of_person**.

17.24 Biological System Component

Figure 17-24 shows the data model for **biological_system_
component**. A **biological_system_component** is a component

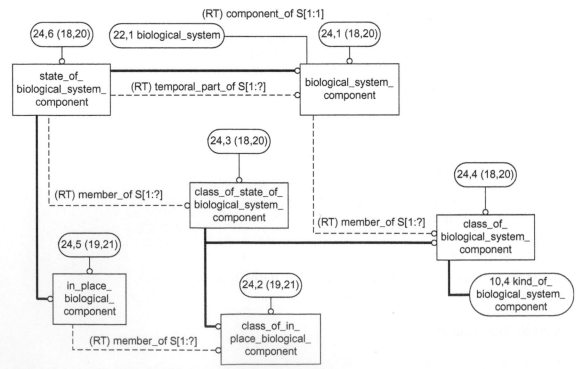

Figure 17-24 HQDM_FRAMEWORK EXPRESS-G diagram 24 of 46.

of a **biological_system**, such as the heart of an animal. A **state_of_biological_system_component** is a **biological_system_component** or a *temporal_part_of* a **biological_system_component**.

A **state_of_biological_system_component** may be a *member_of* one or more **class_of_state_of_biological_system_component** and one or more **kind_of_biological_system_component**.

An **in_place_biological_component** is an **installed_object** that is in a **biological_system**. An **in_place_biological_component** may be a *member_of* one or more **class_of_in_place_biological_component**.

17.24.1 Biological_system_component

A **biological_object,** **state_of_biological_system_component,** and **system_component** that is any **biological_object** that is also a **system_component**.

<u>EXPRESS specification:</u>

```
*)
  ENTITY biological_system_component
    SUBTYPE OF(biological_object, state_of_biological_
           system_component, system_component);
    SELF\system_component.
        component_of             :SET [1:1] OF biological_system;
    SELF\biological_object.
        member_of                :OPTIONAL SET [1:?] OF class_of_
                                  biological_system_component;
  END_ENTITY;
(*
```

<u>Attribute definitions:</u>

component_of   A *component_of* relationship type where a **biological_system_component** is a *component_of* exactly one **biological_system**.

member_of   A *member_of* relationship type where a **biological_system_component** may be a *member_of* one or more **class_of_biological_system_component**.

17.24.2 Class_of_biological_system_component

A **class_of_biological_object,** **class_of_state_of_biological_system_component,** and **class_of_system_component** that is **biological_system_component** or any of its subsets.

EXPRESS specification:

```
*)
ENTITY class_of_biological_system_component
  SUBTYPE OF(class_of_biological_object, class_of_state_of_
            biological_system_component, class_of_system_
            component);
  END_ENTITY;
(*
```

17.24.3 Class_of_in_place_biological_component

A **class_of_state_of_biological_system_component**, that is also a **class_of_state_of_ordinary_biological_object,** and a **class_of_installed_object** that is **in_place_biological_component** or any of its subsets.

EXPRESS specification:

```
*)
ENTITY class_of_in_place_biological_component
  SUBTYPE OF(class_of_state_of_biological_system_component,
            class_of_state_of_ordinary_biological_object,
            class_of_installed_object);
  END_ENTITY;
(*
```

17.24.4 Class_of_state_of_biological_ system_component

A **class_of_state_of_biological_object** and **class_of_state_of_system_component** that is **state_of_biological_system_component** or any of its subsets.

EXPRESS specification:

```
*)
ENTITY class_of_state_of_biological_system_component
  SUBTYPE OF(class_of_state_of_biological_object,
            class_of_state_of_system_component);
  END_ENTITY;
(*
```

17.24.5 In_place_biological_component

An **installed_object** that is also a **state_of_ordinary_biological_object** and a **state_of_system_component**.

EXPRESS specification:

```
*)
  ENTITY in_place_biological_component
    SUBTYPE OF(state_of_biological_system_component, installed_
            object, state_of_ordinary_biological_object);
    SELF\state_of_biological_
        system_component.member_of    :OPTIONAL SET [1:?] OF
                                      class_of_in_place_
                                      biological_component;
  END_ENTITY;
(*
```

Attribute definitions:

member_of   A *member_of* relationship type where an
            in_place_biological_component may be a
            member_of one or more
            class_of_in_place_biological_component.

17.24.6 State_of_biological_system_component

A **state_of_biological_system_component** and **state_of_system_component** that is a **biological_system_component** or a *temporal_part_of* a **biological_system_component**.

EXPRESS specification:

```
*)
  ENTITY state_of_biological_system_component
    SUBTYPE OF(state_of_biological_object,
            state_of_system_component);
    SELF\state_of_biological_
        object.temporal_part_of    :OPTIONAL SET [1:?] OF
                                    biological_system_
                                    component;
    SELF\state_of_biological_
        object.member_of           :OPTIONAL SET [1:?] OF class_
                                    of_state_of_biological_
                                    system_component;
  END_ENTITY;
(*
```

Attribute definitions:

temporal_part_of   A *temporal_part_of* relationship type where
                a **state_of_biological_system_component**
                may be a *temporal_part_of* one or more
                biological_system_component.

member_of A *member_of* relationship type where a **state_of_biological_system_component** may be a *member_of* one or more **class_of_state_of_biological_system_component**.

17.25 Intentionally Constructed Object

Figure 17-25 shows the data model for **intentionally_constructed_object**. An **intentionally_constructed_object** is an **individual** that is intentionally created to be what it is. A **state_of_intentionally_constructed_object** is an **intentionally_constructed_object** or a *temporal_part_of* an **intentionally_constructed_object**.

A **state_of_intentionally_constructed_object** may be a *member_of* one or more **class_of_state_of_intentionally_constructed_object**. An **intentionally_constructed_object** may be a *member_of* one or more **class_of_intentionally_constructed_object** and **kind_of_intentionally_constructed_object**.

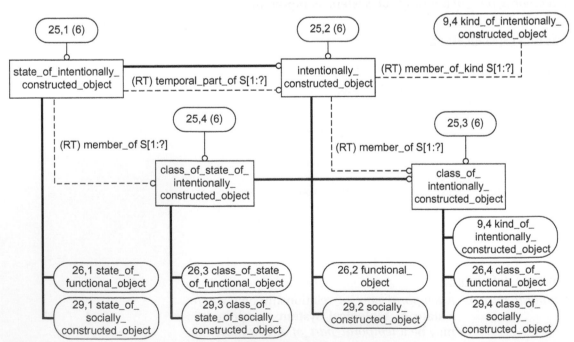

Figure 17-25 HQDM_FRAMEWORK EXPRESS-G diagram 25 of 46.

17.25.1 Class_of_intentionally_constructed_object

A **class_of_individual** that is also a **class_of_state_of_intentionally_constructed_object** that is **intentionally_constructed_object** or any of its subsets.

EXPRESS specification:

```
*)
  ENTITY class_of_intentionally_constructed_object
    SUBTYPE OF(class_of_individual, class_of_state_of_
              intentionally_constructed_object);
  END_ENTITY;
(*
```

17.25.2 Class_of_state_of_intentionally_constructed_object

A **class_of_state** that is **state_of_intentionally_constructed_object** or any of its subsets.

EXPRESS specification:

```
*)
  ENTITY class_of_state_of_intentionally_constructed_object
    SUBTYPE OF(class_of_state);
  END_ENTITY;
(*
```

17.25.3 Intentionally_constructed_object

An **individual** and **state_of_intentionally_constructed_object** that is intentionally constructed.

Note: Being intentionally constructed means that it is an act of will or agreement that makes it what it is.

EXPRESS specification:

```
*)
  ENTITY intentionally_constructed_object
    SUBTYPE OF(individual,
        state_of_intentionally_constructed_object);
    SELF\individual.member_of        :OPTIONAL SET [1:?] OF
                                      class_of_intentionally_
                                      constructed_object;
    SELF\individual.member_of_kind   :OPTIONAL SET [1:?] OF
                                      kind_of_intentionally_
                                      constructed_object;
  END_ENTITY;
(*
```

Attribute definitions:

member_of	A *member_of* relationship type where an **intentionally_constructed_object** may be a *member_of* one or more **class_of_intentionally_constructed_object**.
member_of_kind	A *member_of_kind* relationship type where an **intentionally_constructed_object** may be a *member_of* one or more **kind_of_ intentionally_constructed_object**.

17.25.4 State_of_intentionally_constructed_object

A **state** that is an **intentionally_constructed_object** or a *temporal_part_of* an **intentionally_constructed_object**.

EXPRESS specification:

```
*)
  ENTITY state_of_intentionally_constructed_object
    SUBTYPE OF(state);
    SELF\state.temporal_part_of    :OPTIONAL SET [1:?] OF
                                    intentionally_constructed_
                                    object;
    SELF\state.member_of           :OPTIONAL SET [1:?] OF class_
                                    of_state_of_intentionally_
                                    constructed_object;

  END_ENTITY;
(*
```

Attribute definitions:

temporal_part_of	A *temporal_part_of* relationship type where a **state_of_intentionally_constructed_object** may be a *temporal_part_of* one or more **intentionally_constructed_object**.
member_of	A *member_of* relationship type where a **state_of_intentionally_constructed_object** may be a *member_of* one or more **class_ of_state_of_intentionally_constructed_object**.

17.26 Functional Object

Figure 17-26 shows the data model for **functional_object**. A **functional_object** is a **physical_object** that was intentionally created to be what it is and has an intended **role**. A **state_of_ functional_object** is a **functional_object** or a *temporal_part_of* a **functional_object**.

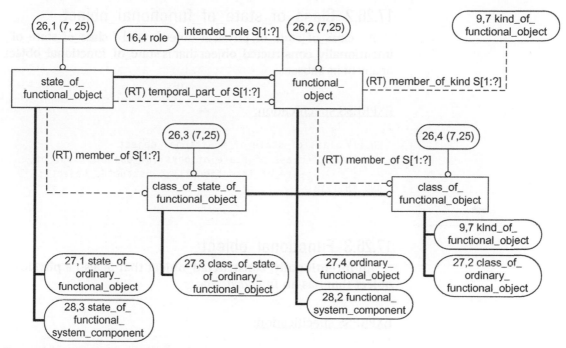

Figure 17-26 HQDM_FRAMEWORK EXPRESS-G diagram 26 of 46.

A **state_of_functional_object** may be a *member_of* one or more **class_of_state_of_functional_object**. A **functional_object** may be a *member_of* one or more **class_of_functional_object** and **kind_of_functional_object**.

17.26.1 Class_of_functional_object

A **class_of_physical_object**, **class_of_intentionally_constructed_object**, and **class_of_state_of_functional_object** that is **functional_object** or any of its subsets.

EXPRESS specification:
```
*)
 ENTITY class_of_functional_object
   SUBTYPE OF(class_of_physical_object, class_of_intentionally_
            constructed_object, class_of_state_of_functional_
            object);
 END_ENTITY;
(*
```

17.26.2 Class_of_state_of_functional_object

A **class_of_state_of_physical_object** and **class_of_state_of_intentionally_constructed_object** that is **state_of_functional_object** or any of its subsets.

<u>EXPRESS specification:</u>

```
*)
  ENTITY class_of_state_of_functional_object
    SUBTYPE OF(class_of_state_of_physical_object, class_of_
            state_of_intentionally_constructed_object);
  END_ENTITY;
(*
```

17.26.3 Functional_object

An **intentionally_constructed_object** that is also a **physical_object** that has an *intended_role*.

<u>EXPRESS specification:</u>

```
*)
  ENTITY functional_object
    SUBTYPE OF(intentionally_constructed_object,
            state_of_functional_object, physical_object);
    SELF\intentionally_
        constructed_object.member_of   :OPTIONAL SET [1:?] OF
                                         class_of_functional_
                                         object;
    intended_role                       :SET [1:?] OF role;
    SELF\intentionally_constructed_
        object.member_of_kind           :OPTIONAL SET [1:?] OF
                                         kind_of_functional_
                                         object;

  END_ENTITY;
(*
```

<u>Attribute definitions:</u>

member_of	A *member_of* relationship type where a **functional_object** may be a *member_of* one or more **class_of_functional_object**.
intended_role	A relationship type where a **functional_object** has one or more intended **role**(s).
member_of_kind	A *member_of_kind* relationship type where a **functional_object** may be a *member_of* one or more **kind_of_functional_object**.

17.26.4 State_of_functional_object

A **state_of_intentionally_constructed_object** and **state_of_physical_object** that is a **functional_object** or a *temporal_part_of* a **functional_object**.

EXPRESS specification:

```
*)
  ENTITY state_of_functional_object
    SUBTYPE OF(state_of_intentionally_constructed_object,
           state_of_physical_object);
    SELF\state_of_intentionally_
        constructed_object.
        temporal_part_of              :OPTIONAL SET [1:?] OF
                                          functional_object;

    SELF\state_of_intentionally_
        constructed_object.
        member_of                     :OPTIONAL SET [1:?] OF class_
                                          of_state_of_functional_
                                          object;

  END_ENTITY;
(*
```

Attribute definitions:

temporal_part_of	A *temporal_part_of* relationship type where a **state_of_functional_object** may be a *temporal_part_of* one or more **functional_object**.
member_of	A *member_of* relationship type where a **state_of_functional_object** may be a *member_of* one or more **class_of_state_of_functional_object**.

17.27 Ordinary Functional Object

Figure 17-27 shows the data model for **ordinary_functional_object**. An **ordinary_functional_object** is a **functional_object** that does not survive the simultaneous replacement of all its parts. A **state_of_ordinary_functional_object** is an **ordinary_functional_object** or a *temporal_part_of* an **ordinary_functional_object**.

A **state_of_ordinary_functional_object** may be a *member_of* one or more **class_of_state_of_ordinary_functional_object**. An **ordinary_functional_object** may be a *member_of* one or more **class_of_ordinary_functional_object** and **kind_of_ordinary_functional_object**.

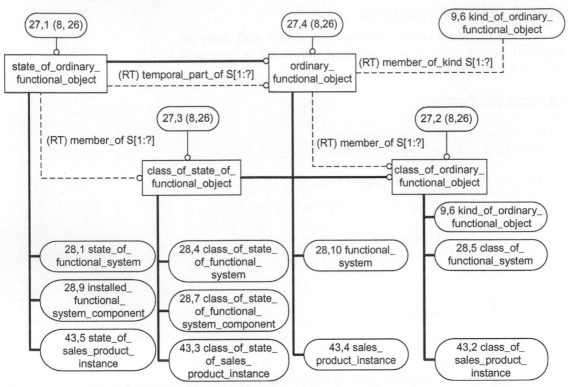

Figure 17-27 HQDM_FRAMEWORK EXPRESS-G diagram 27 of 46.

17.27.1 Class_of_ordinary_functional_object

A **class_of_state_of_ordinary_functional_object**, that is also a **class_of_functional_object**, and a **class_of_ordinary_physical_object** that is **ordinary_functional_object** or any of its subsets.

EXPRESS specification:

```
*)
  ENTITY class_of_ordinary_functional_object
    SUBTYPE OF(class_of_state_of_ordinary_functional_object,
              class_of_functional_object, class_of_ordinary_
              physical_object);
  END_ENTITY;
(*
```

17.27.2 Class_of_state_of_ordinary_functional_object

A **class_of_state_of_functional_object** that is also a **class_of_state_of_ordinary_physical_object** that is **state_of_ordinary_functional_object** or any of its subsets.

EXPRESS specification:

```
*)
  ENTITY class_of_state_of_ordinary_functional_object
    SUBTYPE OF(class_of_state_of_functional_object,
            class_of_state_of_ordinary_physical_object);
  END_ENTITY;
(*
```

17.27.3 Ordinary_functional_object

Any **state_of_ordinary_functional_object** and **ordinary_physical_object** that is a **functional_object**.

EXPRESS specification:

```
*)
  ENTITY ordinary_functional_object
    SUBTYPE OF(functional_object, state_of_ordinary_
            functional_object, ordinary_physical_object);
    SELF\functional_object.
        member_of              :OPTIONAL SET [1:?] OF class_of_
                                ordinary_functional_object;
    SELF\functional_object.
        member_of_kind         :OPTIONAL SET [1:?] OF kind_of_
                                ordinary_functional_object;
  END_ENTITY;
(*
```

Attribute definitions:

member_of A *member_of* relationship type where an **ordinary_functional_object** may be a *member_of* one or more **class_of_ordinary_functional_object**.

member_of_kind A *member_of* relationship type where an **ordinary_functional_object** may be a *member_of* one or more **kind_of_ordinary_functional_object**.

17.27.4 State_of_ordinary_functional_object

Any **state_of_functional_object** that is also a **state_of_ordinary_physical_object**.

EXPRESS specification:

```
*)
  ENTITY state_of_ordinary_functional_object
```

```
SUBTYPE OF(state_of_functional_object,
        state_of_ordinary_physical_object);
SELF\state_of_functional_
    object.temporal_part_of    :OPTIONAL SET [1:?] OF
                                    ordinary_functional_object;

SELF\state_of_functional_
    object.member_of           :OPTIONAL SET [1:?] OF class_
                                    of_state_of_ordinary_
                                    functional_object;

END_ENTITY;
(*
```

Attribute definitions:

temporal_part_of	A *temporal_part_of* relationship type where a **state_of_ordinary_functional_object** may be a *temporal_part_of* one or more **ordinary_functional_object**.
member_of	A *member_of* relationship type where a **state_of_ordinary_functional_object** may be a *member_of* one or more **class_of_state_of_ordinary_functional_object**.

17.28 Functional System

Figure 17-28 shows the data model for **functional_system**. A **functional_system** is a **functional_object** that is also a **system**. A **state_of_functional_system** is a **functional_system** or a *temporal_part_of* a **functional_system**.

A **state_of_functional_system** may be a *member_of* one or more **class_of_state_of_functional_system**. A **functional_system** may be a *member_of* one or more **class_of_functional_system** and **kind_of_functional_system**.

A **functional_system_component** is a **functional_object** that is a **system_component**. A **state_of_functional_system_component** is a **functional_system_component** or a *temporal_part_of* a **functional_system_component**.

A **state_of_functional_system_component** may be a *member_of* one or more **class_of_state_of_functional_system_component**. A **functional_system_component** may be a *member_of* one or more **class_of_functional_system_component** and **kind_of_functional_system_component**.

An **installed_functional_system_component** is a **state_of_functional_system_component**, **installed_object**, and **state_of_ordinary_functional_object** that is the *temporal_part_of* the **ordinary_functional_object** while it is installed.

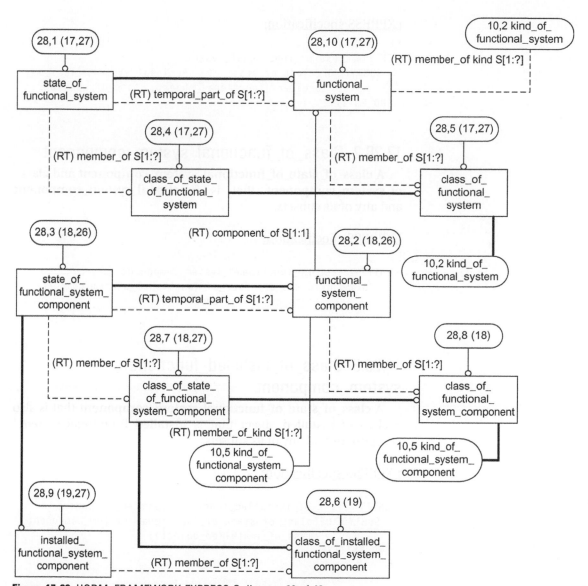

Figure 17-28 HQDM_FRAMEWORK EXPRESS-G diagram 28 of 46.

An **installed_functional_system_component** may be a *member_of* one or more **class_of_installed_functional_system_component**.

17.28.1 Class_of_functional_system

A **class_of_state_of_functional_system**, that is also a **class_of_ordinary_functional_object**, and a **class_of_system** that is **functional_system** or any of its subsets.

EXPRESS specification:

```
*)
  ENTITY class_of_functional_system
    SUBTYPE OF(class_of_state_of_functional_system, class_of_
              ordinary_functional_object, class_of_system);
  END_ENTITY;
(*
```

17.28.2 Class_of_functional_system_component

A **class_of_state_of_functional_system_component** and **class_of_system_component** that is **functional_system_component** and any of its subsets.

EXPRESS specification:

```
*)
  ENTITY class_of_functional_system_component
    SUBTYPE OF(class_of_state_of_functional_system_component,
              class_of_system_component);
  END_ENTITY;
(*
```

17.28.3 Class_of_installed_functional_system_component

A **class_of_state_of_functional_system_component** that is also a **class_of_installed_object** that is **installed_functional_system_component** and any of its subsets.

EXPRESS specification:

```
*)
  ENTITY class_of_installed_functional_system_component
    SUBTYPE OF(class_of_state_of_functional_system_component,
              class_of_installed_object);
  END_ENTITY;
(*
```

17.28.4 Class_of_state_of_functional_system

A **class_of_state_of_ordinary_functional_object** that is also a **class_of_state_of_system** that is **state_of_functional_system** or any of its subsets.

EXPRESS specification:

```
*)
  ENTITY class_of_state_of_functional_system
```

```
      SUBTYPE OF(class_of_state_of_ordinary_functional_object,
              class_of_state_of_system);
   END_ENTITY;
(*
```

17.28.5 Class_of_state_of_functional_ system_component

A **class_of_state_of_ordinary_functional_object** that is also a **class_of_state_of_system_component** that is **state_of_functional_ system_component** or any of its subsets.

<u>EXPRESS specification:</u>

```
*)
   ENTITY class_of_state_of_functional_system_component
     SUBTYPE OF(class_of_state_of_ordinary_functional_object,
              class_of_state_of_system_component);
   END_ENTITY;
(*
```

17.28.6 Functional_system

Any **state_of_functional_system** that is also an **ordinary_ functional_object** and a **system**.

<u>EXPRESS specification:</u>

```
*)
   ENTITY functional_system
     SUBTYPE OF(system, state_of_functional_system,
              ordinary_functional_object);
     SELF\system.member_of        :OPTIONAL SET [1:?] OF
                                    class_of_functional_system;
     SELF\system.member_of_kind   :OPTIONAL SET [1:?] OF
                                    kind_of_functional_system;
   END_ENTITY;
(*
```

<u>Attribute definitions:</u>

member_of   A *member_of* relationship type where a **functional_system** may be a *member_of* one or more **class_of_functional_system**.

member_of_kind   A *member_of_kind* relationship type where a **functional_system** may be a *member_of* one or more **kind_of_functional_system**.

17.28.7 Functional_system_component

An **intentionally_constructed_object** that is a replaceable *component_of* a **functional_system**.

<u>EXPRESS specification:</u>

```
*)
  ENTITY functional_system_component
    SUBTYPE OF(functional_object, state_of_functional_
              system_component, system_component);
    SELF\system_component.
        component_of           :SET [1:1] OF functional_system;
    SELF\functional_object.
        member_of              :OPTIONAL SET [1:?] OF class_of_
                                functional_system_component;
    SELF\functional_object.
        member_of_kind         :SET [1:?] OF kind_of_
                                functional_system_component;
  END_ENTITY;
(*
```

<u>Attribute definitions:</u>

component_of	A *component_of* relationship type where each **functional_system_component** is a component of exactly one **functional_system**.
member_of	A *member_of* relationship type where a **functional_system_component** may be a *member_of* one or more **class_of_functional_system_component**.
member_of_kind	A *member_of_kind* relationship type where a **functional_system_component** is a *member_of* at least one **kind_of_functional_system_component**.

17.28.8 Installed_functional_system_component

Any **installed_object** that is also a **state_of_ordinary_functional_object** and a **state_of_functional_system_component**.

<u>EXPRESS specification:</u>

```
*)
  ENTITY installed_functional_system_component
    SUBTYPE OF(state_of_functional_system_component, installed_
              object, state_of_ordinary_functional_object);
```

```
    SELF\state_of_functional_
        system_component.member_of  :OPTIONAL SET [1:?] OF class_
                                     of_installed_functional_
                                     system_component;
  END_ENTITY;
(*
```

Attribute definitions:

member_of A *member_of* relationship type where an
installed_functional_system_component may be a
member_of one or more **class_of_installed_
functional_system_component**.

17.28.9 State_of_functional_system

Any **state_of_ordinary_functional_object** that is also a
state_of_system.

EXPRESS specification:

```
*)
  ENTITY state_of_functional_system
    SUBTYPE OF(state_of_system,
            state_of_ordinary_functional_object);
    SELF\state_of_system.
        temporal_part_of :OPTIONAL SET [1:?] OF
                            functional_system;
    SELF\state_of_system.
        member_of           :OPTIONAL SET [1:?] OF class_of_state_
                            of_functional_system;
  END_ENTITY;
(*
```

Attribute definitions:

temporal_part_of A *temporal_part_of* relationship type where a
state_of_functional_system may be a
temporal_part_of one or more
functional_system.

member_of A *member_of* relationship type where a
state_of_functional_system may be a
member_of one or more
class_of_state_of_functional_system.

17.28.10 State_of_functional_system_component

A **state_of_intentionally_constructed_object** that is a **system_
component** or a *temporal_part_of* a **system_component**.

EXPRESS specification:

```
*)
  ENTITY state_of_functional_system_component
    SUBTYPE OF(state_of_functional_object, state_of_system_
            component);
    SELF\state_of_functional_
        object.temporal_part_of    :OPTIONAL SET [1:?] OF
                                    functional_system_
                                    component;
    SELF\state_of_functional_
        object.member_of           :OPTIONAL SET [1:?] OF class_
                                    of_state_of_functional_
                                    system_component;
  END_ENTITY;
(*
```

Attribute definitions:

temporal_part_of	A *temporal_part_of* relationship type where a **state_of_functional_system_component** may be a *temporal_part_of* one or more **functional_system_component**.
member_of	A *member_of* relationship type where a **state_of_functional_system_component** may be a *member_of* one or more **class_of_functional_system_component**.

17.29 Socially Constructed Object

Figure 17-29 shows the data model for **socially_constructed_object**. A **socially_constructed_object** is something that is created as the result of an explicit or tacit agreement, for example money or an **organization**. A **state_of_socially_constructed_object** is a **socially_constructed_object** or a *temporal_part_of* a **socially_constructed_object**.

A **state_of_socially_constructed_object** may be a *member_of* one or more **class_of_state_of_socially_constructed_object**. A **socially_constructed_object** may be a *member_of* one or more **class_of_socially_constructed_object** and **kind_of_socially_constructed_object**.

A **state_of_socially_constructed_activity** is any **state_of_socially_constructed_object** that is also a **state_of_activity**. A **class_of_state_of_socially_constructed_activity** is **state_of_socially_constructed_activity** or any of its subsets.

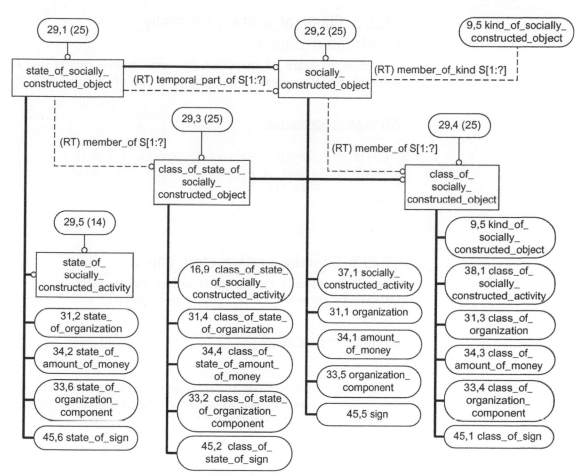

Figure 17-29 HQDM_FRAMEWORK EXPRESS-G diagram 29 of 46.

17.29.1 Class_of_socially_contructed_object

A **class_of_intentionally_constructed_object** that is **socially_constructed_object** or any of its subsets.

EXPRESS specification:

```
*)
 ENTITY class_of_socially_contructed_object
   SUBTYPE OF(class_of_intentionally_constructed_object,
           class_of_state_of_socially_constructed_object);
 END_ENTITY;
(*
```

17.29.2 Class_of_state_of_socially_constructed_object

A **class_of_state_of_intentionally_constructed_object** that is **state_of_socially_constructed_object** or one of its subsets.

<u>EXPRESS specification:</u>

```
*)
  ENTITY class_of_state_of_socially_constructed_object
    SUBTYPE OF(class_of_state_of_intentionally_constructed_
            object);
  END_ENTITY;
(*
```

17.29.3 Socially_constructed_object

An **intentionally_constructed_object** that is necessarily constructed by agreement or at least acquiescence of many people.

<u>EXPRESS specification:</u>

```
*)
  ENTITY socially_constructed_object
    SUBTYPE OF(intentionally_constructed_object,
            state_of_socially_constructed_object);
    SELF\intentionally_constructed_
        object.member_of          :OPTIONAL SET [1:?] OF class_
                                    of_socially_contructed_
                                    object;
    SELF\intentionally_constructed_
        object.member_of_kind     :OPTIONAL SET [1:?] OF kind_
                                    of_socially_constructed_
                                    object;
  END_ENTITY;
(*
```

<u>Attribute definitions:</u>

member_of	A *member_of* relationship type where a **socially_constructed_object** may be a *member_of* one or more **class_of_socially_constructed_object**.
member_of_kind	A *member_of_kind* where a **socially_constructed_object** may be a *member_of* one or more **kind_of_socially_constructed_object**.

17.29.4 State_of_socially_constructed_activity

Any **state_of_socially_constructed_object** that is also a **state_of_activity**.

EXPRESS specification:
```
*)
  ENTITY state_of_socially_constructed_activity
    SUBTYPE OF(state_of_socially_constructed_object,
            state_of_activity);
  END_ENTITY;
(*
```

17.29.5 State_of_socially_constructed_object

A **state_of_intentionally_constructed_object** that is a **socially_constructed_object** or a *temporal_part_of* a **socially_ constructed_object**.

EXPRESS specification:
```
*)
  ENTITY state_of_socially_constructed_object
    SUBTYPE OF(state_of_intentionally_constructed_object);
    SELF\state_of_intentionally_
        constructed_object.
        member_of                    :OPTIONAL SET [1:?] OF class_
                                      of_state_of_socially_
                                      constructed_object;

    SELF\state_of_intentionally_
        constructed_object.
        temporal_part_of             :OPTIONAL SET [1:?] OF
                                      socially_constructed_
                                      object;
  END_ENTITY;
(*
```

Attribute definitions:

member_of   A *member_of* relationship type where a **state_of_socially_constructed_object** may be a *member_of* one or more **class_of_state_ of_socially_constructed_object**.

temporal_part_of A *temporal_part_of* relationship type where a **state_of_socially_constructed_object** may be a *temporal_part_of* one or more **socially_constructed_object**.

17.30 Party

Figure 17-30 shows the data model for **party. party** is an abstract entity (AE), which means that each member must be a *member_of* at least one subtype, in this case **person** or **organization**. A **state_of_party** is also an abstract entity that is a **party** or a *temporal_part_of* a **party**.

A **state_of_party** may be a *member_of* one or more **class_of_state_of_party**. A **party** may be a *member_of* one or more **class_of_party** and **kind_of_party**.

17.30.1 Class_of_party

A **class_of_system** that is **party** or any of its possible subtypes.

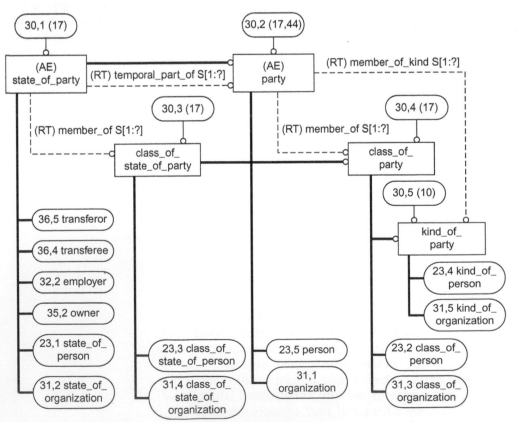

Figure 17-30 HQDM_FRAMEWORK EXPRESS-G diagram 30 of 46.

EXPRESS specification:

```
*)
  ENTITY class_of_party
    SUBTYPE OF(class_of_system, class_of_state_of_party);
  END_ENTITY;
(*
```

17.30.2 Class_of_state_of_party

A **class_of_state_of_system** that is **state_of_party** or any of its possible subtypes.

EXPRESS specification:

```
*)
  ENTITY class_of_state_of_party
    SUBTYPE OF(class_of_state_of_system);
  END_ENTITY;
(*
```

17.30.3 Kind_of_party

A **class_of_party** that is also a **kind_of_system** where all the members are of the same kind.

EXPRESS specification:

```
*)
  ENTITY kind_of_party
    SUBTYPE OF(class_of_party, kind_of_system);
  END_ENTITY;
(*
```

17.30.4 Party

A **state_of_party** that is also a **system** that is a **person** or an **organization**.

EXPRESS specification:

```
*)
  ENTITY party
    ABSTRACT
    SUBTYPE OF(state_of_party, system);
    SELF\state_of_party.member_of      :OPTIONAL SET [1:?] OF
                                         class_of_party;
    SELF\system.member_of_kind         :OPTIONAL SET [1:?] OF
                                         kind_of_party;
  END_ENTITY;
(*
```

Attribute definitions:

member_of	A *member_of* relationship type where a **party** may be a *member_of* one or more **class_of_party**.
member_of_kind	A *member_of_kind* relationship type where each **party** may be a *member_of* one or more **kind_of_party**.

17.30.5 State_of_party

A **state_of_system** that is a **party** or a *temporal_part_of* a **party**.

EXPRESS specification:

```
*)
  ENTITY state_of_party
    ABSTRACT
    SUBTYPE OF(state_of_system);
    SELF\state_of_system.temporal_
        part_of                       :OPTIONAL SET [1:?] OF party;
    SELF\state_of_system.
        member_of                     :OPTIONAL SET [1:?] OF
                                       class_of_state_of_party;
  END_ENTITY;
(*
```

Attribute definitions:

temporal_part_of	A *temporal_part_of* relationship type where a **state_of_party** may be a *temporal_part_of* one or more **party**.
member_of	A *member_of* relationship type where a **state_of_party** may be a *member_of* one or more **class_of_state_of_party**.

17.31 Organization and Language Community

Figure 17-31 shows the data model for **organization**. An **organization** is a **party** that is a group of people organized for a purpose. A **state_of_organization** is an **organization** or a *temporal_part_of* an **organization**.

A **state_of_organization** may be a *member_of* one or more **class_of_state_of_organization**. An **organization** may be a *member_of* one or more **class_of_organization** and **kind_of_organization**.

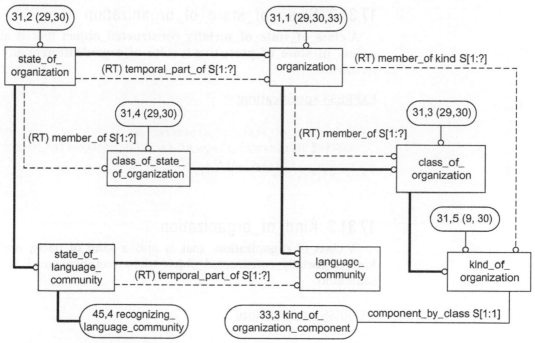

Figure 17-31 HQDM_FRAMEWORK EXPRESS-G diagram 31 of 46.

A **language_community** is an **organization** that shares understanding of a common set of **sign**s, which is not restricted to natural languages, but may include other symbols and names. A **state_of_language_community** is a **language_community** or a *temporal_part_of* a **language_community**.

17.31.1 Class_of_organization

A **class_of_state_of_organization**, that is also a **class_of_socially_constructed_object**, and a **class_of_party** that is **organization** or any of its subsets.

EXPRESS specification:

```
*)
  ENTITY class_of_organization
    SUBTYPE OF(class_of_state_of_organization, class_of_
            socially_contructed_object, class_of_party);
  END_ENTITY;
(*
```

17.31.2 Class_of_state_of_organization

A **class_of_state_of_socially_constructed_object** that is also a **class_of_state_of_party** that is **state_of_organization** or any of its subsets.

<u>EXPRESS specification:</u>

```
*)
  ENTITY class_of_state_of_organization
    SUBTYPE OF(class_of_state_of_socially_constructed_object,
            class_of_state_of_party);
  END_ENTITY;
(*
```

17.31.3 Kind_of_organization

A **class_of_organization**, that is also a **kind_of_party,** and a **kind_of_socially_constructed_object** whose members are all of the same kind.

<u>EXPRESS specification:</u>

```
*)
  ENTITY kind_of_organization
    SUBTYPE OF(class_of_organization, kind_of_party,
            kind_of_socially_constructed_object);
    component_by_class    :SET [1:1] OF kind_of_organization_
                                  component;
  END_ENTITY;
(*
```

17.31.4 Language_community

An **organization** that is a group of people who share a common understanding of a set of **signs**.

Note: This is not restricted to natural languages, but also controlled languages, taxonomies, and so on.

<u>EXPRESS specification:</u>

```
*)
  ENTITY language_community
    SUBTYPE OF(state_of_language_community, organization);
  END_ENTITY;
(*
```

17.31.5 Organization

A **state_of_organization**, that is also a **party**, and a **socially_constructed_object** that is an organized body of people.

EXPRESS specification:

```
*)
  ENTITY organization
    SUBTYPE OF(state_of_organization, party,
             socially_constructed_object);
    SELF\state_of_organization.
        member_of                    :OPTIONAL SET [1:?] OF
                                      class_of_organization;
    SELF\party.member_of_kind        :OPTIONAL SET [1:?] OF
                                      kind_of_organization;
  END_ENTITY;
(*
```

Attribute definitions:

member_of	A *member_of* relationship type where an **organization** may be a *member_of* one or more **class_of_organization**.
member_of_kind	A *member_of_kind* relationship type where an **organization** may be a *member_of* one or more **kind_of_organization**.

17.31.6 State_of_language_community

A **state_of_organization** that is a *temporal_part_of* a **language_community**.

EXPRESS specification:

```
*)
  ENTITY state_of_language_community
    SUBTYPE OF(state_of_organization);
    SELF\state_of_organization.
        temporal_part_of        :OPTIONAL SET [1:?] OF
                                  language_community;
  END_ENTITY;
(*
```

Attribute definitions:

temporal_part_of	A *temporal_part_of* relationship type where a **state_of_language_community** may be a *temporal_part_of* one or more **language_community**.

17.31.7 State_of_organization

A **state_of_party** that is also a **state_of_socially_constructed_object** that is an **organization** or a *temporal_part_of* an **organization**.

EXPRESS specification:

```
*)
  ENTITY state_of_organization
    SUBTYPE OF(state_of_party,
               state_of_socially_constructed_object);
    SELF\state_of_party.temporal_
        part_of            :OPTIONAL SET [1:?] OF organization;
    SELF\state_of_party.
        member_of          :OPTIONAL SET [1:?] OF
                               class_of_state_of_organization;
  END_ENTITY;
(*
```

Attribute definitions:

temporal_part_of   A *temporal_part_of* relationship type where a
                   state_of_organization may be a
                   temporal_part_of one or more **organization**.

member_of   A *member_of* relationship type where a
                   state_of_organization may be a *member_of*
                   one or more **class_of_state_of_organization**.

17.32 Employment

Figure 17-32 shows the data model for **employment**. An **employment** is an **association** that has an **employer** and an **employee** as *participant_in* the **employment**. The **employer** is a *temporal_part_of* a **party**, and the **employee** is a *temporal_part_of* a **person**.

17.32.1 Employee

A **state_of_person** that is a *participant_in* an **employment**.

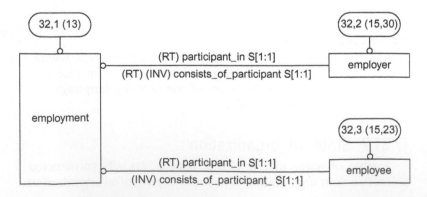

Figure 17-32 HQDM_
FRAMEWORK EXPRESS-G
diagram 32 of 46.

EXPRESS specification:

```
*)
  ENTITY employee
    SUBTYPE OF(state_of_person, participant);
    SELF\participant.participant_in        :SET [1:1] OF
                                              employment;
  END_ENTITY;
(*
```

Attribute definitions:

participant_in   A *participant_in* relationship type where an
employee is a *participant_in* exactly one
employment.

17.32.2 Employer

A **state_of_party** that is a *participant_in* an **employment**.

EXPRESS specification:

```
*)
  ENTITY employer
    SUBTYPE OF(state_of_party, participant);
    SELF\participant.participant_in        :SET [1:1] OF
                                              employment;
  END_ENTITY;
(*
```

Attribute definitions:

participant_in   A *participant_in* relationship type where an
employer is a *participant_in* exactly one
employment.

17.32.3 Employment

An **association** that consists of an **employer** and an **employee**
where the **employer** pays the **employee** to work for them.

EXPRESS specification:

```
*)
  ENTITY employment
    SUBTYPE OF(association);
  INVERSE
    SELF\association.consists_
      of_participant                :SET [1:1] OF employer FOR
                                      participant_in;
```

```
    consists_of_participant_          :SET [1:1] OF employee FOR
                                       participant_in:
  END_ENTITY;
(*
```

Attribute definitions:

consists_of_participant	A *consists_of_participant* relationship type where an **employment** *consists_of* exactly one **employer**.
*consists_of_participant_*	A *consists_of_participant* relationship type where an **employment** *consists_of* exactly one **employee**.

17.33 Organization Component and Position

Figure 17-33 is a data model for **organization_component** and **position**. An **organization_component** is a **state_of_organization_component**, that is also a **system_component**, and a **socially_constructed_object** that is a replaceable *component_of* an **organization** that is existence dependent on the **organization**. A **state_of_organization_component** is an **organization_component** or a *temporal_part_of* an **organization_component**.

A **state_of_organization_component** may be a *member_of* one or more **class_of_state_of_organization_component**. An **organization_component** may be a *member_of* one or more **class_of_organization_component** and **kind_of_organization_component**. A **position** is an **organization_component** that can be filled by one or more **persons**. A **state_of_position** is a **position** or a *temporal_part_of* a **position**.

A **state_of_position** may be a *member_of* one or more **class_of_state_of_position** and a **position** may be a *member_of* one or more **class_of_position** and **kind_of_position**.

A **person_in_position** is a **state_of_person** that is also a **state_of_position** that is the **person** while they are in the **position**, and the **position** while the **person** is in it. A **class_of_person_in_position** is **person_in_position** or any of its subsets. A **person_in_position** may be a *member_of* one or more **class_of_person_in_position**.

17.33.1 Class_of_organization_component

A **class_of_state_of_organization_component**, that is also a **class_of_system_component**, and a **class_of_socially_constructed_object** that is **organization_component** or any of its subsets.

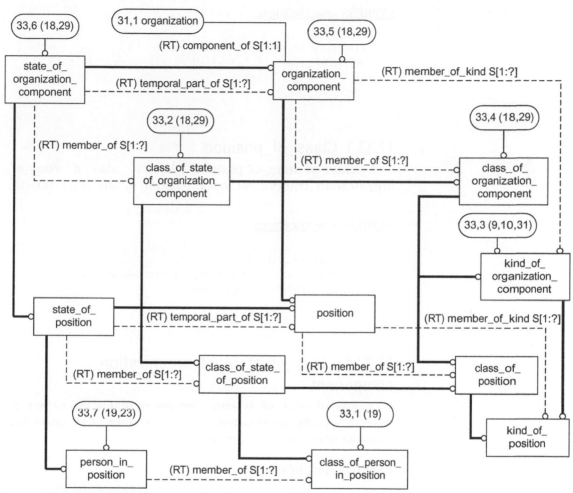

Figure 17-33 HQDM_FRAMEWORK EXPRESS-G diagram 33 of 46.

<u>EXPRESS specification:</u>

```
*)
  ENTITY class_of_organization_component
    SUBTYPE OF(class_of_state_of_organization_component, class_
             of_system_component, class_of_socially_contructed_
             object);
  END_ENTITY;
(*
```

17.33.2 Class_of_person_in_position

A **class_of_installed_object** that is also a **class_of_state_of_ position** that is **person_in_position** or any of its subsets.

EXPRESS specification:
```
*)
  ENTITY class_of_person_in_position
    SUBTYPE OF(class_of_installed_object, class_of_state_
              of_position);
  END_ENTITY;
(*
```

17.33.3 Class_of_position

A **class_of_state_of_position** that is also a **class_of_organization_component** that is **position** or any of its subsets.

EXPRESS specification:
```
*)
  ENTITY class_of_position
    SUBTYPE OF(class_of_state_of_position, class_of_
              organization_component);
  END_ENTITY;
(*
```

17.33.4 Class_of_state_of_organization_component

A **class_of_state_of_system_component** that is also a **class_of_state_of_socially_constructed_object** that is **state_of_organization_component** or any of its subsets.

EXPRESS specification:
```
*)
  ENTITY class_of_state_of_organization_component
    SUBTYPE OF(class_of_state_of_system_component,
              class_of_state_of_socially_constructed_object);
  END_ENTITY;
(*
```

17.33.5 Class_of_state_of_position

A **class_of_state_of_organization_component** that is **state_of_position** or any of its subsets.

EXPRESS specification:
```
*)
  ENTITY class_of_state_of_position
```

```
   SUBTYPE OF(class_of_state_of_organization_component);
 END_ENTITY;
(*
```

17.33.6 Kind_of_organization_component

A **class_of_organization_component** that is also a **kind_of_system_component** whose members are all of the same kind.

<u>EXPRESS specification:</u>

```
*)
 ENTITY kind_of_organization_component
   SUBTYPE OF(class_of_organization_component, kind_of_system_
             component, kind_of_socially_constructed_object);
 END_ENTITY;
(*
```

17.33.7 Kind_of_position

A **class_of_position** that is also a **kind_of_organization_component** where all the members are of the same kind.

<u>EXPRESS specification:</u>

```
*)
 ENTITY kind_of_position
   SUBTYPE OF(class_of_position, kind_of_organization_
             component);
 END_ENTITY;
(*
```

17.33.8 Organization_component

A **state_of_organization_component**, **system_component**, and **socially_constructed_object** that is a *component_of* an **organization** that can be completely replaced without losing its identity.

<u>EXPRESS specification:</u>

```
*)
 ENTITY organization_component
   SUBTYPE OF(state_of_organization_component,
             system_component, socially_constructed_object);
   SELF\system_component.
       component_of              :SET [1:1] OF organization;
   SELF\state_of_organization_
       component.member_of       :OPTIONAL SET [1:?] OF class_
                                  of_organization_component;
```

```
SELF\physical_object.
      member_of_kind        :OPTIONAL SET [1:?] OF kind_of_
                              organization_component;
END_ENTITY;
(*
```

Attribute definitions:

component_of	A *component_of* relationship type where an **organization_component** is a replaceable component of exactly one **organization**.
member_of	A *member_of* relationship type where an **organization_component** may be a *member_of* one or more **class_of_organization_component**.
member_of_kind	A *member_of_kind* relationship type where an **organization_component** may be a *member_of* one or more **kind_of_organization_component**.

17.33.9 Person_in_position

A **state_of_position**, that is also a **state_of_person**, and an **installed_object** that is a **person** while they are in a **position** and also the **position** while it is filled by the **person**.

EXPRESS specification:

```
*)
  ENTITY person_in_position
    SUBTYPE OF(state_of_position, state_of_person,
            installed_object);
    SELF\state_of_position.
        member_of        :OPTIONAL SET [1:?] OF class_of_person_
                            in_position;
  END_ENTITY;
(*
```

Attribute definitions:

member_of	A *member_of* relationship type where a **person_in_position** may be a *member_of* one or more **class_of_person_in_position**.

17.33.10 Position

An **organization_component** that is also a **state_of_position** that may be held by a **person**.

Note: Normally a **position** is held by one **person** at a time, but this does not have to be the case.

EXPRESS specification:

```
*)
  ENTITY position
    SUBTYPE OF(organization_component, state_of_position);
    SELF\organization_component.
        member_of                    :OPTIONAL SET [1:?] OF
                                      class_of_position;
    SELF\organization_component.
        member_of_kind               :OPTIONAL SET [1:?] OF
                                      kind_of_position;
  END_ENTITY;
(*
```

Attribute definitions:

member_of   A *member_of* relationship type where a **position** may be a *member_of* one or more **class_of_position**.

member_of_kind   A *member_of_kind* relationship type where a **position** may be a *member_of* one or more **kind_of_position**.

17.33.11 State_of_organization_component

A **state_of_system_component** that is also a **state_of_socially_constructed_object** that is a *temporal_part_of* an **organization_component**.

EXPRESS specification:

```
*)
  ENTITY state_of_organization_component
    SUBTYPE OF(state_of_system_component,
            state_of_socially_constructed_object);
    SELF\state_of_system_component.
        temporal_part_of             :OPTIONAL SET [1:?] OF
                                      organization_component;
    SELF\state_of_system_component.
        member_of                    :OPTIONAL SET [1:?] OF class_
                                      of_state_of_organization_
                                      component;
  END_ENTITY;
(*
```

Attribute definitions:

temporal_part_of   A *temporal_part_of* relationship type where a **state_of_organization_component** may be a *temporal_part_of* one or more **organization_component**.

member_of	A *member_of* relationship type where a **state_of_organization_component** may be a *member_of* one or more **class_of_state_of_organization_component**.

17.33.12 State_of_position

A **state_of_organization_component** that is a **position** or a *temporal_part_of* a **position**.

<u>EXPRESS specification:</u>

```
*)
  ENTITY state_of_position
    SUBTYPE OF(state_of_organization_component);
    SELF\state_of_organization_
        component.temporal_part_of :OPTIONAL SET [1:?] OF
                                        position;
    SELF\state_of_organization_
        component.member_of         :OPTIONAL SET [1:?] OF class_
                                        of_state_of_position;
  END_ENTITY;
(*
```

<u>Attribute definitions:</u>

temporal_part_of	A *temporal_part_of* relationship type where a **state_of_position** may be a *temporal_part_of* one or more **position**.
member_of	A *member_of* relationship type where a **state_of_position** may be a *member_of* one or more **class_of_state_of_position**.

17.34 Money

Figure 17-34 shows the data model for **amount_of_money**. An **amount_of_money** is a **socially_constructed_object** that is also a **physical_object** that is a means of exchange. A **state_of_amount_of_money** is an **amount_of_money** or a *temporal_part_of* an **amount_of_money**.

A **state_of_amount_of_money** may be a *member_of* one or more **class_of_state_of_amount_of_money**. An **amount_of_money** may be a *member_of* one or more **class_of_amount_of_money** and a *member_of* exactly one **currency**.

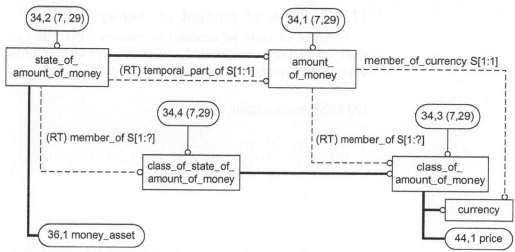

Figure 17-34 HQDM_FRAMEWORK EXPRESS-G diagram 34 of 46.

17.34.1 Amount_of_money

A **state_of_amount_of_money**, that is also a **socially_constructed_object**, and a **physical_object** that is intended and accepted for use as a means of exchange.

EXPRESS specification:

```
*)
  ENTITY amount_of_money
    SUBTYPE OF(state_of_amount_of_money,
            socially_constructed_object, physical_object);
    SELF\state_of_amount_of_
        money.member_of        :OPTIONAL SET [1:?] OF
                                class_of_amount_of_money;
    member_of_currency         :OPTIONAL SET [1:1] OF currency;
  END_ENTITY;
(*
```

Attribute definitions:

member_of	A *member_of* relationship type where an **amount_of_money** may be a *member_of* one or more **class_of_amount_of_money**.
member_of_currency	A *member_of* relationship type where an **amount_of_money** may be a *member_of* exactly one **currency**.

17.34.2 Class_of_amount_of_money

A **class_of_state_of_amount_of_money**, that is also a **class_of_socially_constructed_object,** and a **class_of_physical_object** that is **amount_of_money** or any of its subsets.

EXPRESS specification:
```
*)
  ENTITY class_of_amount_of_money
    SUBTYPE OF(class_of_state_of_amount_of_money, class_of_
             socially_contructed_object, class_of_physical_
             object);
  END_ENTITY;
(*
```

17.34.3 Class_of_state_of_amount_of_money

A **class_of_state_of_socially_constructed_object** that is also a **class_of_state_of_physical_object** that is **state_of_amount_of_money** or one of its subsets.

EXPRESS specification:
```
*)
  ENTITY class_of_state_of_amount_of_money
    SUBTYPE OF(class_of_state_of_socially_constructed_object,
             class_of_state_of_physical_object);
  END_ENTITY;
(*
```

17.34.4 Currency

A **class_of_amount_of_money** that is the subset of **amount_of_money** that has as members all the money issued by an issuing authority.

EXPRESS specification:
```
*)
  ENTITY currency
    SUBTYPE OF(class_of_amount_of_money);
  END_ENTITY;
(*
```

17.34.5 State_of_amount_of_money

A **socially_constructed_object** that is also a **state_of_physical_object** that is a *temporal_part_of* an **amount_of_money**.

EXPRESS specification:

```
*)
  ENTITY state_of_amount_of_money
    SUBTYPE OF(state_of_socially_constructed_object,
               state_of_physical_object);
    SELF\state_of_socially_constructed_
         object.temporal_part_of       :OPTIONAL SET [1:1] OF
                                        amount_of_money;
    SELF\state_of_socially_
         constructed_object.member_of  :OPTIONAL SET [1:?] OF
                                        class_of_state_of_
                                        amount_of_money;
  END_ENTITY;
(*
```

Attribute definitions:

temporal_part_of A *temporal_part_of* relationship type where a **state_of_amount_of_money** may be a *temporal_part_of* one or more **amount_of_money**.

member_of A *member_of* relationship type where a **state_of_amount_of_money** may be a *member_of* one or more **class_of_state_of_amount_of_money**.

17.35 Ownership

Figure 17-35 shows the data model for **ownership**. An **ownership** is an **association** of an **owner** and an **asset** where the **owner** owns the **asset**. An **owner** is a **state_of_party** that is also a **participant** that owns the **asset**. An **asset** is a **participant** that is a **state_of_physical_object** that is owned. A **beginning_of_ownership** is an **event** that marks the *beginning* of an **ownership**, and an **ending_of_ownership** marks the *ending* of an **ownership**.

17.35.1 Asset

A **state_of_physical_object** that is also a **participant** that is the *participant_in* an **ownership** that is owned.

EXPRESS specification:

```
*)
  ENTITY asset
    SUBTYPE OF(participant);
    SELF\participant.participant_in    :SET [1:1] OF ownership;
  END_ENTITY;
(*
```

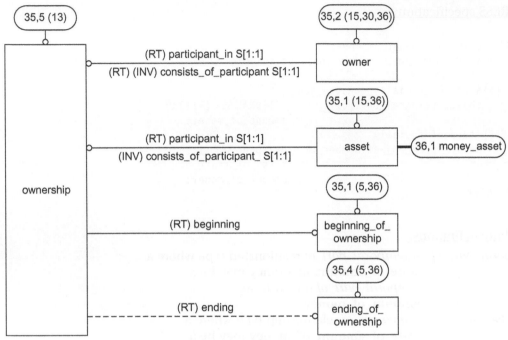

Figure 17-35 HQDM_FRAMEWORK EXPRESS-G diagram 35 of 46.

Attribute definitions:

participant_in   A *participant_in* relationship type where an **asset** is a *participant_in* exactly one **ownership**.

17.35.2 Beginning_of_ownership

An **event** that is the *beginning* of an **ownership**.

EXPRESS specification:

```
*)
  ENTITY beginning_of_ownership
    SUBTYPE OF(event);
  END_ENTITY;
(*
```

17.35.3 Ending_of_ownership

An **event** that is the *ending* of an **ownership**.

EXPRESS specification:

```
*)
  ENTITY ending_of_ownership
    SUBTYPE OF(event);
  END_ENTITY;
(*
```

17.35.4 Owner

A **state_of_party** that is also a **participant** that is a *participant_in* an **ownership**.

EXPRESS specification:

```
*)
  ENTITY owner
    SUBTYPE OF(state_of_party, participant);
    SELF\participant.participant_in    :SET [1:1] OF ownership;
  END_ENTITY;
(*
```

Attribute definitions:

participant_in   A *participant_in* relationship type where an **owner** is a *participant_in* exactly one **ownership**.

17.35.5 Ownership

An **association** that *consists_of* an **owner** and an **asset** where the **owner** owns the **asset**.

EXPRESS specification:

```
*)
  ENTITY ownership
    SUBTYPE OF(association);
    SELF\spatio_temporal_
        extent.ending            :OPTIONAL ending_of_ownership;
    SELF\spatio_temporal_
        extent.beginning         :beginning_of_ownership;
  INVERSE
    SELF\association.consists_
        of_participant           :SET [1:1] OF owner FOR
                                  participant_in;
    consists_of_participant_     :SET [1:1] OF asset FOR
                                  participant_in;
  END_ENTITY;
(*
```

Attribute definitions:

ending	An *ending* relationship type where an **ownership** has as *ending* not more than one **ending_of_ownership**.
beginning	A *beginning* relationship type where an **ownership** has as *beginning* exactly one **beginning_of_ownership**.
consists_of_participant	A *consists_of_participant* relationship type where an **ownership** *consists_of_participant* exactly one **owner**.
*consists_of_participant_*	A *consists_of_participant* relationship type where an **ownership** *consists_of_participant* exactly one **asset**.

17.36 Transfer of Ownership

Figure 17-36 shows the data model for **transfer_of_ownership**. A **transfer_of_ownership** is a **socially_constructed_activity** that *causes* the **ending_of_ownership** for one **ownership** and *causes* the **beginning_of_ownership** of another. The **participants** in the **activity** are the **transferor**, which is a *temporal_part_of* the current **owner**, and the **transferee**, who will become the new **owner** and the **transfer_of_ownership** *references* the **asset** which is to be transferred. A **transfer_of_ownership** may be *part_of* an **exchange_of_goods_and_money**.

One kind of **transfer_of_ownership** is when a **money_asset** is transferred.

17.36.1 Money_asset

An **asset** that is a **state_of_amount_of_money**.

EXPRESS specification:

```
*)
  ENTITY money_asset
    SUBTYPE OF(asset, state_of_amount_of_money);
  END_ENTITY;
(*
```

17.36.2 Transfer_of_ownership

A **socially_constructed_activity** that ends one **ownership** and begins another for **asset**s that are a *temporal_part_of* the same **physical_object**.

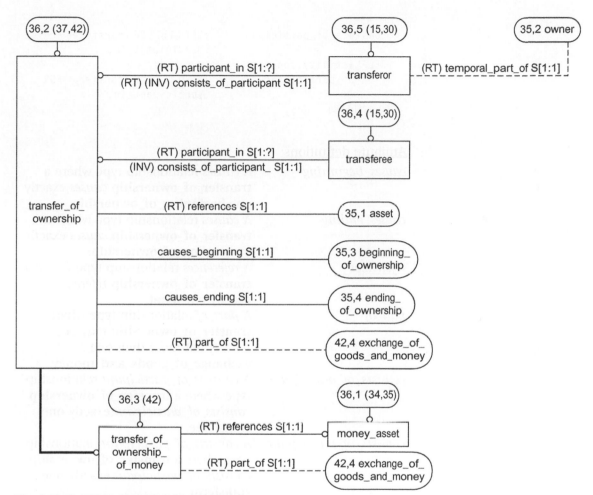

Figure 17-36 HQDM_FRAMEWORK EXPRESS-G diagram 36 of 46.

EXPRESS specification:

```
*)
 ENTITY transfer_of_ownership
   SUBTYPE OF(socially_constructed_activity);
   causes_beginning           :SET [1:1] OF
                               beginning_of_ownership;
   causes_ending              :SET [1:1] OF ending_of_
                               ownership;
   SELF\activity.references   :SET [1:1] OF asset;
   SELF\socially_constructed_
       activity.part_of       :OPTIONAL SET [1:1] OF
                               exchange_of_goods_and_money;
```

```
INVERSE
  consists_of_participant_    :SET [1:1] OF transferee FOR
                                      participant_in;

  SELF\activity.consists_
      of_participant          :SET [1:1] OF transferor FOR
                                      participant_in;

END_ENTITY;
(*
```

<u>Attribute definitions:</u>

causes_beginning	A *causes* relationship type where a **transfer_of_ownership** *causes* exactly one **beginning_of_ownership**.
causes_ending	A *causes* relationship type where a **transfer_of_ownership** *causes* exactly one **ending_of_ownership**.
references	A *references* relationship type where a **transfer_of_ownership** *references* exactly one **asset**.
part_of	A *part_of* relationship type where a **transfer_of_ownership** may be *part_of* not more than one **exchange_of_goods_and_money**.
*consists_of_participant_*	A *consists_of_participant* relationship type where a **transfer_of_ownership** *consists_of_participant* exactly one **transferee**.
consists_of_participant	A *consists_of_participant* relationship type where a **transfer_of_ownership** *consists_of_participant* exactly one **transferor**.

17.36.3 Transfer_of_ownership_of_money

A **transfer_of_ownership** where the **asset** is a **money_asset**.

<u>EXPRESS specification:</u>

```
*)
  ENTITY transfer_of_ownership_of_money
    SUBTYPE OF(transfer_of_ownership);
    SELF\transfer_of_ownership.
        references               :SET [1:1] OF money_asset;
    SELF\transfer_of_ownership.
        part_of                  :OPTIONAL SET [1:1] OF
                                      exchange_of_goods_and_money;
  END_ENTITY;
(*
```

Attribute definitions:

references A *references* relationship type where a
transfer_of_ownership_of_money *references* exactly
one **money_asset**.

part_of A *part_of* relationship type where a
transfer_of_ownership_of_money may be a *part_of*
at most one **exchange_of_goods_and_money**.

17.36.4 Transferee

A **state_of_party** and **participant** receiving **ownership** in a
transfer_of_ownership.

EXPRESS specification:

```
*)
  ENTITY transferee
    SUBTYPE OF(state_of_party, participant);
    SELF\participant.
        participant_in    :SET [1:?] OF transfer_of_ownership;
  END_ENTITY;
(*
```

Attribute definitions:

participant_in A *participant_in* relationship type where a
transferee is a *participant_in* one or more
transfer_of_ownership.

17.36.5 Transferor

A **state_of_party** that is also a **participant** that is a *temporal_
part_of* an **owner** that is a *participant_in* one or more **transfers_
of_ownership**.

EXPRESS specification:

```
*)
  ENTITY transferor
    SUBTYPE OF(state_of_party, participant);
    SELF\state_of_party.temporal_
        part_of           :OPTIONAL SET [1:1] OF owner;
    SELF\participant.
        participant_in    :SET [1:?] OF transfer_of_ownership;
  END_ENTITY;
(*
```

Attribute definitions:

temporal_part_of   A *temporal_part_of* relationship type where a **transferor** is a *temporal_part_of* exactly one **owner**.

participant_in   A *participant_in* relationship type where a **transferor** is *participant_in* one or more **transfer_of_ownership**.

17.37 Socially Constructed Activity

Figure 17-37 shows the data model for **socially_constructed_activity**. A **socially_constructed_activity** is an intentional **activity** that is socially constructed; that is, it involves the agreement of several parties.

A **socially_constructed_activity** may be a *member_of* one or more **class_of_socially_constructed_activity**, may be *part_of* a **reaching_agreement**, or may be *part_of* an **agreement_execution**.

17.37.1 Socially_constructed_activity

Any **socially_constructed_object** that is also an **activity**.

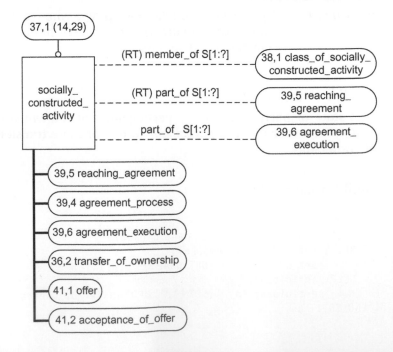

Figure 17-37 HQDM_FRAMEWORK
EXPRESS-G diagram 37 of 46.

EXPRESS specification:

```
*)
  ENTITY socially_constructed_activity
    SUBTYPE OF(activity, socially_constructed_object);
    SELF\activity.member_of   :OPTIONAL SET [1:?] OF class_of_
                                  socially_constructed_activity;
    SELF\activity.part_of     :OPTIONAL SET [1:?] OF reaching_
                                  agreement;
    part_of_                  :OPTIONAL SET [1:?] OF agreement_
                                  execution;
  END_ENTITY;
(*
```

Attribute definitions:

member_of A *member_of* relationship type where a **socially_constructed_activity** may be a *member_of* one or more **class_of_socially_constructed_activity**.

part_of A *part_of* relationship type where a **socially_constructed_activity** may be a *part_of* one or more **reaching_agreement**.

*part_of_* A *part_of* relationship type where a **socially_constructed_object** may be a *part_of* one or more **agreement_execution**.

17.38 Class of Socially Constructed Activity

Figure 17-38 shows the data model for **class_of_socially_constructed_activity**. A **class_of_socially_constructed_activity** is **socially_constructed_activity** or any of its subsets. A *member_of* a **class_of_socially_constructed_activity** may be a *part_of* a *member_of* a **class_of_reaching_agreement** or of a **class_of_agreement_execution**.

17.38.1 Class_of_socially_constructed_activity

A **class_of_socially_constructed_object** and **class_of_activity** that is **socially_constructed_activity** or any of its subsets.

EXPRESS specification:

```
*)
  ENTITY class_of_socially_constructed_activity
```

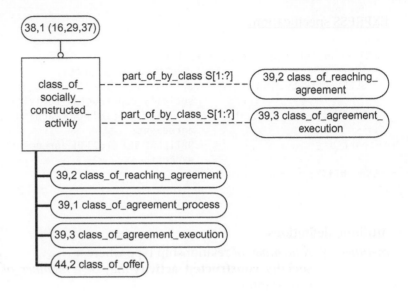

Figure 17-38 HQDM_FRAMEWORK EXPRESS-G diagram 38 of 46.

```
SUBTYPE OF(class_of_activity,
           class_of_socially_contructed_object);
part_of_by_class       :OPTIONAL SET [1:?] OF
                        class_of_reaching_agreement;
part_of_by_class_      :OPTIONAL SET [1:?] OF
                        class_of_agreement_execution;
 END_ENTITY;
(*
```

Attribute definitions:

part_of_by_class   A *part_of_by_class* where a *member_of* a **class_of_socially_constructed_activity** may be a *part_of* a *member_of* a **class_of_reaching_agreement**.

*part_of_by_class_*   A *part_of_by_class* relationship type where a *member_of* a **class_of_socially_ constructed_activity** may be a *part_of* a *member_of* a **class_of_agreement_execution**.

17.39 Agreement

Figure 17-39 shows the data model for agreement. An **agreement_process** is an **activity** that consists of a **reaching_agreement** and an **agreement_execution**, where the **reaching_agreement** agrees the **agreement_execution**.

A **reaching_agreement** may be a *member_of* one or more **class_of_reaching_agreement**. An **agreement_process** may be a

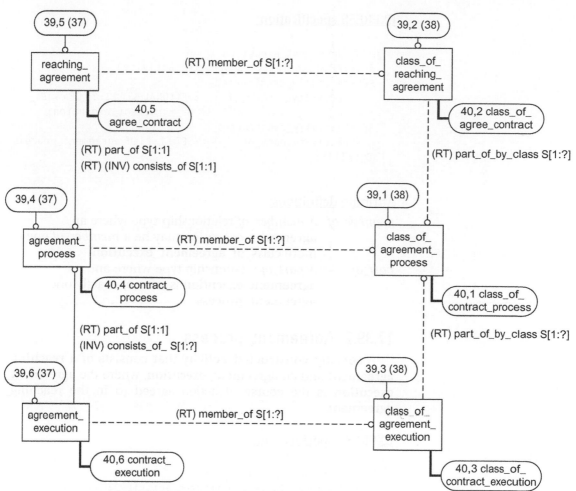

Figure 17-39 HQDM_FRAMEWORK EXPRESS-G diagram 39 of 46.

member_of one or more **class_of_agreement_process**, and an **agreement_execution** may be a *member_of* one or more **class_of_agreement_execution**.

A *member_of* **class_of_agreement_process** may have members of a **class_of_reaching_agreement** and a **class_of_agreement_execution** as parts.

17.39.1 Agreement_execution

A **socially_constructed_activity** where two or more parties carry out a course of action previously agreed upon.

<u>EXPRESS specification:</u>

```
*)
  ENTITY agreement_execution
    SUBTYPE OF(socially_constructed_activity);
    SELF\socially_constructed_
        activity.member_of      :OPTIONAL SET [1:?] OF class_
                                   of_agreement_execution;
    SELF\socially_constructed_
        activity.part_of        :SET [1:1] OF agreement_process;
  END_ENTITY;
(*
```

<u>Attribute definitions:</u>

member_of A *member_of* relationship type where an
               agreement_execution may be a *member_of* one or
               more **class_of_agreement_execution.**

part_of A *part_of* relationship type where an
               agreement_execution is *part_of* exactly one
               agreement_process.

17.39.2 Agreement_process

A **socially_constructed_activity** that consists of a **reaching_agreement** and an **agreement_execution**, where the **agreement_execution** is the course of action agreed to in the **reaching_agreement.**

<u>EXPRESS specification:</u>

```
*)
  ENTITY agreement_process
    SUBTYPE OF(socially_constructed_activity);
    SELF\socially_constructed_
        activity.member_of      :OPTIONAL SET [1:?] OF
                                   class_of_agreement_process;
  INVERSE
    consists_of_                :SET [1:?] OF agreement_
                                   execution FOR part_of;

    SELF\activity.consists_of   :SET [1:1] OF reaching_
                                   agreement FOR part_of;
  END_ENTITY;
(*
```

<u>Attribute definitions:</u>

member_of A *member_of* relationship type where an
               agreement_process may be a *member_of* one or
               more **class_of_agreement_process.**

*consists_of_*   A *consists_of* relationship type where an **agreement_process** consists of at least one **agreement_execution**.

consists_of   A *consists_of* relationship type where an **agreement_process** consists of exactly one **reaching_agreement**.

17.39.3 Class_of_agreement_execution

A **class_of_socially_constructed_activity** that is **agreement_execution** or any of its subsets.

EXPRESS specification:

```
*)
  ENTITY class_of_agreement_execution
    SUBTYPE OF(class_of_socially_constructed_activity);
    SELF\class_of_socially_constructed_
        activity.part_of_by_class      :OPTIONAL SET [1:?] OF
                                        class_of_agreement_
                                        process;
  END_ENTITY;
(*
```

Attribute definitions:

part_of_by_class   A *part_of_by_class* relationship type where a *member_of* the **class_of_agreement_execution** may be a *part_of* a *member_of* the **class_of_agreement_process**.

17.39.4 Class_of_agreement_process

A **class_of_socially_constructed_activity** that is **agreement_process** or any of its subsets.

EXPRESS specification:

```
*)
  ENTITY class_of_agreement_process
    SUBTYPE OF(class_of_socially_constructed_activity);
  END_ENTITY;
(*
```

17.39.5 Class_of_reaching_agreement

A **class_of_socially_constructed_activity** that is **reaching_agreement** or any of its subsets.

EXPRESS specification:

```
*)
  ENTITY class_of_reaching_agreement
    SUBTYPE OF(class_of_socially_constructed_activity);
    SELF\class_of_socially_constructed_
        activity.part_of_by_class        :OPTIONAL SET [1:?] OF
                                          class_of_agreement_
                                          process;

  END_ENTITY;
(*
```

Attribute definitions:

part_of_by_class   A *part_of_by_class* relationship type where a *member_of* a **class_of_reaching_agreement** may be a *part_of* a *member_of* a **class_of_agreement_process**.

17.39.6 Reaching_agreement

A **socially_constructed_activity** where two or more parties determine a course of action.

EXPRESS specification:

```
*)
  ENTITY reaching_agreement
    SUBTYPE OF(socially_constructed_activity);
    SELF\socially_constructed_
        activity.member_of      :OPTIONAL SET [1:?] OF class_of_
                                   reaching_agreement;
    SELF\socially_constructed_
        activity.part_of        :SET [1:1] OF agreement_process;
  END_ENTITY;
(*
```

Attribute definitions:

member_of   A *member_of* relationship type where a **reaching_agreement** may be a *member_of* one or more **class_of_reaching_agreement**.

part_of   A *part_of* relationship type where a **reaching_agreement** is a *part_of* exactly one **agreement_process**.

17.40 Contract

Figure 17-40 shows the data model for contract. A **contract_process** is an **agreement_process** where the **reaching_agreement**

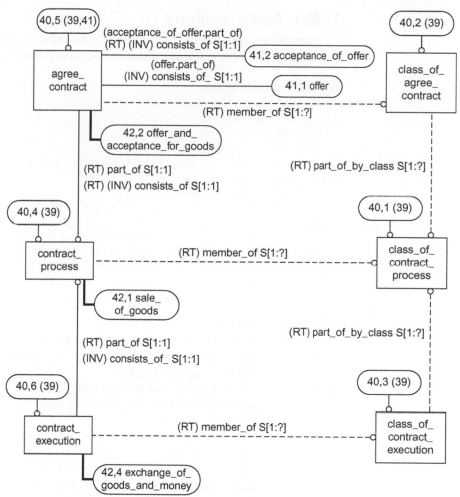

Figure 17-40 HQDM_FRAMEWORK EXPRESS-G diagram 40 of 46.

is an **agree_contract** and the **agreement_execution** is a **contract_execution**. An **agree_contract** is an **activity** in which one or more parties make offers, and the other **party** accepts an **offer**.

An **agree_contract** may be a *member_of* one or more **class_of_agree_contract**. A **contract_process** may be a *member_of* one or more **class_of_contract_process** and a **contract_execution** may be a *member_of* one or more **class_of_contract_execution**.

A *member_of* a **class_of_contract_process** may have a *member_of* a **class_of_agree_contract** and a **class_of_agree_contract** as part.

17.40.1 Agree_contract

A **reaching_agreement** that consists of an **offer** of some **thing** in exchange for some consideration and an **acceptance_of_offer**.

EXPRESS specification:

```
*)
  ENTITY agree_contract
    SUBTYPE OF(reaching_agreement);
    SELF\reaching_agreement.
        member_of                :OPTIONAL SET [1:?] OF
class_of_agree_contract;
    SELF\reaching_agreement.
        part_of                  :SET [1:1] OF contract_process;
  INVERSE
    consists_of_             :SET [1:1] OF offer FOR part_of;
    SELF\activity.consists_of  :SET [1:1] OF acceptance_
                                  of_offer FOR part_of;
  END_ENTITY;
(*
```

Attribute definitions:

member_of   A *member_of* relationship type where an **agree_contract** may be a *member_of* one or more **class_of_agree_contract**.

part_of   A *part_of* relationship type where an **agree_contract** is *part_of* exactly one **contract_process**.

*consists_of_*   A *consists_of* relationship type where an **agree_contract** *consists_of* exactly one **offer**.

consists_of   A *consists_of* relationship type where the **agree_contract** *consists_of* exactly one **acceptance_of_offer**.

17.40.2 Class_of_agree_contract

A **class_of_reaching_agreement** that is **agree_contract** or any of its subsets.

EXPRESS specification:

```
*)
  ENTITY class_of_agree_contract
    SUBTYPE OF(class_of_reaching_agreement);
    SELF\class_of_reaching_
        agreement.part_of_by_class  :OPTIONAL SET [1:?] OF class_
                                          of_contract_process;
  END_ENTITY;
(*
```

<u>Attribute definitions:</u>

part_of_by_class   A *part_of_by_class* relationship type where a *member_of* the **class_of_agree_contract** may be a *part_of* a *member_of* one or more **class_of_contract_process**.

17.40.3 Class_of_contract_execution

A **class_of_agreement_execution** that is **contract_execution** or any of its subsets.

<u>EXPRESS specification:</u>

```
*)
  ENTITY class_of_contract_execution
    SUBTYPE OF(class_of_agreement_execution);
    SELF\class_of_agreement_
        execution.part_of_by_class    :OPTIONAL SET [1:?] OF
                                       class_of_contract_
                                       process;
  END_ENTITY;
(*
```

<u>Attribute definitions:</u>

part_of_by_class   A *part_of_by_class* relationship type where a *member_of* the **class_of_contract_execution** may be a *part_of* a *member_of* the **class_of_contract_process**.

17.40.4 Class_of_contract_process

A **class_of_agreement_process** that is **contract_process** or any of its subsets.

<u>EXPRESS specification:</u>

```
*)
  ENTITY class_of_contract_process
    SUBTYPE OF(class_of_agreement_process);
  END_ENTITY;
(*
```

17.40.5 Contract_execution

An **agreement_execution** that is the provision of some **thing** in exchange for some consideration.

<u>EXPRESS specification:</u>

```
*)
  ENTITY contract_execution
    SUBTYPE OF(agreement_execution);
    SELF\agreement_execution.
        member_of          :OPTIONAL SET [1:?] OF
                              class_of_contract_execution;
    SELF\agreement_execution.
        part_of            :SET [1:1] OF contract_process;
  END_ENTITY;
(*
```

<u>Attribute definitions:</u>

member_of   A *member_of* relationship type where a **contract_execution** may be a *member_of* one or more **class_of_contract_execution**.

part_of   A *part_of* relationship type where a **contract_execution** is *part_of* exactly one **contract_process**.

17.40.6 Contract_process

An **agreement_process** that consists of an **agree_contract** and a **contract_execution**.

<u>EXPRESS specification:</u>

```
*)
  ENTITY contract_process
    SUBTYPE OF(agreement_process);
    SELF\agreement_process.
        member_of          :OPTIONAL SET [1:?] OF class_of_
                              contract_process;
  INVERSE
    SELF\agreement_process.
        consists_of_       :SET [1:1] OF contract_execution
                            FOR part_of;
    SELF\agreement_process.
        consists_of        :SET [1:1] OF agree_contract FOR
                            part_of;
  END_ENTITY;
(*
```

<u>Attribute definitions:</u>

member_of   A *member_of* relationship type where a contract process may be a *member_of* one or more **class_of_contract_process**.

*consists_of_* A *consists_of_* relationship type where a
contract_process *consists_of* exactly one
contract_execution.

consists_of A *consists_of* relationship type where a **contract_
process** *consists_of* exactly one **agree_contract**.

17.41 Offer and Acceptance of Offer

Figure 17-41 shows the data model for **offer** and **acceptance_
of_offer**. An **offer** is a **socially_constructed_activity** that proposes an exchange of some **thing** for some consideration. An
offer may be a *member_of* one or more **class_of_offer**, and may
be *part_of* an **agree_contract**.

An **acceptance_of_offer** is the acceptance of a particular
offer, and is *part_of* an **agree_contract**.

17.41.1 Acceptance_of_offer

A **socially_constructed_activity** that is the acceptance of an
offer as *part_of* an **agree_contract**.

EXPRESS specification:
```
*)
  ENTITY acceptance_of_offer
    SUBTYPE OF(socially_constructed_activity);
```

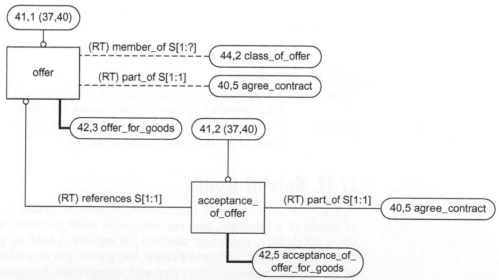

Figure 17-41 HQDM_FRAMEWORK EXPRESS-G diagram 41 of 46.

```
        SELF\activity.references       :SET [1:1] OF offer;
        SELF\socially_constructed_
              activity.part_of         :SET [1:1] OF agree_contract;
     END_ENTITY;
   (*
```

<u>Attribute definitions:</u>

references   A *references* relationship type where an **acceptance_ of_offer** *references* exactly one **offer** that is accepted.

part_of   A *part_of* relationship type where an **acceptance_of_offer** is *part_of* just one **agree_contract**.

17.41.2 Offer

A **socially_constructed_activity** that proposes an exchange of some **thing** for some consideration.

<u>EXPRESS specification:</u>

```
*)
  ENTITY offer
    SUBTYPE OF(socially_constructed_activity);
    SELF\socially_constructed_
          activity.member_of        :OPTIONAL SET [1:?] OF
                                      class_of_offer;
    SELF\socially_constructed_
          activity.part_of          :OPTIONAL SET [1:1] OF
                                      agree_contract;
  END_ENTITY;
(*
```

<u>Attribute definitions:</u>

member_of   A *member_of* relationship type where an **offer** may be a *member_of* one or more **class_of_offer**.

part_of   A *part_of* relationship type where an **offer** may be *part_of* at most one **agree_contract**.

17.42 Sale of Goods

Figure 17-42 shows the data model for **sale_of_goods**. A **sale_ of_goods** is a **contract_process** where an **offer** is made to sell some goods for a particular **amount_of_money**. A **sale_of_goods** consists of an **offer_and_acceptance_for_goods** and an **exchange_ of_goods_and_money**. An **offer_and_acceptance_for_goods** is an **agree_contract** that consists of an **offer_for_goods** and an

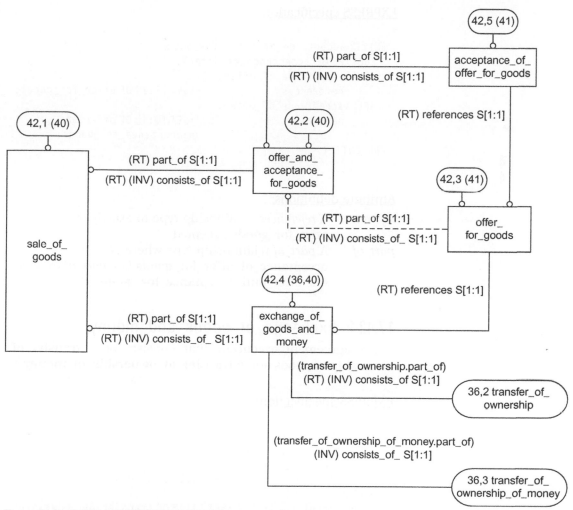

Figure 17-42 HQDM_FRAMEWORK EXPRESS-G diagram 42 of 46.

acceptance_of_offer_for_goods. The **offer_for_goods** *references* the offered **exchange_of_goods_and_money**.

An **exchange_of_goods_and_money** is a **contract_execution** that consists of a **transfer_of_ownership**, and a **transfer_of_ownership_of_money**.

17.42.1 Acceptance_of_offer_for_goods

A **reaching_agreement** that consists of one or more **offers** of a **transfer_of_ownership_of_money** for a **transfer_of_ownership** of goods where one **offer** is accepted.

<u>EXPRESS specification:</u>

```
*)
  ENTITY acceptance_of_offer_for_goods
    SUBTYPE OF(acceptance_of_offer);
    SELF\acceptance_of_offer.
         references              :SET [1:1] OF offer_for_goods;
    SELF\acceptance_of_offer.
         part_of                 :SET [1:1] OF offer_and_
                                   acceptance_for_goods;
  END_ENTITY;
(*
```

<u>Attribute definitions:</u>

references A *references* relationship type to exactly one **offer_for_goods** accepted.

part_of A *part_of* relationship type where an **acceptance_of_offer_for_goods** is a *part_of* exactly one **offer_and_acceptance_for_goods**.

17.42.2 Exchange_of_goods_and_money

An **agreement_execution** that consists of a **transfer_of_ownership** of goods and a **transfer_of_ownership_of_money**.

<u>EXPRESS specification:</u>

```
*)
  ENTITY exchange_of_goods_and_money
    SUBTYPE OF(contract_execution);
    SELF\contract_execution.
         part_of           :SET [1:1] OF sale_of_goods;
  INVERSE
    consists_of_           :SET [1:1] OF transfer_of_ownership_
                            of_money FOR part_of;
    SELF\activity.
         consists_of       :SET [1:1] OF transfer_of_ownership
FOR part_of;
  END_ENTITY;
(*
```

<u>Attribute definitions:</u>

part_of A *part_of* relationship type where an **exchange_of_goods_and_money** is a *part_of* exactly one **sale_of_goods**.

*consists_of_* A *consists_of* relationship type where an **exchange_of_goods_and_money** consists of exactly

one **transfer_of_ownership_of_money**.
Note: This entity type has another *consists_of*
relationship type. EXPRESS requires relationship type
names to be unique, so I have renamed this one.

consists_of   A *consists_of* relationship type where an
exchange_of_goods_and_money consists of
exactly one **transfer_of_ownership** as a part.

17.42.3 Offer_and_acceptance_for_goods

A **reaching_agreement** that *consists_of* exactly one **offer** of a
transfer_of_ownership_of_money for exactly one **transfer_of_ownership** that is accepted.

<u>EXPRESS specification:</u>

```
*)
  ENTITY offer_and_acceptance_for_goods
    SUBTYPE OF(agree_contract);
    SELF\agree_contract.
        part_of              :SET [1:1] OF sale_of_goods;
  INVERSE
    SELF\agree_contract.
        consists_of_         :SET [1:1] OF offer_for_goods FOR
                              part_of;

    SELF\agree_contract.
        consists_of          :SET [1:1] OF acceptance_of_offer_
                              for_goods FOR part_of;
  END_ENTITY;
(*
```

<u>Attribute definitions:</u>

part_of   A *part_of* relationship type where an
offer_and_acceptance_for_goods is a *part_of*
exactly one **sale_of_goods**.

*consists_of_*   A *consists_of_* relationship type where an
offer_and_acceptance_for_goods *consists_of*
exactly one **offer_for_goods**.

consists_of   A *consists_of* relationship type where an
offer_and_acceptance_for_goods consists of
exactly one **acceptance_of_offer_for_goods**.

17.42.4 Offer_for_goods

An **offer** of an **exchange_of_goods_and_money**.

<u>EXPRESS specification:</u>

```
*)
 ENTITY offer_for_goods
   SUBTYPE OF(offer);
   SELF\activity.references    :SET [1:1] OF
                                exchange_of_goods_and_money;
       SELF\offer.part_of       :OPTIONAL SET [1:1] OF offer_
                                and_acceptance_for_goods;
   END_ENTITY;
(*
```

<u>Attribute definitions:</u>

references A *references* relationship type to exactly one **exchange_of_goods_and_money** offered.

part_of A *part_of* relationship type where an **offer_for_goods** may be *part_of* no more than one **offer_and_acceptance_for_goods**.

17.42.5 Sale_of_goods

An **agreement_process** that consists of an **offer_and_acceptance_for_goods** and an **exchange_of_goods_and_money**.

<u>EXPRESS specification:</u>

```
*)
 ENTITY sale_of_goods
   SUBTYPE OF(contract_process);
 INVERSE
   SELF\contract_process.
       consists_of_        :SET [1:1] OF exchange_of_goods_
                            and_money FOR part_of;
   SELF\contract_process.
       consists_of         :SET [1:1] OF offer_and_acceptance_
                            for_goods FOR part_of;
   END_ENTITY;
(*
```

<u>Attribute definitions:</u>

*consists_of_* A *consists_of* relationship type where a **sale_of_goods** *consists_of* exactly one **exchange_of_goods_and_money**.

consists_of A *consists_of* relationship type where a **sale_of_goods** *consists_of* exactly one **offer_and_acceptance_for_goods**.

17.43 Sales Product, Product Brand, and Sales Product Version

Figure 17-43 shows the data model for **sales_product**, **product_ brand**, and **sales_product_version**. A **sales_product_instance** is an **ordinary_functional_object** that is a particular article intended for sale. A **state_of_sales_product_instance** is a **sales_product_instance** or a *temporal_part_of* a **sales_product_instance**.

A **state_of_sales_product_instance** may be a *member_of* one or more **class_of_state_of_sales_product_instance**, and a **sales_product_instance** may be a *member_of* one or more **class_of_sales_product_instance**.

A **sales_product** is a **class_of_sales_product_instance** that is a set of **sales_product_instance** sold under the same product

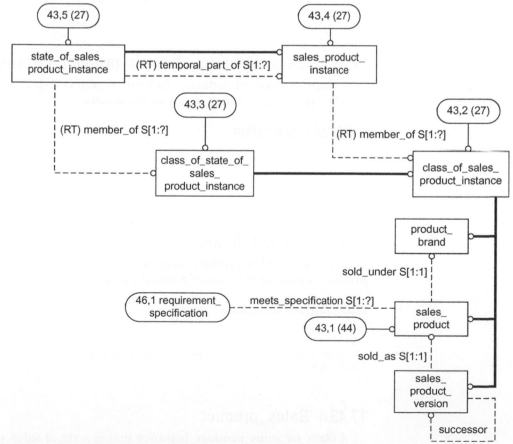

Figure 17-43 HQDM_FRAMEWORK EXPRESS-G diagram 43 of 46.

name. A **sales_product_version** is a **class_of_sales_product_instance** that is the customer facing specification of a version of a **sales_product**. A **product_brand** is a **class_of_sales_product_instance** that is a set of **sales_product_instance** sold under a brand name.

17.43.1 Class_of_sales_product_instance

A **class_of_state_of_sales_product_instance** that is also a **class_of_ordinary_functional_object** that is **sales_product_instance** or any of its subsets.

EXPRESS specification:
```
*)
  ENTITY class_of_sales_product_instance
    SUBTYPE OF(class_of_state_of_sales_product_instance,
             class_of_ordinary_functional_object);
  END_ENTITY;
(*
```

17.43.2 Class_of_state_of_sales_product_instance

A **class_of_state_of_ordinary_functional_object** that is **state_of_sales_product_instance** or any of its subsets.

EXPRESS specification:
```
*)
  ENTITY class_of_state_of_sales_product_instance
    SUBTYPE OF(class_of_state_of_ordinary_functional_object);
  END_ENTITY;
(*
```

17.43.3 Product_brand

A **class_of_sales_product_instance** that is a set of **sales_product_instance** sold under a brand name.

EXPRESS specification:
```
*)
  ENTITY product_brand
    SUBTYPE OF(class_of_sales_product_instance);
  END_ENTITY;
(*
```

17.43.4 Sales_product

A **class_of_sales_product_instance** that is a set of **sales_product_instances** sold under the same product name.

EXPRESS specification:

```
*)
  ENTITY sales_product
    SUBTYPE OF(class_of_sales_product_instance);
    sold_under       :OPTIONAL SET [1:1] OF product_brand;
  END_ENTITY;
(*
```

Attribute definitions:

sold_under A **specialization** where the **sales_product** is sold
under a **product_brand**.

17.43.5 Sales_product_instance

An **ordinary_functional_object** that is produced in order to
be sold.

EXPRESS specification:

```
*)
  ENTITY sales_product_instance
    SUBTYPE OF(state_of_sales_product_instance,
            ordinary_functional_object);
    SELF\state_of_sales_
        product_instance.member_of       :OPTIONAL SET [1:?]
                                          OF class_of_sales_
                                          product_instance;
  END_ENTITY;
(*
```

Attribute definitions:

member_of A *member_of* relationship type where a
sales_product_instance may be a *member_of* one
or more **class_of_sales_product_instance**.

17.43.6 Sales_product_version

A **class_of_sales_product_instance** that is the customer facing
specification of a version of a **sales_product**.

EXPRESS specification:

```
*)
  ENTITY sales_product_version
    SUBTYPE OF(class_of_sales_product_instance);
    sold_as         :OPTIONAL SET [1:1] OF sales_product;
    successor       :OPTIONAL sales_product_version;
  END_ENTITY;
(*
```

Attribute definitions:

sold_as	A **specialization** where the **sales_product**_version may be sold as a **sales_product**.
successor	A relationship type where a **sales_product_version** may have exactly one successor.

17.43.7 State_of_sales_product_instance

A **state_of_ordinary_functional_object** that is a **sales_product_instance** or a *temporal_part_of* one.

EXPRESS specification:

```
*)
  ENTITY state_of_sales_product_instance
    SUBTYPE OF(state_of_ordinary_functional_object);
    SELF\state_of_ordinary_functional_
         object.temporal_part_of    :OPTIONAL SET [1:?] OF
                                         sales_product_instance;
    SELF\state_of_ordinary_functional_
         object.member_of           :OPTIONAL SET [1:?] OF
                                         class_of_state_of_sales_
                                         product_instance;

  END_ENTITY;
(*
```

Attribute definitions:

temporal_part_of	A *temporal_part_of* relationship type where a **state_of_sales_product_instance** may be a *temporal_part_of* one or more **sales_product_instance**.
member_of	A *member_of* relationship type where a **state_of_sales_product_instance** may be a *member_of* one or more **class_of_state_of_sales_product_instance**.

17.44 Offering

Figure 17-44 shows the data model for **offering**. An **offering** is a **class_of_offer** where what is offered is a *member_of* a **class_of_individual** for a **price** by a **party** during a **period_of_time**. A **product_offering** is an **offering** where what is offered is a *member_of* a **sales_product**.

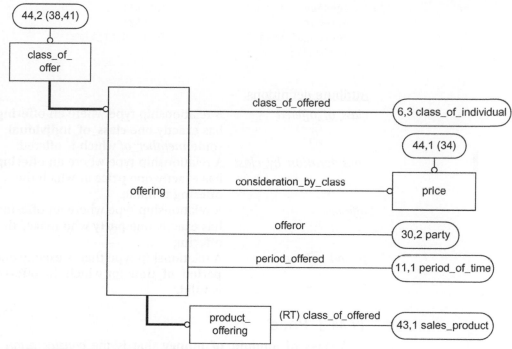

Figure 17-44 HQDM_FRAMEWORK EXPRESS-G diagram 44 of 46.

17.44.1 Class_of_offer

A **class_of_socially_constructed_activity** that is **offer** or any
of its subsets.

EXPRESS specification:

```
*)
  ENTITY class_of_offer
    SUBTYPE OF(class_of_socially_constructed_activity);
  END_ENTITY;
(*
```

17.44.2 Offering

A **class_of_offer** that is for a **class_of_individual**, at a **price**,
by a **party**, for a **period_of_time**.

EXPRESS specification:

```
*)
  ENTITY offering
    SUBTYPE OF(class_of_offer);
    class_of_offered            :class_of_individual;
```

```
    consideration_by_class       :price;
    offeror                      :party;
    period_offered               :period_of_time;
  END_ENTITY;
(*
```

Attribute definitions:

class_of_offered	A relationship type where an **offering** has exactly one **class_of_individual** some *member_of* which is offered.
consideration_by_class	A relationship type where an **offering** has exactly one **price** at which the **offering** is made.
offeror	A relationship type where an **offering** has exactly one **party** who makes the **offering**.
period_offered	A relationship type that is exactly one **period_of_time** for which the **offering** is valid.

17.44.3 Price

A **class_of_amount_of_money** that is the *consideration_by_class* in an **offering**.

EXPRESS specification:

```
*)
  ENTITY price
    SUBTYPE OF(class_of_amount_of_money);
  END_ENTITY;
(*
```

17.44.4 Product_offering

An **offering** that is for a **sales_product**.

EXPRESS specification:

```
*)
  ENTITY product_offering
    SUBTYPE OF(offering);
    SELF\offering.class_of_offered       :sales_product;
  END_ENTITY;
(*
```

Attribute definitions:

class_of_offered A *class_of_offered* relationship type where a *member_of* a **sales_product** is offered.

17.45 Sign and Pattern

Figure 17-45 shows the data model for **sign** and **pattern**. A **sign** is a **socially_constructed_object** that is used by some **recognizing_language_community** to represent some **thing**. A **state_of_sign** is a **sign** or a *temporal_part_of* a **sign**.

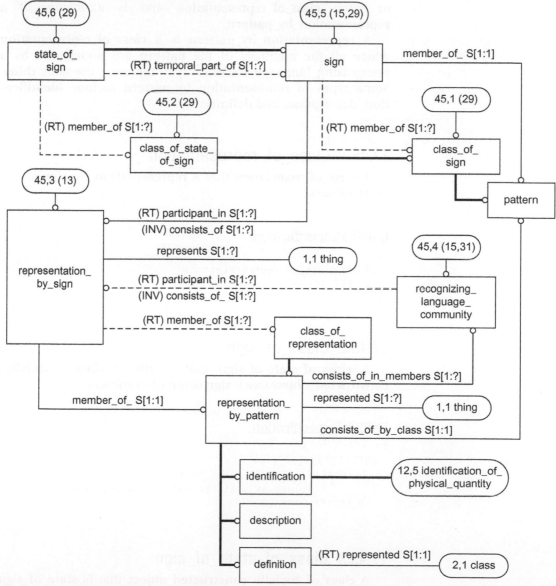

Figure 17-45 HQDM_FRAMEWORK EXPRESS-G diagram 45 of 46.

A **state_of_sign** may be a *member_of* one or more **class_ of_state_of_sign** and a **sign** may be a *member_of* one or more **class_of_sign**. A **sign** is a *member_of* a **pattern**, which governs its intended meaning.

A **representation_by_sign** is an **association** between a **recog- nizing_language_community** and a **sign** in which it represents some **thing**. A **representation_by_sign** may be a *member_of* one or more **class_of_representation** and is a *member_of* a **representation_by_pattern**.

A **representation_by_pattern** is a **class_of_representation** where all the members of the **pattern** are understood by a **recognizing_language_community** to represent the same **thing**. Some types of **representation_by_pattern** include **identifica- tion**, **description**, and **definition**.

17.45.1 Class_of_representation

A **class_of_association** that is **representation_by_sign** or any of its subsets.

EXPRESS specification:
```
*)
  ENTITY class_of_representation;
  END_ENTITY;
(*
```

17.45.2 Class_of_sign

A **class_of_state_of_sign** that is also a **class_of_socially_ constructed_object** that is **sign** or any of its subsets.

EXPRESS specification:
```
*)
  ENTITY class_of_sign
    SUBTYPE OF(class_of_state_of_sign,
            class_of_socially_contructed_object);
  END_ENTITY;
(*
```

17.45.3 Class_of_state_of_sign

A **class_of_socially_constructed_object** that is **state_of_sign** or any of its subsets.

EXPRESS specification:
```
*)
  ENTITY class_of_state_of_sign
    SUBTYPE OF(class_of_state_of_socially_constructed_object);
  END_ENTITY;
(*
```

17.45.4 Definition

A **representation_by_pattern** that defines a **class**.

EXPRESS specification:
```
*)
  ENTITY definition
    SUBTYPE OF(representation_by_pattern);
    SELF\representation_by_pattern.
        represented                    :SET [1:1] OF class;
  END_ENTITY;
(*
```

Attribute definitions:

represented A relationship type where exactly one **class** is defined by the **definition**.

17.45.5 Description

A **representation_by_pattern** that describes some **thing**.

EXPRESS specification:
```
*)
  ENTITY description
    SUBTYPE OF(representation_by_pattern);
  END_ENTITY;
(*
```

17.45.6 Identification

A **representation_by_pattern** that is a surrogate for the **thing** *represented*.

EXPRESS specification:
```
*)
  ENTITY identification
    SUBTYPE OF(representation_by_pattern);
  END_ENTITY;
(*
```

17.45.7 Pattern

A **class_of_sign** where all the **signs** are of the same **pattern**.

EXPRESS specification:

```
*)
  ENTITY pattern
    SUBTYPE OF(class_of_sign);
  END_ENTITY;
(*
```

17.45.8 Recognizing_language_community

A **state_of_language_community** that recognizes what a **pattern** is intended to represent.

EXPRESS specification:

```
*)
  ENTITY recognizing_language_community
    SUBTYPE OF(state_of_language_community, participant);
    SELF\participant.
        participant_in   :OPTIONAL SET [1:?] OF representation_
                               by_sign;
  END_ENTITY;
(*
```

Attribute definitions:

participant_in   A *participant_in* relationship type where a **recognizing_language_community** is a *participant_in* one or more **representation_by_sign**.

17.45.9 Representation_by_pattern

A **class_of_representation** where the **sign** in all the members are members of the **pattern** specified.

EXPRESS specification:

```
*)
  ENTITY representation_by_pattern
    SUBTYPE OF(class_of_representation);
    represented              :SET [1:?] OF thing;
    consists_of_by_class     :SET [1:1] OF pattern;
    consists_of_in_members   :SET [1:?] OF recognizing_
                               language_community;
  END_ENTITY;
(*
```

Attribute definitions:

represented	A relationship type where the **thing** is *represented* by each *member_of* the **representation_by_pattern**.
consists_of_by_class	A *consists_of_by_class* relationship type where a *member_of* the **representation_by_pattern** has a **sign** that is a *member_of* the **pattern**.
consists_of_in_members	A relationship type where a **recognizing_language_community** is a *participant_in* each *member_of* one or more **representation_by_pattern**.

17.45.10 Representation_by_sign

An **association** of a **sign** and a **recognizing_language_community** that recognizes the **sign** as representing some **thing**.

EXPRESS specification:

```
*)
  ENTITY representation_by_sign
    SUBTYPE OF(association);
    represented            :SET [1:?] OF thing;
    SELF\association.
        member_of          :OPTIONAL SET [1:?] OF
                            class_of_representation;
    member_of_             :SET [1:1] OF representation_
                            by_pattern;
  INVERSE
    consists_of_           :SET [1:?] OF recognizing_language_
                            community FOR participant_in;
    consists_of            :SET [1:?] OF sign FOR participant_in;
  END_ENTITY;
(*
```

Attribute definitions:

represented	A relationship type where a **representation_by_sign** represents one or more **thing**.
member_of	A *member_of* relationship type where the **representation_by_sign** may be a *member_of* one or more **class_of_representation**.
*member_of_*	A *member_of* relationship type where the **representation_by_sign** must be a *member_of* exactly one **representation_by_pattern**.

*consists_of_*   A *consists_of* relationship type where a **representation_by_sign** consists of one or more **recognizing_language_community**.

consists_of   A *consists_of* relationship type where one or more **sign** is used in the **representation_by_sign**.

17.45.11 Sign

A **state_of_sign**, that is also a **socially_constructed_object**, and a **participant** that represents some **thing** for some community in one or more **representations_by_sign**.

<u>EXPRESS specification:</u>

```
*)
  ENTITY sign
    SUBTYPE OF(socially_constructed_object, state_of_sign,
            participant);
    SELF\socially_constructed_
        object.member_of        :OPTIONAL SET [1:?] OF
                                 class_of_sign;
    member_of_                  :SET [1:1] OF pattern;
    SELF\participant.
        participant_in          :SET [1:?] OF representation_
                                 by_sign;
  END_ENTITY;
(*
```

<u>Attribute definitions:</u>

member_of   A *member_of* relationship type where a **sign** may be a *member_of* one or more **class_of_sign**.

*member_of_*   A *member_of* relationship type where a **sign** is a *member_of* one or more **pattern**.

participant_in   A *participant_in* relationship type where a **sign** is a *participant_in* one or more **representation_by_sign**.

17.45.12 State_of_sign

A **state_of_socially_constructed_object** that is a **sign** or a *temporal_part_of* a **sign**.

<u>EXPRESS specification:</u>

```
*)
  ENTITY state_of_sign
    SUBTYPE OF(state_of_socially_constructed_object);
```

```
SELF\state_of_socially_constructed_
     object.temporal_part_of        :OPTIONAL SET [1:?] OF
                                     sign;
SELF\state_of_socially_
     constructed_object.member_of   :OPTIONAL SET [1:?]
                                     OF class_of_state_
                                     of_sign;
END_ENTITY;
(*
```

<u>Attribute definitions:</u>

temporal_part_of A *temporal_part_of* relationship type where a **state_of_sign** may be a *temporal_part_of* one or more **sign**.

member_of A *member_of* relationship type where a **state_of_sign** may be a *member_of* one or more **class_of_state_of_sign**.

17.46 Requirement and Requirement Specification

Figure 17-46 shows the data model for **requirement** and **requirement-specification**.

A **plan** is a **possible_world** that some **party** would like to bring about.

A **requirement** is a **spatio_temporal_extent** that is *part_of_plan* of at least one **plan** and is *defined_by* exactly one **requirement_specification**, where the *part_of_plan* relationship type is a subtype of the *part_of* relationship type and the *defined_by* relationship type is a subtype of the *member_of* relationship type.

A **requirement_specification** is a **class_of_spatio_temporal_extent** that is the *intersection_of* one or more **class_of_state**.

A **physical_property_range** is a **class_of_state** that *ranges_over* (is a superset of) one or more **physical_property** of the same **kind_of_physical_property**. A **state** is a *member_of* a **property_range** when its value for the **kind_of_physical_property** falls within the range.

A **physical_quantity_range** is a **physical_property_range** where the **kind_of_physical_property** is a **kind_of_physical_quantity** and where the **physical_quantity_range** has an *upper_bound* and a *lower_bound* that are a **physical_quantity**.

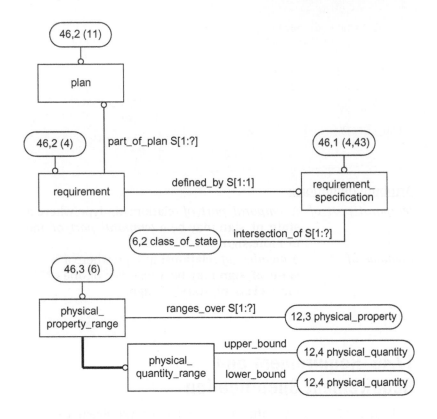

Figure 17-46 HQDM_
FRAMEWORK EXPRESS-G
diagram 46 of 46.

17.46.1 Physical_property_range

A **class_of_state** where each member of the set is a member of a **physical_property** within the range.

Note: The **physical_property_range** is the supertype of each **physical_property** in the range.

<u>EXPRESS specification:</u>

```
*)
  ENTITY physical_property_range
    SUBTYPE OF(class_of_state);
    ranges_over        :SET [1:?] OF physical_property;
  END_ENTITY;
(*
```

<u>Attribute definitions:</u>

ranges_over   A *supertype_of* relationship type where the members
               of each **physical_property** in
               the **physical_property_range** are members of the
               physical_property_range.

17.46.2 Physical_quantity_range

A **physical_property_range** that ranges over **physical_quantity** values.

<u>EXPRESS specification:</u>

```
*)
  ENTITY physical_quantity_range
    SUBTYPE OF(physical_property_range);
    upper_bound        :physical_quantity;
    lower_bound        :physical_quantity;
  END_ENTITY;
(*
```

<u>Attribute definitions:</u>

upper_bound   A *supertype_of* relationship type where each **physical_quantity_range** must have as *upper_bound* exactly one **physical_quantity**.

lower_bound   A *supertype_of* relationship type where each **physical_quantity_range** must have as *lower_bound* exactly one **physical_quantity**.

17.46.3 Plan

A **possible_world** that some party would like to bring about.

<u>EXPRESS specification:</u>

```
*)
  ENTITY plan
    SUBTYPE OF(possible_world);
  END_ENTITY;
(*
```

17.46.4 Requirement

A **spatio_temporal_extent** that is *part_of_plan* at least one **plan** and is *defined_by* exactly one **requirement_specification**.

<u>EXPRESS specification:</u>

```
*)
  ENTITY requirement
    SUBTYPE OF(spatio_temporal_extent);
    defined_by        :SET [1:1] OF requirement_specification;
    part_of_plan      :SET [1:?] OF plan;
  END_ENTITY;
(*
```

Attribute definitions:

defined_by   A *member_of* relationship type where a
requirement is *defined_by* exactly one
requirement_specification.

part_of_plan A *part_of* relationship type where a **requirement**
must be *part_of* one or more **plans**.

17.46.5 Requirement_specification

A **class_of_spatio_temporal_extent** that is the *intersection_of*
one or more **class_of_state**.

EXPRESS specification:

```
*)
  ENTITY requirement_specification
    SUBTYPE OF(class_of_spatio_temporal_extent);
    intersection_of        :SET [1:?] OF class_of_state;
  END_ENTITY;
(*
```

Attribute definitions:

intersection_of A *subtype_of* relationship type where each
requirement_specification is the *intersection_of*
one or more **class_of_state**.
Note: the **requirement_specification** is a
subtype of each of the related **class_of_state**.

```
*)
  END_SCHEMA;
```

A MAPPING BETWEEN THE HQDM SCHEMA AND ISO 15926-2

A.1 Introduction

This book presents a data model that is a different take on the same ontological principles behind the ISO 15926-2 data model. As I explained earlier, the reason for the different take is the different purpose that this book has from the ISO standard. In developing the ISO standard, there was considerable pressure to keep the number of entity types as small as possible. This perhaps led to the standard being harder to interpret and use than a larger, more explicit model. By contrast, in the HQDM schema, I present the same ontological principles in such a way that my data model makes it easier to see how the data model should be populated. This produces a data model with a larger entity type count but that covers only the core of the ISO 15926-2 data model.

The purpose of this appendix is to show how the entity types in the two data models relate to each other. I do this both graphically and textually. The graphical conventions are illustrated in Figure A-1, where the double-ended lollypop shows the entity types are equivalent, the subtype symbol shows that an HQDM entity type is a subtype of an ISO 15926-2 entity type, and the arrow shows the ISO 15926-2 entity type of which the HQDM entity type is an instance (so the entity type can be placed in the ISO 15926 RDL). An instance of relationship is required unless the entity types are equivalent.

Not all entity types are mapped, but those that are critical to understanding the relationship between the HQDM data model and the ISO 15926-2 data model are.

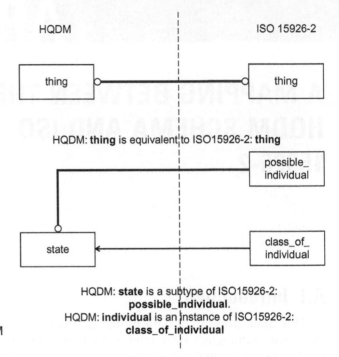

Figure A-1 Example notation for mapping HQDM entity types to ISO 15926-2 entity types.

A.2 Thing

Figure A-2 Mapping for **thing**.

- HQDM: **thing** is equivalent to ISO15926-2: **thing**.

A.3 Spatio_temporal_extent

Figure A-3 Mapping for **spatio_temporal_extent**.

- HQDM: **spatio_temporal_extent** is equivalent to ISO15926-2: **possible_individual**.

A.4 Abstract_object

Figure A-4 Mapping for **abstract_object**.

- HQDM: **abstract_object** is equivalent to ISO15926-2: **abstract_object**.

A.5 Class

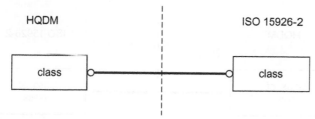

Figure A-5 Mapping for **class**.

- HQDM: **class** is equivalent to ISO15926-2: **class**.

A.6 Class_of_spatio_temporal_extent

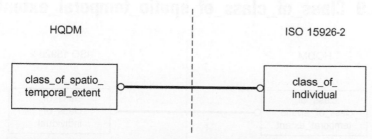

Figure A-6 Mapping for **class_of_spatio_temporal_extent**.

- HQDM: **class_of_spatio_temporal_extent** is equivalent to ISO15926-2: **class_of_individual**.

A.7 Class_of_abstract_object

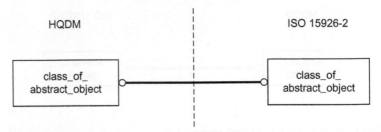

Figure A-7 Mapping for **class_of_abstract_object**.

- HQDM: **class_of_abstract_object** is equivalent to ISO15926-2: **class_of_abstract_object**.

A.8 Class_of_class

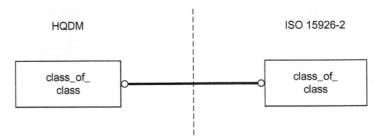

Figure A-8 Mapping for **class_of_class**.

- HQDM: **class_of_class** is equivalent to ISO15926-2: **class_of_class**.

A.9 Class_of_class_of_spatio_temporal_extent

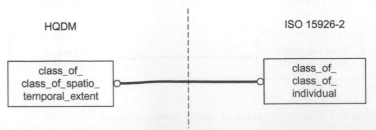

Figure A-9 Mapping for class_of_**class_of_class_of_spatio_temporal_extent**.

- HQDM: **class_of_class_of_spatio_temporal_extent** is equivalent to ISO15926-2: **class_of_class_of_individual**.

A.10 Event

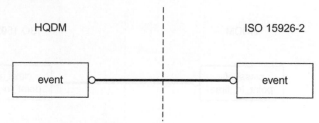

Figure A-10 Mapping for **event**.

- HQDM: **event** is equivalent to ISO15926-2: **event**.

A.11 Point_in_time

Figure A-11 Mapping for **point_in_time**.

- HQDM: **point_in_time** is equivalent to ISO15926-2: **point_in_time**.

A.12 Class_of_event

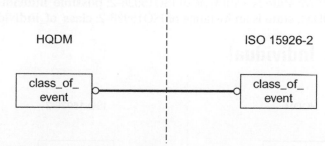

Figure A-12 Mapping for **class_of_event**.

- HQDM: **class_of_event** is equivalent to ISO15926-2: **class_of_event**.

A.13 Class_of_point_in_time

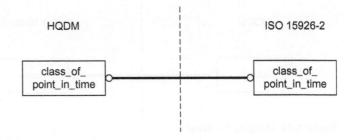

Figure A-13 Mapping for **class_of_point_in_time**.

- HQDM: **class_of_point_in_time** is equivalent to ISO15926-2: **class_of_point_in_time**.

A.14 State

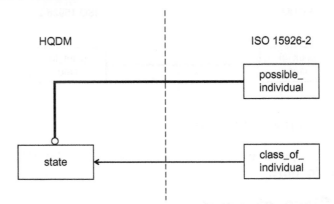

Figure A-14 Mapping for **state**.

- HQDM: **state** is a subtype of ISO15926-2: **possible_individual**.
- HQDM: **state** is an instance of ISO15926-2: **class_of_individual**.

A.15 Individual

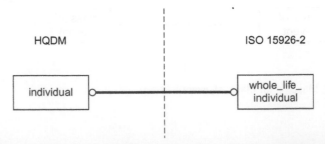

Figure A-15 Mapping for **individual**.

- HQDM: **individual** is equivalent to ISO15926-2: **whole_life_individual**.

A.16 Class_of_state

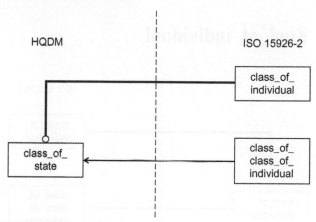

Figure A-16 Mapping for **class_of_state**.

- HQDM: **class_of_state** is a subtype of ISO15926-2: **class_of_individual**.
- HQDM: **class_of_state** is an instance of ISO15926-2: **class_of_class_of_individual**.

A.17 Class_of_individual

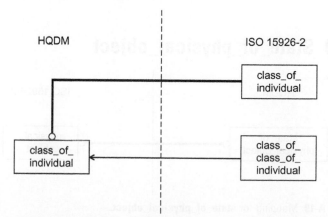

Figure A-17 Mapping for **class_of_individual**.

- HQDM: **class_of_individual** is a subtype of ISO15926-2: **class_of_individual**.
- HQDM: **class_of_individual** is an instance of ISO15926-2: **class_of_class_of_individual**.

A.18 Kind_of_individual

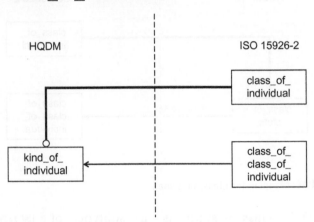

Figure A-18 Mapping for **kind_of_individual**.

- HQDM: **kind_of_individual** is a subtype of ISO15926-2: **class_of_individual**.
- HQDM: **kind_of_individual** is an instance of ISO15926-2: **class_of_class_of_individual**.

A.19 State_of_physical_object

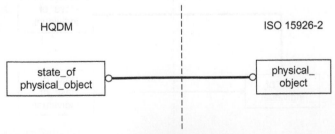

Figure A-19 Mapping for **state_of_physical_object**.

- HQDM: **state_of_physical_object** is equivalent to ISO15926-2: **physical_object**.

A.20 Physical_object

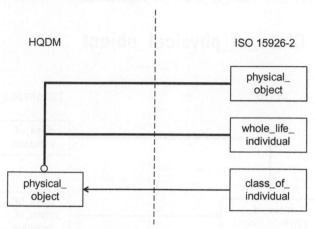

Figure A-20 Mapping for **physical_object**.

- HQDM: **physical_object** is a subtype of ISO15926-2: **physical_object**.
- HQDM: **physical_object** is a subtype of ISO15926-2: **whole_life_individual**.
- HQDM: **physical_object** is an instance of ISO15926-2: **class_of_individual**.

A.21 Class_of_state_of_physical_object

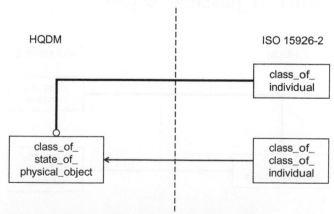

Figure A-21 Mapping for **class_of_state_of_physical_object**.

- HQDM: **class_of_state_of_physical_object** is a subtype of ISO15926-2: **class_of_individual**.

- HQDM: **class_of_state_of_physical_object** is an instance of ISO15926-2: **class_of_class_of_individual**.

A.22 Class_of_physical_object

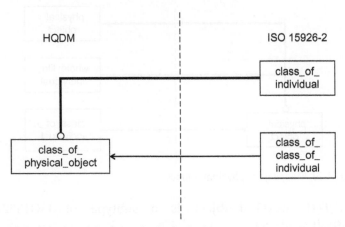

Figure A-22 Mapping for **class_of_physical_object**.

- HQDM: **class_of_physical_object** is a subtype of ISO15926-2: **class_of_individual**.
- HQDM: **class_of_physical_object** is an instance of ISO15926-2: **class_of_class_of_individual**.

A.23 Kind_of_physical_object

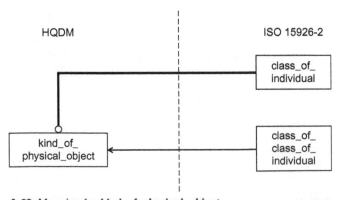

Figure A-23 Mapping for **kind_of_physical_object**.

- HQDM: **kind_of_physical_object** is a subtype of ISO15926-2: **class_of_individual**.

- HQDM: **kind_of_physical_object** is an instance of ISO15926-2: **class_of_class_of_individual**.

A.24 State_of_ordinary_physical_object

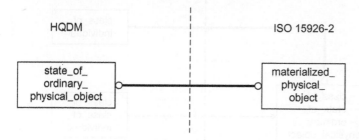

HQDM

ISO 15926-2

state_of_ordinary_physical_object

materialized_physical_object

Figure A-24 Mapping for **state_of_ordinary_physical_object**.

- HQDM: **state_of_ordinary_physical_object** is equivalent to ISO15926-2: **materialized_physical_object**.

A.25 Ordinary_physical_object

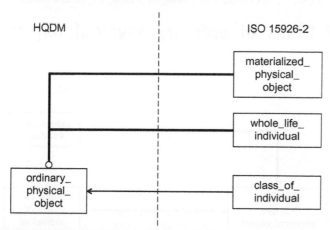

HQDM

ISO 15926-2

materialized_physical_object

whole_life_individual

ordinary_physical_object

class_of_individual

Figure A-25 Mapping for **ordinary_physical_object**.

- HQDM: **ordinary_physical_object** is a subtype of ISO15926-2: **materialized_physical_object**.
- HQDM: **ordinary_physical_object** is a subtype of ISO15926-2: **whole_life_individual**.
- HQDM: **ordinary_physical_object** is an instance of ISO15926-2: **class_of_individual**.

A.26 Class_of_state_of_ ordinary_physical_object

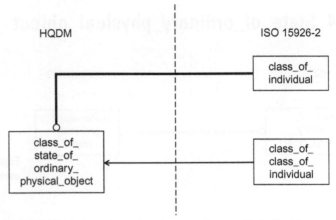

Figure A-26 Mapping for **class_of_state_of_ordinary_physical_object**.

- HQDM: **class_of_state_of_ordinary_physical_object** is a subtype of ISO15926-2: **class_of_individual**.
- HQDM: **class_of_state_of_ordinary_physical_objec**t is an instance of ISO15926-2: **class_of_class_of_individual**.

A.27 Class_of_ordinary_physical_object

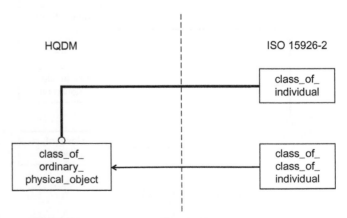

Figure A-27 Mapping for **class_of_ordinary_physical_object**.

- HQDM: **class_of_ordinary_physical_object** is a subtype of ISO15926-2: **class_of_individual**.
- HQDM: **class_of_ordinary_physical_object** is an instance of ISO15926-2: **class_of_class_of_individual**

A.28 Kind_of_ordinary_physical_object

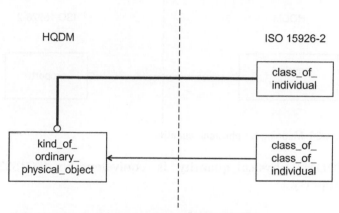

Figure A-28 Mapping for **kind_of_ordinary_physical_object**.

- HQDM: **kind_of_ordinary_physical_object** is a subtype of ISO15926-2: **class_of_individual.**
- HQDM: **kind_of_ordinary_physical_object** is an instance of ISO15926-2: **class_of_class_of_individual**.

A.29 Physical_property

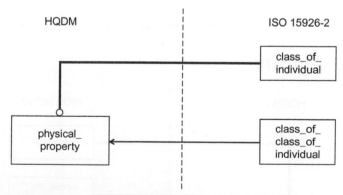

Figure A-29 Mapping for **physical_property**.

- HQDM: **physical_property** is a subtype of ISO15926-2: **class_of_individual**.
- HQDM: **physical_property** is an instance of ISO15926-2: **class_of_class_of_individual**.

A.30 Physical_quantity

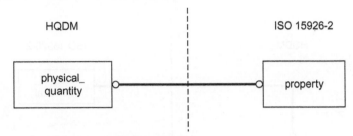

HQDM

ISO 15926-2

Figure A-30 Mapping for **physical_quantity**.

- HQDM: **physical_quantity** is equivalent to ISO15926-2: **property**.

A.31 State_of_activity

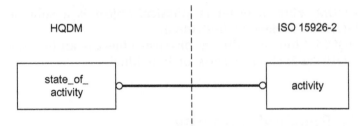

HQDM

ISO 15926-2

Figure A-31 Mapping for **state_of_activity**.

- HQDM: **state_of_activity** is equivalent to ISO15926-2: **activity**.

A.32 Activity

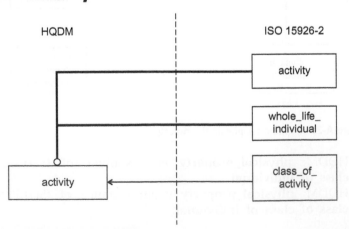

HQDM

ISO 15926-2

Figure A-32 Mapping for **activity**.

- HQDM: **activity** is a subtype of ISO15926-2: **activity**.
- HQDM: **activity** is a subtype of ISO15926-2: **whole_life_individual**.
- HQDM: **activity** is an instance of ISO15926-2: **class_of_activity**.

A.33 Class_of_activity

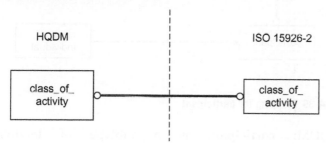

Figure A-33 Mapping for **class_of_activity**.

- HQDM: **class_of_activity** is equivalent to ISO15926-2: **class_of_activity**.

A.34 Kind_of_activity

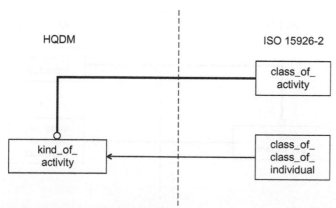

Figure A-34 Mapping for **kind_of_activity**.

- HQDM: **kind_of_activity** is a subtype of ISO15926-2: **class_of_activity**.
- HQDM: **kind_of_activity** is an instance of ISO15926-2: **class_of_class_of_individual**.

A.35 Participant

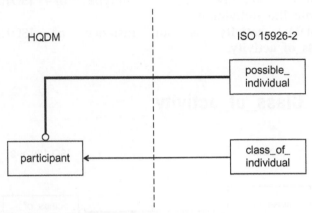

Figure A-35 Mapping for **participant**.

- HQDM: **participant** is a subtype of ISO15926-2: **possible_individual**.
- HQDM: **participant** is an instance of ISO15926-2: **class_of_individual**.

A.36 Class_of_participant

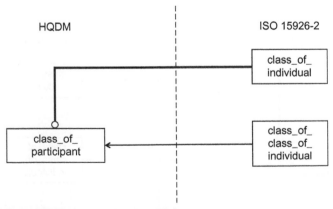

Figure A-36 Mapping for **class_of_participant**.

- HQDM: **class_of_participant** is a subtype of ISO15926-2: **class_of_individual**.
- HQDM: **class_of_participant** is an instance of ISO15926-2: **class_of_class_of_individual**.

A.37 Role

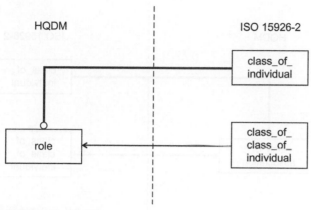

Figure A-37 Mapping for **role**.

- HQDM: **role** is a subtype of ISO15926-2: **class_of_individual**.
- HQDM: **role** is an instance of ISO15926-2: **class_of_class_of_individual**.

A.38 Association

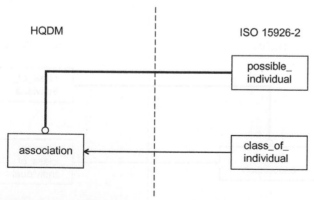

Figure A-38 Mapping for **association**.

- HQDM: **association** is a subtype of ISO15926-2: **possible_individual**.
- HQDM: **association** is an instance of ISO15926-2: **class_of_individual**.

A.39 Class_of_association

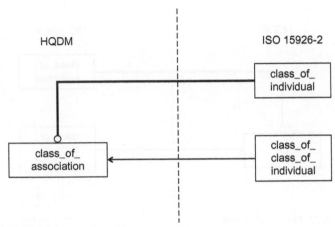

Figure A-39 Mapping for **class_of_association**.

- HQDM: **class_of_association** is a subtype of ISO15926-2: **class_of_individual**.
- HQDM: **class_of_association** is an instance of ISO15926-2: **class_of_class_of_individual**.

A.40 Kind_of_association

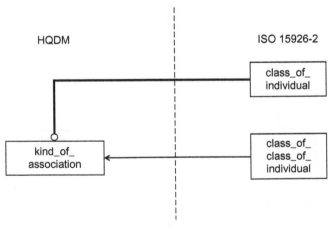

Figure A-40 Mapping for **kind_of_association**.

- HQDM: **kind_of_association** is a subtype of ISO15926-2: **class_of_individual**.
- HQDM: **kind_of_association** is an instance of ISO15926-2: **class_of_class_of_individual**.

A.41 State_of_system

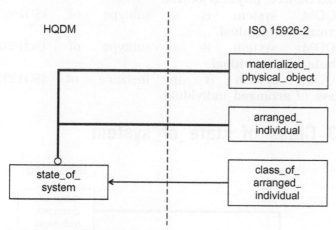

Figure A-41 Mapping for **state_of_system**.

- HQDM: **state_of_system** is a subtype of ISO15926-2: **materialized_physical_object**.
- HQDM: **state_of_system** is a subtype of ISO15926-2: **arranged_individual**.
- HQDM: **state_of_system** is an instance of ISO15926-2: **class_of_arranged_individual**.

A.42 System

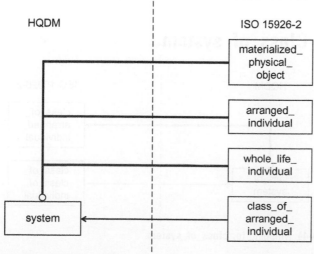

Figure A-42 Mapping for **system**.

- HQDM: **system** is a subtype of ISO15926-2: **materialized_physical_object**.
- HQDM: **system** is a subtype of ISO15926-2: **arranged_individual**.
- HQDM: **system** is a subtype of ISO15926-2: **whole_life_individual**.
- HQDM: **system** is an instance of ISO15926-2: **class_of_arranged_individual**.

A.43 Class_of_state_of_system

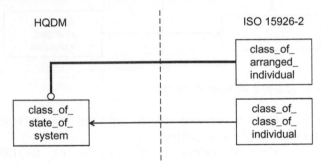

Figure A-43 Mapping for **class_of_state_of_system**.

- HQDM: **class_of_state_of_system** is a subtype of ISO15926-2: **class_of_arranged_individual**.
- HQDM: **class_of_state_of_system** is an instance of ISO15926-2: **class_of_class_of_individual**.

A.44 Class_of_system

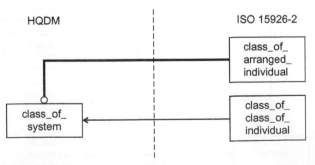

Figure A-44 Mapping for **class_of_system**.

- HQDM: **class_of_system** is a subtype of ISO15926-2: **class_of_arranged_individual**.
- HQDM: **class_of_system** is an instance of ISO15926-2: **class_of_class_of_individual**.

A.45 Kind_of_system

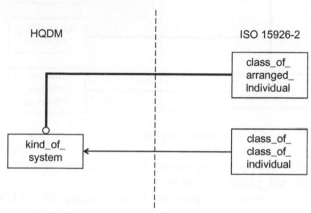

Figure A-45 Mapping for **kind_of_system**.

- HQDM: **kind_of_system** is a subtype of ISO15926-2: **class_of_arranged_individual**.
- HQDM: **kind_of_system** is an instance of ISO15926-2: **class_of_class_of_individual**.

A.46 State_of_system_component

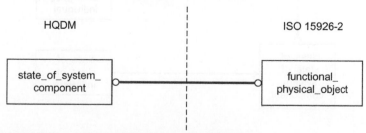

Figure A-46 Mapping for **state_of_system_component**.

- HQDM: **state_of_system_component** is equivalent to ISO15926-2: **functional_physical_object**.

A.47 System_component

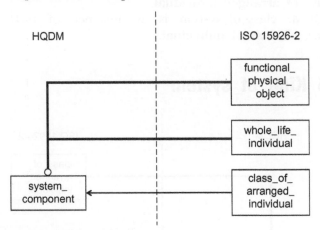

Figure A-47 Mapping for **system_component**.

- HQDM: **system_component** is a subtype of ISO15926-2: **functional_physical_object**.
- HQDM: **system_component** is a subtype of ISO15926-2: **whole_life_individual**.
- HQDM: **system_component** is an instance of ISO15926-2: **class_of_arranged_individual**.

A.48 Class_of_state_of_system_component

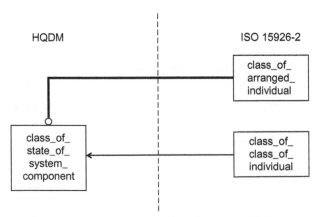

Figure A-48 Mapping for **class_of_state_of_system_component**.

- HQDM: **class_of_state_of_system_component** is a subtype of ISO15926-2: **class_of_arranged_individual**.
- HQDM: **class_of_state_of_system_component** is an instance of ISO15926-2: **class_of_class_of_individual.**

A.49 Class_of_system_component

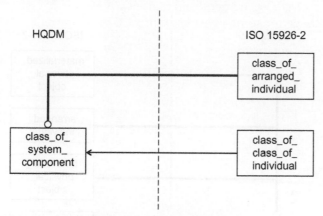

Figure A-49 Mapping for **class_of_system_component**.

- HQDM: **class_of_system_component** is a subtype of ISO15926-2: **class_of_arranged_individual**.
- HQDM: **class_of_system_component** is an instance of ISO15926-2: **class_of_class_of_individual**.

A.50 Kind_of_system_component

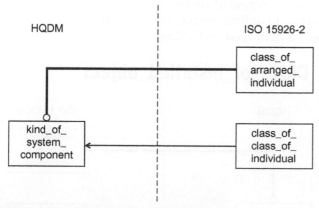

Figure A-50 Mapping for **kind_of_system_component**.

- HQDM: **kind_of_system_component** is a subtype of ISO15926-2: **class_of_arranged_individual**.
- HQDM: **kind_of_system_component** is an instance of ISO15926-2: **class_of_class_of_individual**.

A.51 Installed_object

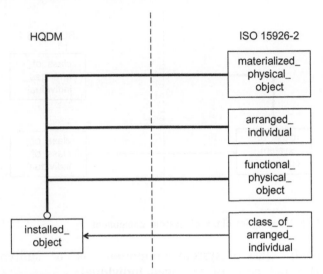

Figure A-51 Mapping for **installed_object**.

- HQDM: **installed_object** is a subtype of ISO15926-2: **materialized_physical_object**.
- HQDM: **installed_object** is a subtype of ISO15926-2: **arranged_individual**.
- HQDM: **installed_object** is a subtype of ISO15926-2: **functional_physical_object**.
- HQDM: **installed_object** is an instance of ISO15926-2: **class_of_arranged_individual**.

A.52 Class_of_installed_object

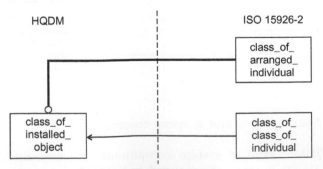

Figure A-52 Mapping for **class_of_installed_object**.

- HQDM: **class_of_installed_object** is a subtype of ISO15926-2: **class_of_arranged_individual**.
- HQDM: **class_of_installed_object** is an instance of ISO15926-2: **class_of_class_of_individual**.

A.53 State_of_biological_object

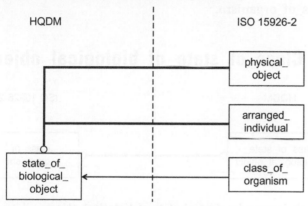

Figure A-53 Mapping for **state_of_biological_object**.

- HQDM: **state_of_biological_object** is a subtype of ISO15926-2: **physical_object**.
- HQDM: **statc_of_biological_object** is a subtype of ISO15926-2: **arranged_individual**.
- HQDM: **state_of_biological_object** is an instance of ISO15926-2: **class_of_organism**.

A.54 Biological_object

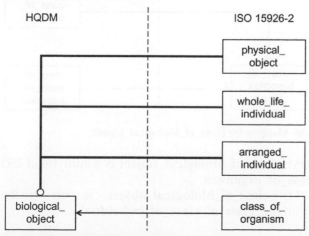

Figure A-54 Mapping for **biological_object**.

- HQDM: **biological_object** is a subtype of ISO15926-2: **physical_object**.
- HQDM: **biological_object** is a subtype of ISO15926-2: **whole_life_individual**.
- HQDM: **biological_object** is a subtype of ISO15926-2: **arranged_individual**.
- HQDM: **biological_object** is an instance of ISO15926-2: **class_of_organism**.

A.55 Class_of_state_of_biological_object

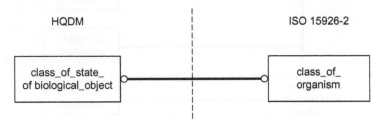

Figure A-55 Mapping for **class_of_state_of_biological_object**.

- HQDM: **class_of_state_of_biological_object** is equivalent to ISO15926-2: **class_of_organism**.

A.56 Class_of_biological_object

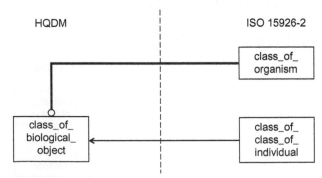

Figure A-56 Mapping for **class_of_biological_object**.

- HQDM: **class_of_biological_object** is a subtype of ISO15926-2: **class_of_organism**.
- HQDM: **class_of_biological_object** is an instance of ISO15926-2: **class_of_class_of_individual**.

A.57 Kind_of_biological_object

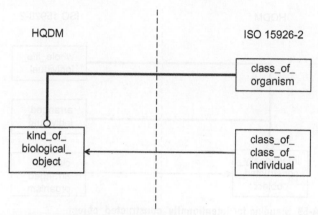

Figure A-57 Mapping for **kind_of_biological_object**.

- HQDM: **kind_of_biological_object** is a subtype of ISO15926-2: **class_of_organism**.
- HQDM: **kind_of_biological_object** is an instance of ISO15926-2: **class_of_class_of_individual**.

A.58 State_of_intentionally_constructed_ object

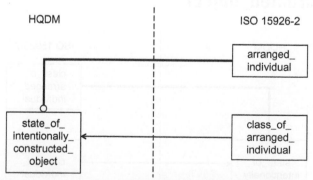

Figure A-58 Mapping for **state_of_intentionally_constructed_object**.

- HQDM: **state_of_intentionally_constructed_object** is a subtype of ISO15926-2: **arranged_individual**.
- HQDM: **state_of_intentionally_constructed_object** is an instance of ISO15926-2: **class_of_arranged_individual**.

A.59 Intentionally_constructed_object

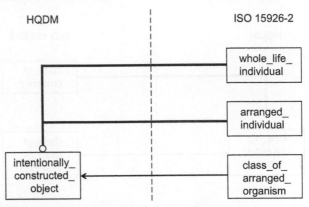

Figure A-59 Mapping for **intentionally_constructed_object**.

- HQDM: **intentionally_constructed_object** is a subtype of ISO15926-2: **whole_life_individual**.
- HQDM: **intentionally_constructed_object** is a subtype of ISO15926-2: **arranged_individual**.
- HQDM: **intentionally_constructed_object** is an instance of ISO15926-2: **class_of_arranged_individual**.

A.60 Class_of_state_of_intentionally_constructed_object

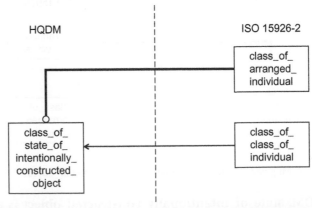

Figure A-60 Mapping for **class_of_state_of_intentionally_constructed_object**.

- HQDM:**class_of_state_of_intentionally_constructed_object** is a subtype of ISO15926-2: **class_of_arranged_individual**.

- HQDM: **class_of_state_of_intentionally_constructed_object** is an instance of ISO15926-2: **class_of_class_of_individual**.

A.61 Class_of_intentionally_ constructed_object

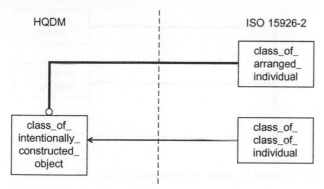

Figure A-61 Mapping for **class_of_intentionally_constructed_object**.

- HQDM: **class_of_intentionally_constructed_object** is a subtype of ISO15926-2: **class_of_arranged_individual**.
- HQDM: **class_of_intentionally_constructed_object** is an instance of ISO15926-2: **class_of_class_of_individual**.

A.62 Kind_of_intentionally_ constructed_object

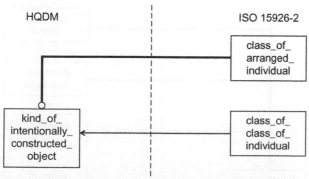

Figure A-62 Mapping for **kind_of_intentionally_constructed_object**.

- HQDM: **kind_of_intentionally_constructed_object** is a subtype of ISO15926-2: **class_of_arranged_individual**.

- HQDM: **kind_of_intentionally_constructed_object** is an instance of ISO15926-2: **class_of_class_of_individual**.

A.63 State_of_functional_object

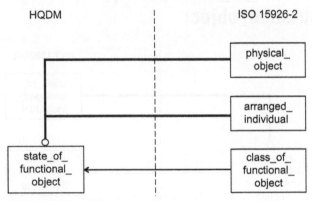

Figure A-63 Mapping for **state_of_functional_object**.

- HQDM: **state_of_functional_object** is a subtype of ISO15926-2: **physical_object**.
- HQDM: **state_of_functional_object** is a subtype of ISO15926-2: **arranged_individual**.
- HQDM: **state_of_functional_object** is an instance of ISO15926-2: **class_of_functional_object**.

A.64 Functional_object

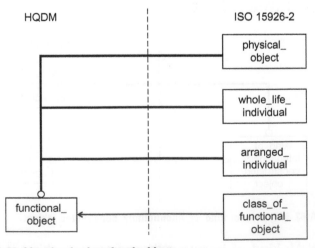

Figure A-64 Mapping for **functional_object**.

- HQDM: **functional_object** is a subtype of ISO15926-2: **physical_object**.
- HQDM: **functional_object** is a subtype of ISO15926-2: **whole_life_individual**.
- HQDM: **functional_object** is a subtype of ISO15926-2: **arranged_individual**.
- HQDM: **functional_object** is an instance of ISO15926-2: **class_of_functional_object**.

A.65 Class_of_state_of_functional_object

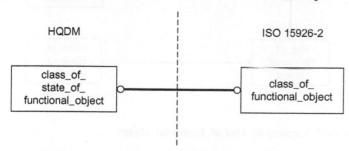

Figure A-65 Mapping for **class_of_state_of_functional_object**.

- HQDM: **class_of_state_of_functional_object** is equivalent to ISO15926-2: **class_of_functional_object**.

A.66 Class_of_functional_object

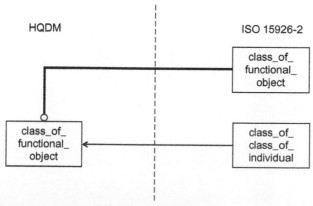

Figure A-66 Mapping for **class_of_functional_object**.

- HQDM: **class_of_functional_object** is a subtype of ISO15926-2: **class_of_functional_object**.

- HQDM: **class_of_functional_object** is an instance of ISO15926-2: **class_of_class_of_individual**.

A.67 Kind_of_functional_object

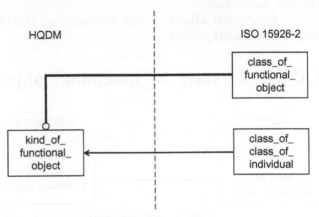

Figure A-67 Mapping for **kind_of_functional_object**.

- HQDM: **kind_of_functional_object** is a subtype of ISO15926-2: **class_of_functional_object**.
- HQDM: **kind_of_functional_object** is an instance of ISO15926-2: **class_of_class_of_individual**.

INDEX

Note: Page numbers followed by *f* and *t* refer to figures and tables, respectively

Printed and bound by CPI Group (UK) Ltd, Croydon, CR0 4YY

03/10/2024

01040310-0003